Accidental SEO Manager

Managing SEO Teams and Agencies

Third Edition

Ash Nallawalla

Twitter/X: @ashnallawalla

Keywords: Search Engine Optimization (SEO), Search Marketing, Digital Marketing, Web Governance, Organic Search, Marketing Management, Content Strategy

658.872 Technology and Application of Knowledge > Management and auxiliary services > Management > Of Marketing

BISAC:

- BUS090050 BUSINESS & ECONOMICS / E-Commerce / Search Engine Optimization
- BUS104000 BUSINESS & ECONOMICS / Corporate Governance

Disclaimer: All information has been presented in good faith, using information believed to be accurate at the time of publication. Use the information at your own risk. Errors and omissions are excepted.

ISBN: 978-0-6455232-3-2

FOREWORD

I first met Ash Nallawalla on our SEO forum websites. Later we invited Ash as a lead speaker at our long-running Search related conference Pubcon. Ash's many presentations quickly earned him a reputation as a world-renowned expert in the area of SEO. So, it is not surprising to me that he would choose to share his experiences with us in these pages.

When I started working professionally as an SEO in 1997, all of our clients would all start by asking, "What's SEO?" By the time I won the US Search Awards Lifetime Achievement Award twenty years later, the room was full of expert international SEO practitioners, and hardly a businessperson alive didn't understand the importance of SEO. That transition has moved SEO from a fringe "one size fits all" model to a multidisciplinary team of specialists.

Managing those teams and processes requires a deep understanding of the internet, marketing, and the technology that builds websites. Until now, few existing books have the knowledge and credibility that Ash Nallawalla brings to the subject. After more than two decades building websites and managing in-house and agency teams, Ash shares a wealth of expertise I've not encountered in other SEO-related books.

The content related to building and managing an SEO team is unique among educational materials available today. Previously, the only place to get such knowledge was at an industry conference or association-sponsored events. At our own conferences, it is very difficult to get people to share their hard-earned experiences the way Ash freely does in this book.

While so many SEO documents are dated before they are even released due to changes in the industry, Ash lays out policy, SEO process, and best practices that will be as at home in five years as they are today.

Brett Tabke

Founder and CEO, Pubcon Inc

Austin, Texas

TABLE OF CONTENTS

PREFACE

Not all organizations can have an in-house SEO team, or even a single person in that role. Others are more fortunate. Small, medium, and large organizations alike use SEO agencies. There aren't any "bad" agencies in the main, but there are good and bad fits, good and bad choices. Make the right choice, and you will create a great partnership. Large companies use a mix of in-house SEOs and external consultants.

This book is for:

- The "accidental SEO manager" who has just been handed the organization's website and is wondering what this SEO stuff is and why it matters. They now have to manage an in-house SEO team or an external agency.
- Some digital agencies that offer SEO services are using this book as a part of a sales pitch or in an existing relationship. It will better inform the client, and you might get additional work.

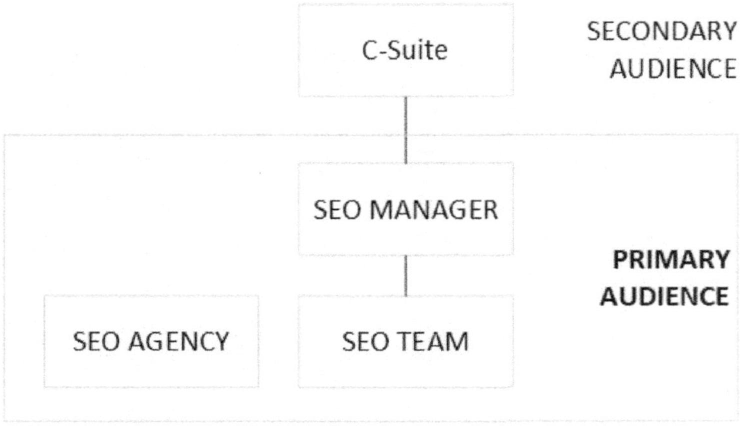

Figure 1 Audience of this book.

If you are an SEO practitioner, this book will make a perfect gift for your manager, perhaps making your work life easier and giving you less "noise" to take home. Please read it thoroughly before you give it to them.

This is not a "how-to-perform-SEO" textbook. Instead, it is a "what" and "why" backgrounder for the ones who manage SEO managers or SEO teams. Many "how-to perform SEO" books quickly go out of date – this one will likely have a longer shelf life. This book covers many of the same topics as the "how-to" books, but they are presented differently and go into detail that is omitted here by design.

This book encourages positive conversations between the various players in an SEO ecology. Although it mentions many concepts siloed in large enterprises, where expertise is spread across many teams, the message will be apparent to smaller entities, where a single person makes all decisions.

The term "SEO" is used interchangeably in this book, in context, to mean the process of Search Engine Optimization or to the people who perform it, namely, the Search Engine Optimizers.

WHY LEAVE MONEY ON THE TABLE?

This is the book I have long *wanted* to write.

For many years, I joked to my team that my next book would be *In Praise of Ignorance*. This is that book, although it does not bear that cheeky title. Ignorance can be a good thing because people with the answers make a living from their knowledge. We hire lawyers, plumbers, electricians, and mechanics because they know their subject matter better than we do (and often because the law requires us to employ registered professionals for specific tasks). Perhaps we are all leveraging this ignorance?

SEO was initially an esoteric specialty because search engines didn't reveal much about their algorithms. SEO involves reverse engineering, trial-and-error, observation, refinement, comparing notes, taking risks, and indulging in some guesswork. Opinions abound, but context matters, so two people can contradict each other and be right at the same time.

Did you notice that word I just used – risks? SEO requires taking calculated risks, as you will see in these pages.

The risk for SEO agency customers is that they are ignorant about the provider's knowledge (or their ignorance). There are horror stories and success stories. Through this book, I hope to highlight SEO best practices as they exist today.

My SEO Journey

I built my first website for my computer user group in late 1995 and several commercial ones for my then-employer, Hayes Microcomputer Products Inc (the inventor of the consumer dial-up modems) around 1996, and became aware of SEO a couple of years later. Naturally, I devoured every word I could find on this new specialty.

Following a remarkably successful lead-generation campaign at Macromedia (now part of Adobe) in 2002, the regional head office in Melbourne moved to Singapore, leaving the staff behind. I was the CRM Manager, managing a database of several million customer and prospect records. I decided to become a "CRM consultant" and built my own business site, crm911.com. It ranked #1 for that keyword for years until Google's algorithm favored other sites. I never worked as a CRM consultant because my SEO skills were spotted and led to this 20-plus-year career in search marketing.

SEO Is a Commodity Now

Since 2002, I have made a good living from SEO. When I joined a digital agency in 2005, business owners were ignorant about SEO. Many had no website. We had to educate them. Today, it is rare to find a business owner who has not heard of SEO, but rarer still to find one who gives it the due focus. SEO has become a commodity, and everybody seems to be an expert, at least in their mind.

On the other hand, paid search, known as Pay-per-Click (PPC) but mistakenly referred to as Search Engine Marketing (SEM), receives significant focus from management because it costs tens of millions in a large enterprise. Most online sales come from advertising campaigns, direct visits, email campaigns, and repeat customers. Here are some breakdowns in large enterprises I have worked in or consulted to:

	Sales from SEO	Sales from PPC	Other
Company A	32%	40%	28%
Company B	48%	28%	24%
Company C	60%	5%	35%

In this book, I will remind the reader that conversion-oriented businesses need to check how many conversions come through SEO and whether they have allowed this team to maximize their potential.

Consumers Have Evolved

Consumers are increasingly resistant to push marketing. They use filters to divert your direct email to their Junk folder, or unsubscribe if the frequency is excessive and the content is irrelevant. They use ad blockers in their web browsers. They don't take calls from unknown or blocked numbers.

On the other hand, consumers are happy to use a search engine to find answers. This is where SEO plays a leading role.

THE BUSINESS CASE FOR SEO

Today's SEO ignorance is costly. Even though a tool tells you the opportunity cost of speeding up a page, are you going to do anything about it? Many people prefer not to deal with it – it's not even a problem known to senior management. Perhaps this is when you need to engage an agency to say it for you?

"SEO is always the lowest priority until it's not." This is an observation by consultant Andrew Shotland, based on his experience with certain businesses. I have noticed this in successful small businesses, such as restaurants, that claim to be "happy" with the sales generated by food delivery apps – as though maintaining their website isn't a priority.

Slow websites not only annoy visitors but can also cost sales. A now-deprecated Google tool once estimated that a site could halve its page load time from three to 1.5 seconds and make an extra $1.6 Million US Dollars, based on 50,000 monthly visitors, an average order value of $500, and an 8 percent conversion rate. The best business case for SEO is to show the impact on revenue if you neglect SEO.

In a climate where headcount is decreasing and the pressure to increase sales is high, SEO is a low-cost weapon in your sales arsenal.

I spent most of my online career in banking and insurance, but often had no procedural contact with the product design, compliance, delivery, and claims teams. The product was something described on the website. There are literally hundreds of people working on the product, but they work in small groups and are sometimes insulated from the customer and purchase behavior.

Search engines exist to serve users and not website managers who seek to manipulate search results, so they change their algorithms all the time. As a result, SEO practitioners cannot assume that their knowledge will remain complete or up to date. This book will help you check their understanding and get the best out of them.

Why Is Managing SEO so Hard?

The book covers many situations you might recognize from your past or present reality. The painful truth for some companies is that their websites are lemons in a search-friendly sense. It has possibly taken many years of effort to build the lemon, and nobody wants to throw it away and start afresh. They would rather spend some more years rectifying it gingerly, rejecting unpalatable SEO advice. After all, it "works" as it is, and who's to say that the SEO recommendations are well-informed? Are shareholders going to know they may be getting a lower return? No.

NEW CHALLENGES FOR SEO

The search landscape has expanded far beyond the traditional blue links.

Generative AI systems such as **Google AI Overviews**, **Bing Copilot**, and **ChatGPT** now summarize content directly within results, often quoting or paraphrasing from optimized sources.

As a manager, you must ensure that your content is technically accessible, accurately represented, and properly attributed in these emerging "AI answers."

This book's core principles—discoverability, governance, and measurement—remain unchanged, but they now apply across both **search engines** and **AI surfaces**.

BUSY READERS

If you are skimming this book, look at the paragraphs marked with a gray border, such as this one.

HOW THIS BOOK IS USED

This book is used as preparatory material for the Visibility Governance Maturity Workshop (VGMM). It establishes shared language, scope, and context before the workshop, ensuring participants approach governance questions from a common baseline. The workshop itself is a facilitated executive session that produces a current-state governance determination; this book supports that process but does not replace the workshop or function as an assessment, audit, or scoring tool.

HOW THIS BOOK FITS INTO THE SERIES

This is the second volume in the *Managing SEO* series. It introduces the essentials of managing SEO within an organization—how to select and evaluate agencies, build productive internal teams, and connect search strategy to business objectives. Written for those who have inherited SEO responsibility rather than trained for it, it simplifies complex ideas into clear managerial guidance.

- ***Book 1, Managing SEO***, distills the series into a concise, manager-ready guide that integrates governance, measurement, and execution without repeating material from the subsequent books.
- ***Book 3, AI Visibility Playbook,*** expands the conversation from management to accountability—how to govern digital and AI-driven systems responsibly.

- ***Book 4, Is Our SEO Working?***, equips managers with measurement frameworks and diagnostic tools to evaluate whether their SEO investment is delivering value.
- ***Book 5, The C-Suite Blind Spot,*** speaks directly to executives, demonstrating how to embed SEO into organizational governance and strategic decision-making.
- ***12 Habits of Successful SEOs,*** although not part of this series, will inspire you and your team.

– Melbourne, Australia

Chapter 1

SO, WHAT IS SEO?

"Ranking high for outcomes that matter to the website owner" is the aim of SEO. In practical terms, this means ensuring that relevant pages are visible where prospective customers search—whether that visibility appears as a classic link, a rich result, or an AI-mediated answer. Those searches should contribute to business outcomes rather than vanity rankings. You need to anticipate how people express their needs, based on evidence rather than assumptions, and adapt as those patterns change. There are effective and ineffective ways to approach SEO, and success depends on understanding current practices and discarding outdated techniques.

WHAT IS SEO TODAY?

It is essential to keep up with the current consensus on what constitutes search engine optimization and what does not. SEO is no longer limited to ranking pages in a list of links. It now encompasses how content is discovered, interpreted, evaluated, and presented across multiple search surfaces.

At this point in the book, the main components of SEO are:

1. Content (including AI-assisted content)
2. Technical foundations
3. Links and citations
4. Search engine guidelines

Search Engine Guidelines

Search engine guidelines are a critical element of SEO. Major search providers publish these guidelines to describe acceptable practices and quality expectations. While they are necessarily broad and do not disclose ranking formulas, they establish boundaries within which sites must operate to avoid adverse visibility impacts.

Compliance with these guidelines does not guarantee success, but ignoring them increases risk. Note the absence of "keywords" in the illustration below. Keywords still matter as analytical constructs, but they are no longer the primary organizing principle of SEO.

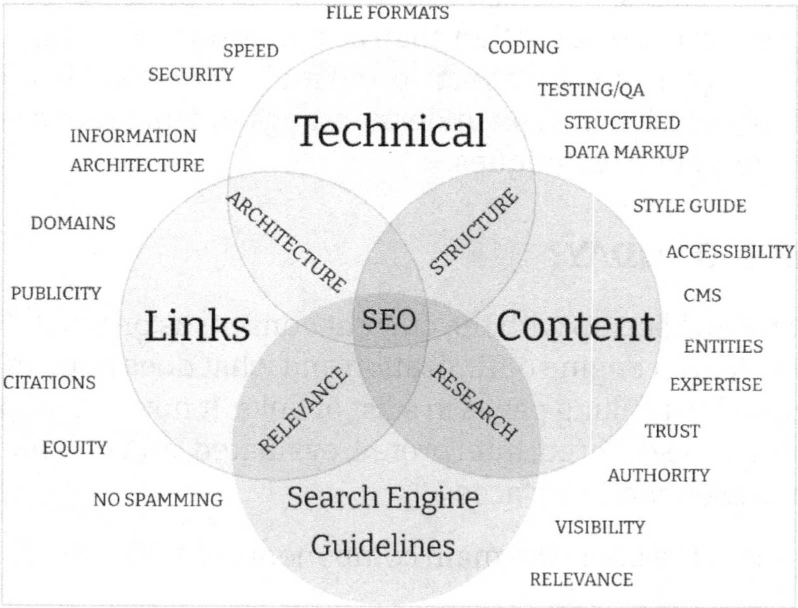

Figure 2. Some components of SEO.

Search engines provide such guidance to web designers, developers, and business owners. Unfortunately, they are broad and sometimes omit specific details because search engines treat them as trade secrets. SEOs make it their business to observe website conversion behavior and second-guess the unwritten rules.

Some key guideline resources include:

- Google Search Central
- Bing Webmaster Guidelines
- Yandex Webmaster

Pillars of SEO?

You may encounter articles that describe the "three pillars of SEO." These models vary because SEO changes over time and because authors emphasize different aspects based on experience. Most frameworks converge on relevance as a central theme.

In this book, SEO is treated as resting on three practical pillars: Technical foundations, Content, and Links. These are not rigid categories, but a way to organize responsibilities and risks. As search systems evolve, additional considerations—such as AI-mediated retrieval—become embedded within these pillars rather than replacing them.

SEO is not an exact science. There is no governing body that arbitrates disputed interpretations, and consensus emerges through shared observation rather than formal agreement. The number and nature of "pillars" change over time, but the need for disciplined interpretation does not.

Figure 3 Which three pillars of SEO?

SOME TERMINOLOGY

Search System

A search system is the complete, end-to-end infrastructure responsible for discovering, storing, evaluating, and presenting information. Google Search and Bing Search are examples.

Algorithm

An algorithm is a specific method or model used within a search system to solve a particular problem. They are used to rank results, assess quality, detect spam, or determine how content is summarized or cited.

PRACTICAL SEO CONTEXT

When SEO practitioners refer to a "Google update," they are usually describing changes to one or more components of the search system. Core updates, for example, involve adjustments to ranking and evaluation systems rather than isolated rules.

From a practical perspective, SEO interacts with the full search system lifecycle:

1. Crawl: The system sends bots to find content.
2. Index: The system stores the content in its database.
3. Rank (Algorithm): The system uses a complex algorithm to decide the order of results.
4. Display: The system presents the results, which now include classic links, image packs, and AI-generated answers.

AI-MEDIATED SEO = GEO

Today, AI-related activities are part of SEO and do not strictly require a new label, although many practitioners use the term Generative Engine Optimization (GEO).

GEO is the practice of optimizing content specifically for **Generative AI search surfaces**—such as Google's AI Overviews (formerly SGE), Perplexity, and ChatGPT—rather than just traditional search engines like Google Search or Microsoft Bing.

While traditional SEO focuses on getting your website to rank at the top of search results, GEO focuses on ensuring your content is cited, summarized, and recommended by AI models when they generate answers for users.

The shift from SEO to GEO is a move from "Ranking" to "Retrieval." I prefer the broad term **"Visibility**."

Be careful of someone who guarantees visibility in AI surfaces. That is a large topic, but suffice it to say that you don't need to pay someone for such a guarantee. Make a mental note of "RAG." We will go deeper into Book 4, "*Is Our SEO Working?*"

AI Crawlers and Large Language Models

SEO visibility now extends to how Large Language Models (LLMs) discover and use your site's content. Crawlers such as GPTBot, OAI-SearchBot, and Anthropic-ClaudeBot behave much like search-engine spiders—but their goal is to feed conversational systems. From time to time, they read billions of websites containing all types of content – text, images, and multimedia.

The llms.txt File

The optional llms.txt file lives in the website's root folder, along with robots.txt and sitemap.xml.

It is mentioned in many industry articles, but managers should note that it is a **proposed standard** for the attention of LLM crawlers that might or might not visit your site. Here is the reality:

- There is no agreed format or canonical vocabulary for its contents. Site owners are relying on the LLM to understand the contents.
- An LLM crawler might not ever visit your site.
- There is no way to summon one for the express purpose of educating it about your offerings.
- There is no need to mirror all website content into corresponding "markdown" (.md) files.

For now, llms.txt implementation should be kept as a short, manual task and does not merit a large investment.

WHAT ISN'T SEO

Unprofessional agencies are either ignorant of outdated SEO techniques or deliberately using them to have something tangible to give the unsuspecting customer. Many of those tasks are a waste of time, and some will contravene the guidance in Google Search Essentials. The customer will cancel after complaining about not receiving any improvements. For the SEO provider, this is a "churn and burn" model, and they don't lose any sleep over it.

Some SEO practitioners are unaware of changes to search engine algorithms and may continue to use tactics that no longer work. Many potential customers are unaware of those changes or how much the provider knows.

Blackmail SEO

Smaller organizations might be victims of "Blackmail SEO," a broad term that can manifest in various ways. However, it is not scalable, so it is usually targeted and carefully planned.

One scenario involves accusing the victim of copyright infringement for an image on their website, but an "easy" way out would be to provide a link to the "owner's" website. The threatening email might come from a website that appears to be a legitimate law firm, and a cursory check might show that the domain has been used for many years. The victim might comply and provide the link, with no further issues on this topic. Such a scam might be perpetrated, say, on a niche industry site that has difficulty getting links from the same industry. Links from the same industry are considered more valuable than links from other industries, so the scammer might be an agency desperate to get its client to rank higher. If you get such an approach, investigate the matter thoroughly before complying with the demand.

Hidden Text

An early SEO trick involved placing hidden text on a page, usually white or near-white text on a white background. Sometimes, it was placed with a negative offset, so it was beyond the screen and would not be seen with a Ctrl+A command. This trick still seems to work (or the page would not have ranked without it), but it is an open invitation for search engines to penalize the page or for a competitor to report it. My reaction to this trick is, "If they had the time to write those words, then why don't they make those words visible?"

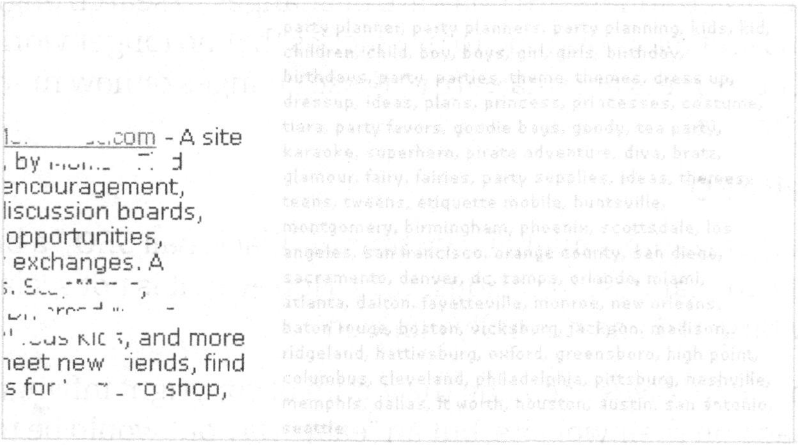

Figure 4 Pale pink text against a white background.

A variation of hidden text is "tiny text" that uses a microscopic font that humans might miss.

Doorway Pages

Google offers three examples of Doorway Pages and advises not to use this tactic:

- Multiple domain names or pages targeted at specific regions or cities that funnel users to one page. Nowadays, Google will ignore such pages and might issue a manual penalty, usually a removal from the index.

- Pages generated to funnel visitors into the actual usable or relevant portion of your site(s).
- Substantially similar pages that are closer to search results than a clearly defined, browsable hierarchy.

Spun Content

A lazy way to create content is to plagiarize a high-ranking page and then put it through an article "spinner," which comes in several grades of sophistication. It consists of using a synonym dictionary, and the search engines can spot them easily.

Artificial Intelligence-Generated Content

Modern tools such as ChatGPT or Copilot can generate very realistic content, but because they rely on existing human knowledge, a search engine might choose to ignore it.

Stuffing Keywords

You might have seen "SEO pages" where the same or similar phrase is used in almost every sentence on the page. It is unlikely to improve the page's ranking.

The Meta Keywords Tag

Any agency that still fills out this long-defunct Meta Keywords tag needs to find a new line of work. Using it won't hurt you, but that time could be better spent on writing content in the body of the page.

Cloaked Pages

A cloaked page would appear in the search engine as "X," but when you clicked this result, it took you to "Y." For example, humans were shown a minimal page, while search engine spiders were shown a text-heavy page with lots of keywords. This stopped working long ago. Some well-known brands were named and shamed and wholly removed from the index until they named their SEO agency and eliminated their bad tactics.

Keyword Density

There was once a notion that keyword density relative to the whole page helped with ranking. It refers to the number of times a phrase or word appears on a page compared to the total number of words on that page. However, pay no attention to keyword density, as Google has said for many years.

Now, search engines use artificial intelligence to understand a page without needing such turgid text. When I worked in insurance, a small page containing nothing but a form ranked on page 1 for a long time.

Footer Links

There was once a belief that placing your keywords at the bottom of the page or making them into links would give you a ranking boost. It no longer works – if it ever did.

Abused Anchor Text

The underlined words on some webpages that are links to another page are the "anchor text." Using a keyword as the anchor text (as opposed to "Click Here") was once a valid ranking trick. It no longer has the same value. There is no harm in using it, but don't have any ranking expectations.

Article Directories

Some low-end agencies still create pages that cover the same topic as the website, but submit them to "article directories." They contain links to the website, but search engines stopped following such links over a decade ago.

Backlinks from .gov and .edu Sites

The theory was that links from government and education sites carried more weight than other sites. In reality, the .edu links were from students making pocket money. Still, the links were disregarded by search engines, and they disappeared when the student graduated, and the account was deleted. The .gov links were from obscure pages where links were available. However, the principle of relevance never went away, even though both .edu and .gov are reputable domains. They won't get you banned or demoted, but don't pay a premium for them.

Content Farms

It's good to have a lot of pages, but not if they are substantially similar to one another because they use slightly different keywords. This is near-duplicate content and will work against all the content, as it cannibalizes itself.

Dedicated IP Address

Low-budget websites are often hosted on shared servers, where the same IP address can host thousands of other websites. In some extreme cases and probably in jurisdictions beyond the reach of the law, such a server might host every kind of nefarious website the law cannot touch. Every website on that address might have been removed from the index.

Domain/Page Authority Links

Someone offering a "High DA/PA" link isn't doing you a favor. Setting aside that these are not Google ranking metrics but are from a third party, the link from a page with a supposed high Page Authority in a foreign language is worthless, unless it is, by coincidence, highly relevant. Moz's DA, Ahrefs' DR, and Semrush's AS are still useful comparative metrics but are also not Google ranking factors—this nuance is now part of most enterprise SEO reporting standards (2024+).

Link Exchange

An early method of obtaining reciprocal links was, "You link to my site, and I'll link to yours." When search engines deprecated this tactic, it was replaced by 3-way links, where you linked to a site and got a link back from a third site. However, this trick could be picked up by search engine algorithms in due course.

Site Submission

Once upon a time, we had to submit our website URL to search engines. There were a few search engines, so it was an actual task. There were thousands of directories, but they were rendered obsolete by search engines. Until that day, one needed to submit URLs. Today, this is a time-wasting practice.

Spammy Links

Some agencies would use a tool to discover pages on any topic in any language that accept comments with no moderation. The tool would drop inane comments such as "Nice post, thanks," with links to the client's website. Such links have long been worthless.

Latent Semantic Indexing

"Latent Semantic Indexing (LSI) keywords" are often seen in the feature list of low-end agencies. LSI tries to understand a human query and returns a result that satisfies it. It requires performing statistical calculations across all the pages on the web, which change millions of times each day. This 30-year-old patent, built for the offline world, is impractical for live search. Google has confirmed repeatedly that there is no such thing as LSI keywords in modern search systems. Google's semantic understanding now comes from transformer-based models (e.g., BERT, MUM, Gemini).

Thin Content

Pages with relatively little content or substantial similarity with other sites are usually not indexed. The search engines call this "thin content." In the early 2000s, many of us built "instant" websites using scripts that replicated the look and feel of catalog websites such as Amazon or eBay. It reached a point where the first 100 results for a product query were the same listing from Amazon and 99 affiliate marketing sites, including mine. Google had enough; overnight, most of the 99 others disappeared from the high ranking.

RANKING

Ranking is the raison d'être of SEO. Ranking refers to the position in a search engine results page (SERP), and the holy grail is to rank #1 or at least appear on the first page for a phrase that converts. Ranking for vanity is pointless.

A position on subsequent pages is considered less valuable for a casual searcher who is happy to choose a result on the first page, but some people will keep looking deeper if they are keen. There's a joke that the best place to hide a dead body is on page 2 of Google results.

Ranking Factors

For over a decade, Google used to say there were "over 200 ranking factors." Some writers would compile a crowd-sourced list of those factors and ask them to rank them in order of importance. Lately, Google has stopped counting them, and it's fair to say there are many more. I have no inside knowledge, but I view a ranking factor as a complex set of rules, where each well-known ranking factor depends on many others.

For example, we know that Google prefers fresh content and dislikes copied content. In theory, a news agency such as Reuters or AP is the first to publish some news item, so you'd expect it to rank #1 for all news searches, yet that is rarely the case. Instead, the powerhouse news publishers usually rank at the top – depending on the user's location – and the wire agency is nowhere to be seen, at least not on the first page.

Another example is well-known to many SEOs. As part of an audit, I identify all images without Alternative Text (Alt attributes, colloquially called "Alt tags") and ask that they be added. This is a mundane task; hence, it is avoided in the first place. Undoubtedly, Alt attributes are essential for Accessibility purposes, but some also believe that they're a Google ranking factor. In all my years of adding them (I also added them to images in this book manuscript), I had never seen a noticeable rise in rankings after adding them.

This book includes the top-ranking factors, so I am not providing a handy list of 200 factors here, as it can be a distraction. Focus on relevance, quality, and the user.

Can SEO Ranking Work for Everyone?

Usually, there are 7 to 9 positions in a SERP (there used to be 10). Even those results are personalized, so two people might see slightly differing results. A hundred or a thousand competing businesses can't appear on page 1, particularly when the results include news, magazine, or reference pages. Google also experiments with continuous scrolling, so there is no "Page 1" in those periods.

So, this is the time to ask, "What is ranking?"

Ranking refers to a keyword's placement in search results. That's an important point. If you don't rank (page 1 is implied) for the most valuable keyword, you will most certainly rank for many others. Let's take the example of the motel industry, where you want to rank for "Orlando motel." If you don't rank for that phrase, you might want to optimize your page for applicable alternatives, such as:

- Orlando motel near Disney

- Orlando motel near Universal
- Orlando motel near airport
- (Brand name) motel in Orlando
- Orlando motel with a gym

Ranking Outside the Box (Long-tail SEO)

Long-tail keywords are the Plan B. They are obscure search terms that few people use, and few websites use language that will surface them. Your business might be able to use this tactic without abandoning the primary keywords. Examples include:

- Winter Park, FL (a suburb near Disney)
- Six-bed motel room in Orlando (to attract large groups, say, if three adjoining rooms can be joined)
- Orlando motel near (name of a specific restaurant)

SEO HATS

You might have heard the expressions that place SEO into three tactical categories, known as "hats."

Black Hat SEO

A simple way to think of Black Hat SEO is tactics that violate Google or Bing webmaster guidelines and could result in a manual penalty, potentially leading to removal from the search engine index.

Gray Hat SEO

Gray Hat SEO is a hazy term used by individuals to describe their working style. It might include some borderline tactics that Google explicitly bans but does not enforce.

White Hat SEO

White Hat SEO is what all responsible organizations will want to perform. They include strict adherence to the guidelines of all relevant search engines.

TYPES OF SEO ACTIVITIES

One could forgive business leaders for thinking of SEO as a tick on a checklist, something best delegated or outsourced. I have seen a leading bank's high rankings decline after eliminating its in-house SEO team and outsourcing the task to an agency. Are you outsourcing your SEO to an agency? Do you know the revenue impact of that step? It might improve or it might not, but it is worth conducting some due diligence. It's also worth reviewing the range of SEO tasks and deciding which can be outsourced.

SEO Audits

Any website assessment for its search engine friendliness begins with an SEO audit. An initial audit of a large site may take weeks, with deeper analysis continuing iteratively as issues are uncovered. An audit is not merely running a tool against the website and concluding from those findings. It includes observing workflows and blockers. After initial remediation, auditing shifts toward continuous monitoring rather than discrete review cycles.

Monitoring, Analysis, and Reporting

You cannot improve something if you cannot measure it. Websites can generate a lot of data, so the challenge is looking at the right data set and learning from it. Large companies might have a team to manage website analytics, while a small organization might ask the SEO person to do it. Regular reporting should cover visibility, technical health, and outcomes such as conversions.

Visibility as Governance

Treat visibility discussions as part of governance reviews, not marketing updates. Encourage your leadership to include SEO and AI-mediated visibility indicators in quarterly digital-risk meetings. When senior executives see visibility as infrastructure, funding and accountability naturally follow.

Business-As-Usual SEO

The SEO team's daily routine involves "business-as-usual" (BAU) activity. New pages are added, and defunct pages are removed. Additionally, there are numerous meetings where the SEO operative needs to be involved, lest decisions be taken that undermine visibility or technical integrity.

ELEVATING THE TEAM TO AGENTIC SEO

As an SEO manager, your primary value lies in **vision and strategy**, not in task execution.

The transition to **Agentic SEO** is the key to reducing drudgery. You are not replacing your specialists, but are equipping them with AI-assisted agents that automate well-defined tasks under human oversight.

The Pain Point: Repetitive Tasks

Your team members often face essential but tedious tasks. This time could be better spent on, for example, reading SEO news:

- **Content Specialist:** Spending hours manually checking aging high-traffic blog posts for outdated statistics, broken links, or expired product mentions, rather than developing cornerstone content.
- **Technical SEO Analyst:** Running weekly crawls to identify new errors, status code anomalies, or orphaned pages, rather than

engineering a site-wide migration or complex schema implementation.

- **Link Builder/Analyst:** Reviewing hundreds of newly published articles and manually going back into 10-20 relevant older posts to insert necessary internal links, rather than developing high-value external outreach strategies.

The Agentic Solution: Deploying Google Gem for the Team

Consider a conceptual internal AI platform (for example, a 'Gem'-style agent framework). Each team member defines the objective for their dedicated agent, and the agent executes it autonomously in multiple steps. The SEO team lead checks all agents for accuracy.

A Gem is a collection of prompts to perform all the steps of the SEO tasks in this example. Gem supports the project by integrating diagnostics, drafting changes, and surfacing actions for controlled execution. It provides the team member with precise data and project completion reports, allowing them to see the impact of their agent's work instantly.

Note that Gem is still in an **experimental** stage and needs human oversight. It may be possible later to let it run in autonomous mode, such as a daily task at a fixed time.

Example Gem

Gem, initiate an Alt Tag Remediation Project.

1. Crawl & Diagnose: Perform a full deep crawl of the entire domain and identify all <img> elements where the 'alt' attribute is either missing or empty (alt="“).
2. Contextual Analysis: For each missing alt tag, analyze the immediate page content (H1s, surrounding paragraph text, and figure captions) and the image's source file name to determine its context and primary subject.

3. Alt Tag Generation: Using a maximum length of 125 characters, generate a descriptive and contextually relevant alt tag that adheres to accessibility best practices (describes the image, avoids keyword stuffing).
4. Implementation: Once all alt tags are generated, execute the change directly within the CMS via API integration. Implement a roll-out limit of 1,000 tags per hour to avoid overloading the system.
5. Reporting: After implementation, run a final verification crawl to confirm the new alt tags are live. Provide a final summary report detailing the total number of images updated and the overall crawl health score change.

Guardrail: Exclude all logo files and social icons whose file names contain 'logo' or 'icon' from the generation step.

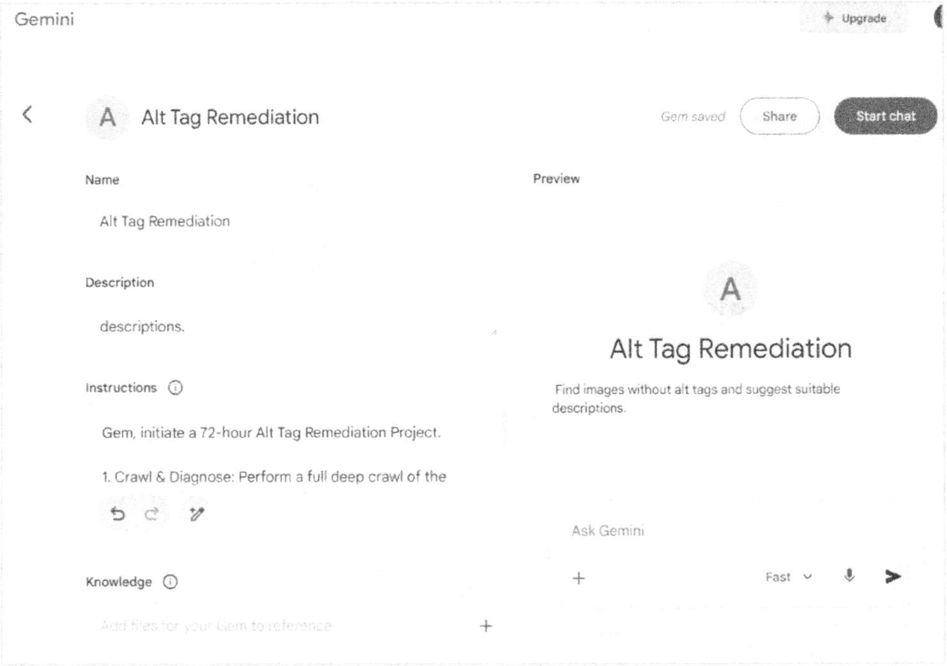

Figure 5 Google Gem is designed to find labels for Alt tags.

Your New Managerial Mandate: Strategy and Oversight

As the manager, your expertise is elevated. You reduce manual checking of routine tasks and focus on validating outcomes.

Your focus shifts entirely to:

1. **Defining the Strategic Horizon:** You set the overarching organizational SEO goals and interpret complex data to pivot the entire team's direction.
2. **Team Enablement:** You ensure your team members are effectively using their agents, validating that the high-level projects they now undertake (e.g., core site migrations, advanced content architecture) align with your vision.
3. **Creative and Ethical Governance:** You oversee the agent's actions for compliance, ethical soundness, and brand consistency, ensuring human accountability and quality standards aligned with E-E-A-T remain paramount.

SEO STRATEGY

SEO strategy is often confused with planning documents; real strategy emerges through alignment, prioritization, and execution.

Real SEO Strategy

A real SEO strategy must begin in the C-Suite boardroom and involve active input from SEO experts. The board needs to share its vision, both short-term and long-term. The SEO team should know who the board considers competitors, as they might not be the ones identified by SEO tools.

This long-term SEO strategy can only be documented at a high level and should span several years.

Implementing Strategy

The SEO Strategic Plan must be implemented within a timeline to deliver the expected sales figures. In addition to the BAU tasks, there might be an overarching business strategy for the year to deliver, as well as any housekeeping tasks to address issues identified in a site audit.

Implementing the Tasks

Other people in the company or by external providers must complete many SEO tasks. Therefore, the SEO team must supervise those tasks to the organization's satisfaction.

TYPES OF SEO PRACTITIONERS

There are no definitions of types of SEOs, but here are some I can identify. Of course, some people will be a blend of these.

Solo SEOs

Solo entrepreneurs work for themselves. They optimize their personal websites that might sell products or services, be they affiliate links or actual products.

Self-Employed SEOs

Self-employed SEOs are like any other business person who wants to work alone for clients on a contractual basis. They might or might not have staff, or they might subcontract.

Employee SEOs

An employee SEO works for an employer for a salary. They are called In-House SEOs.

EARNED MEDIA, OWNED MEDIA, PAID MEDIA, SHARED MEDIA

An excellent way to summarize what we will cover in this book is to examine the digital marketing landscape and identify where SEO fits. You can break it down into four areas:

- **Owned Media** – Assets we own and control, such as the website and syndicated content on other platforms.
- **Earned Media** – We earn exposure from our publicity efforts and reviews. This is also known as Leveraged Media
- **Shared Media** – Our proactive content on social media platforms includes user-generated content. Search engines are in this category. It is also known as Managed Media.
- **Paid Media** – Our ads and sponsored content, which we pay for to appear on other platforms. This has little to no impact on search rankings.

SEO lives in the first two areas – there's no doubt about Owned Media because we optimize our assets, but it can be argued that some aspects of Earned Media are the result of SEO. For example, getting links through outreach, write-ups, or citations in news media could be part of SEO. Working with our social media team could lead to blog mentions and links. Search engines are outside SEO control because their ranking and inclusion algorithms are a secret. Good SEO governance is the magic glue that binds it all together.

SEO IN THE MARKETING FUNNEL

Beyond technical tactics, SEO plays a critical role throughout the marketing conversion funnel, helping marketing teams turn awareness into revenue.

The Marketing Conversion Funnel

All businesses use a model resembling a conversion funnel with three divisions:

- Top of Funnel (ToFu) – Awareness stage
- Middle of Funnel (MoFu) – Consideration stage
- Bottom of Funnel (BoFu) – Decision stage

Although the marketing team owns the funnel, the SEO function plays a major role in driving qualified leads to the content across all three funnel stages.

SEO and ToFu	The SEO team can guide content creators on using the best keywords for textual web and PDF content, as well as for video and audio podcasts.
SEO and MoFu	Optimizing calculators, reviews. And case studies are examples of content that can push leads toward conversion.
SEO and BoFu	Special tagging of offers and pricing is one of many SEO techniques available.

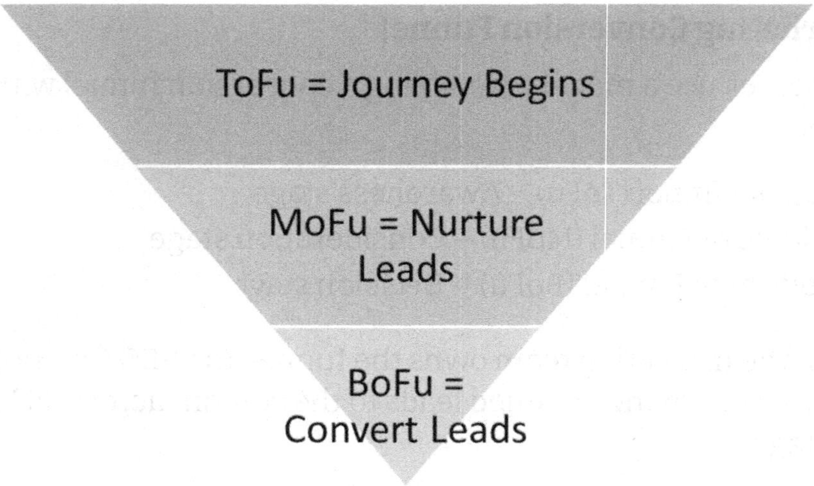

Figure 6 Customer Conversion Funnel.

Given the nature of search engine visitors, not all of them go through the three stages of your funnel. Many will have done their research elsewhere and land in the middle or bottom of the funnel.

Search Marketing

Many SEOs agree that SEO is part of Search Marketing. I think of myself as a search marketer, yet I have never worked as an SEO in a marketing team. One reason for that could be that traditional marketers who have done a Marketing degree have no training in HTML markup, PHP, Java, .NET, CSS, JavaScript, and web servers, so they think it isn't their domain. Technical SEOs speak that language and can feel they don't belong in Marketing.

A Hybrid Specialization

SEO, therefore, is best called a hybrid specialization, which makes it an unwanted orphan. As seen in the replies to my question above, it's a lottery where SEO ends up in a given organization.

Looking Ahead: AI and Governance

SEO practitioners are increasingly aware of how artificial intelligence can both support and disrupt their objectives. Generative AI tools are now producing text and images at scale, influencing content strategies and governance priorities. While Google does not object to AI-generated content as long as it's useful, its rise underscores the need for well-defined governance structures. SEO teams, already familiar with the realities of website management, are well-positioned to contribute to broader governance discussions — including AI and website governance, which are explored in more depth in Book 3, *AI Visibility Playbook*.

FREQUENTLY NEEDED RESOURCES FOR YOUR TEAM

Before we get into the practical aspects of SEO, here is a list of essential tools, platforms, and resources that your team will use regularly. Bookmark or maintain your own updated version of this list, as URLs and product names may change over time.

Official Platforms and Dashboards

- Bing Webmaster Tools
- Google Search Console
- Google Search Central
- Google Ads Keyword Planner
- Google Analytics (GA4)
- Google Looker Studio
- Google Trends
- Google Business Profile
- Google Structured Data Testing Tool
- Google PageSpeed Insights
- Google Developers
- Google Web Vitals

Chapter 2

SEO ESSENTIALS

Perhaps you're an accidental manager of the SEO function in your organization and are trying to make sense of this profession. Let's go over the basics quickly by looking at the larger picture.

"Big picture SEO" addresses the entire e-commerce ecosystem, not just high-value keywords or rankings. All enterprises, large or small, want to maximize earnings (or an equivalent non-monetary goal).

In practice, this is manifested every quarter as an emphasis on new business acquisition, followed by customer retention. At the same time, the rest of the company needs to do "what it takes" to keep money coming in. So, at this point in the book, ask yourself if the SEO team is notified of the new sales targets and is asked, "What resources do you need to help the company reach this target?"

I thought so.

While SEO in a traditional (bricks-and-mortar plus online) business can bring in a substantial share of new online business, it rarely gets funded as well as pay-per-click (PPC) search. For example, in one company, SEO costs 1/20th of the PPC advertising budget and drives 30 to 35 percent of online confirmed sales, while PPC drives 40 percent.

Why? Marketing has a seat at the senior leadership table; SEO does not. I will cover that later, hoping that this book will help change that state of affairs. There's also a perception that PPC works "instantly," while SEO can take a long time to work, or it might not work at all.

WEBSITES AND WEBPAGES

Let's begin with the core assets of concern to organizations and the SEO profession. A website is a collection of web pages (Google sometimes spells it as "webpages") organized to suit its purpose. The underlying technology is beyond the scope of this book. However, it's important to know that a "web server" serves pages to users and that there are several types of web servers, depending on the software stack and configuration. As an extreme example, your laptop computer could be a web server (but please don't do that).

Webpages consist of ingredients that can live in different containers on the server. For example, the text might live within a Content Management System (CMS), which is a special-purpose database similar to a word processor. The images and code are in folders – we let the technical teams look after the details. The CMS displays webpages differently depending on the user's browser – whether on a mobile phone, a tablet, or a desktop/laptop computer. More precisely, the device at the user's end formats them differently.

Using the analogy of a restaurant meal that is plated differently for a take-out customer, a web page is "plated" differently if the viewport (window) is very narrow on the phone, so that a multi-column table might be displayed as successive rows on the phone.

URL

A Uniform Resource Locator (URL) is simply the address of a page on the World Wide Web (WWW). It specifies where the page can be found and how to open it (e.g., the protocol, such as https). A URL might include a parameter at the end.

URL example = https://www.example.com/index.html

Reputation of Author, Site, and Page

In its *Search Quality Evaluator Guidelines,* Google uses the word "reputation" to describe the whole website, webpage, and author.

Later, we will discuss experience, expertise, authoritativeness, and trustworthiness (EEAT). These abstract concepts are easy to understand, but do not have numeric values that Google shares. Third-party tools try to assign proprietary numeric scores, such as "domain authority" and "page authority," but use them with care and a pinch of salt.

WEBMASTER

In the early days of the web, a single person would design, build, and maintain the website. They were known as a webmaster, which is now a dated job title. As websites became complex, additional people were added to the web(site) team. Nowadays, the web team is sometimes hard to locate, as its functions are spread across groups with less obvious names, such as Product, DevOps, Network Security, Data Analytics, Testing, etc. They could be scattered over floors, cities, or countries. Today, the job title of Webmaster is often found in small companies, where one person handles all website work.

PURPOSE OF A WEBSITE

While built for many purposes, websites are the same as a retail outlet's front door or counter – an environment designed to engage with its audience. Here are some examples:

- To give answers, such as search engines, encyclopedias;
- To entertain, such as music, gaming, and video services;
- To provide storage, such as document repositories, archives, and personal files;

- To provide a social platform for personal expression, such as blogs, Twitter, Facebook, or Instagram;
- As a transactional platform for e-commerce, such as eBay, Amazon, stock trading, and other kinds of buying and selling; and
- As a corporate or organizational presence to enable it to perform its operations and inform its audience.

SEARCH ENGINES

These days, a small handful of search engines matter for SEO purposes. In the English-speaking context, that is Google, followed by Bing; in South Korea, it is Naver; in Russia, it is Yandex; and in China, it is Baidu. They discover new web pages and websites by following links on known sites, but they can also be pointed to brand-new content that lacks links. Therefore, I will only describe a few high-level concepts you need to understand about search engines.

Figure 7 Four stages of a search result.

Discovery

A search engine first needs to become aware of a website, that is, "discover" it before it can index it. If you "build it," the search engines might not necessarily come. They will come eventually, but why not make it as early as possible? This discovery might come from a link on another website or through a file called sitemap.xml that you submit to the search engine.

Like scanning a new department store, when you enter, you need to find the section you are interested in. The search engine needs to "look around" to get the lay of the land and note the location of the main departments.

Crawling

The search engine next sends a spider or robot to visit a discovered webpage and explore one or more pages. It might follow links to external websites and find one it has not known of before. It will revisit as often as it determines necessary. It notes anything that has broken or has changed in a database. The spider has a limited crawl budget for your site, so use it wisely.

Search engines have cute names for their spiders. Some are:

- Googlebot – Google Search
- Googlebot-News – Google News
- Googlebot-Image – Google Images
- Bingbot – powers Bing and Yahoo results in many markets
- DuckDuckBot – DuckDuckGo Search
- Baiduspider – Baidu Search (Chinese)
- Yandexbot – Yandex Search (Russian)

You can also deny crawlers from all parts of your website or a specific part with a file called robots.txt. Unfortunately, there are also "bad" bots that, at best, waste your bandwidth and, at worst, copy your content or are otherwise of no benefit. You can try to block them, but there is no guarantee they will obey robots.txt.

An example of blocking crawlers is for your "action URLs" such as "Add to cart," "Go to cart," "Add to wish list," and so on. Those pages are not useful for the search index and will be ignored, anyway.

If the website content seldom changes, the crawlers will visit less frequently. If the content is judged to be of low quality, the page might be crawled but not indexed, or it might lose visibility over time. Avoid changing file names unless absolutely unavoidable because Googlebot might not pick them up immediately. Images, in particular, are revisited infrequently.

Google primarily uses mobile-first crawling and indexing. If a site is inaccessible to mobile Googlebot, indexing and visibility can be severely limited, even if a desktop version exists. A site that is merely search-unfriendly to mobile browsers will not affect indexing.

Rendering

Rendering is a process of "assembling" web pages to make their final appearance. The web server fetches text, data, images, media, style sheets, JavaScript code, and other resources to render a page. This is a technical topic, and at this point in the book, we note that we should make this process easy for search engines so they can see exactly what our users see.

Indexing

The Uniform Resource Locator (URL) of a page and its filtered components are stored in the search engine's index, ready to be returned when a searcher submits a query. If a crawled page is not admitted into the index, it might as well not exist. Many large companies can find themselves in this predicament, so attention to SEO principles is required.

Retrieval (Serving)

When someone queries a search engine, the URL is retrieved from the index and displayed ("served") on a Search Engine Results Page (SERP). The concept of Relevancy is quite important here. The algorithms find the most relevant pages and order them in descending order of relevance, within a results layout that varies by query, device, and result features.

Today, this interpretation increasingly includes AI-generated summaries and blended result formats, not just ranked links."

Log File Analysis for Visibility Diagnostics

In addition to tools such as Google Search Console and crawl simulators, **server log files** provide the only definitive record of how search engine crawlers actually interact with a site. Log files show which URLs are requested, how frequently they are accessed, and what response codes are returned. This makes them particularly useful for investigating crawl prioritization, wasted crawl activity, or pages that are technically available but rarely or never fetched by search engines.

For large enterprise websites, however, log file analysis must be used selectively. High-traffic sites can generate enormous volumes of log data, making continuous collection, storage, and analysis costly and operationally complex. In practice, log files are best generated **periodically or for specific investigations**, such as after a major site migration, platform change, or when unexplained indexing or visibility issues arise. Used this way, log analysis becomes a targeted diagnostic tool rather than an ongoing reporting dependency.

GOOGLE KNOWLEDGE GRAPH

In 2012, Google introduced the concept of a Knowledge Graph and the phrase "things, not strings." It is a collection of knowledge about objects and their relationships. It enables Google to show related information that should help the searcher, and it also contributes to entity understanding that can influence features such as knowledge panels and related-question modules. This was not previously possible with keywords.

If I search for "George Washington," I get a "People also search for" panel showing the early Presidents and Martha Washington.

Figure 8 A search for George Washington.

If I search for “Barack Obama,” I get a “People also search for” panel showing Bruce Springsteen, Michelle Obama, Joe Biden, and Donald Trump.

If I search for “Donald Trump,” I get a “People also search for” panel showing Joe Biden, Donald Trump Jr., Melania Trump, and Barack Obama.

The Knowledge Graph also powers the Knowledge Panel on the right of a desktop SERP.

Most search engines offer “Instant Answers,” which might work for some websites but not others. As the name suggests, the searcher gets their answer in the SERP without having to click on any result. However, if the user does not click through to the website, then a conversion opportunity might be lost.

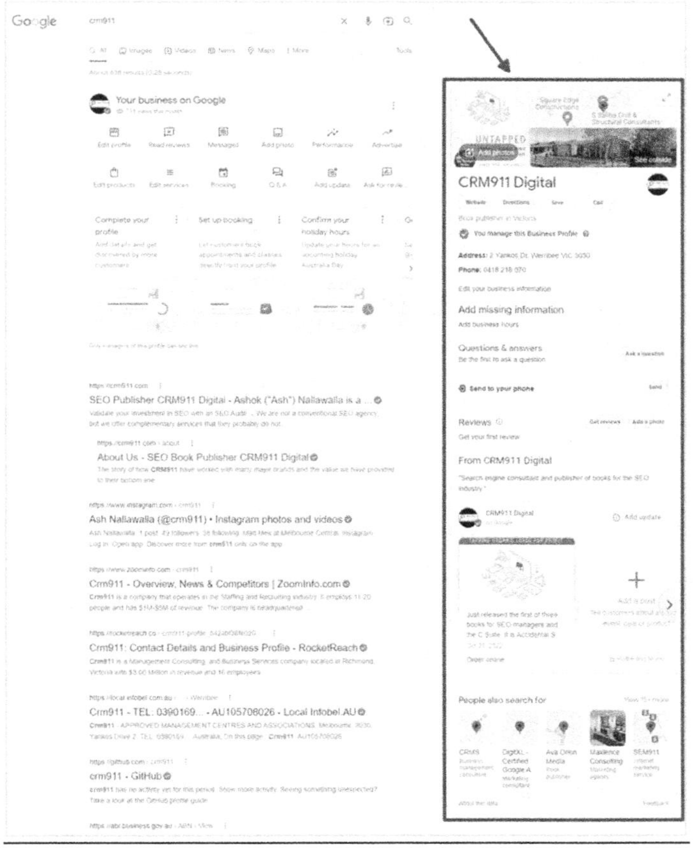

Figure 9 Google Business Profile for this book's publisher.

RESULTS

The relevant results presented on the SERP are ranked according to a best-fit basis, as determined by proprietary ranking systems. Nowadays, two people might not see the same sequence of URLs for the same query, depending on prior search history, location, and other factors.

The major search engines offer a customized version in many countries, and users are taken to their national version by default. They are shown results from their country before those from another country. This improves the user experience – someone in New Zealand who sees a phone priced in Dollars might not realize they are looking at US or Canadian Dollars on a major online retailer. Thus, when two results are equally relevant but are from two countries, the page geographically closest to the user will be shown first.

Figure 10 A Search Engine Results Page (SERP)

Your goal is for your pages to appear on the first page of search results and rank higher than your competitors. We shall see later that such competitors are not necessarily your business competitors.

ENTITIES, NOT KEYWORDS

According to a Google patent, US20160371385A1 (Google, 2019), an entity is a thing or concept that is singular, unique, well-defined, and distinguishable. For example, an entity may be a person, place, item, idea, abstract concept, concrete element, other suitable thing, or any combination thereof.

Entities

Let's say an entity is a "concept" that one might search for. New York City is also known as:

- The Big Apple

- Manhattan
- NYC
- Metropolis
- The Five Boroughs
- (There are at least 20 other labels)

You will get pages about that concept if you search by any of those labels.

Many searches relate to such an entity or entities. Sometimes the presence of one near another creates a connotation that can make the page more relevant to a query. For example, the concepts of "home" and "insurance" in proximity (such as the phrase "home insurance") make the content more likely to be about home insurance than a page about insurance that mentions several concepts, such as car, health, home, boat, etc. That page might be a category page that leads to detailed pages about car insurance, health insurance, home insurance, boat insurance, etc.

A good example of how Google finds an entity is to search for the names of three actors. If you search their names individually, you get their knowledge panels. If you search for two of the names together, you will get the name of the movie if they worked together. Perhaps they worked on two movies, and Google might show both. If you search for all three names together, Google will narrow it down further. In each case, you did not search for the movie's name, which is the entity consisting of all three actors.

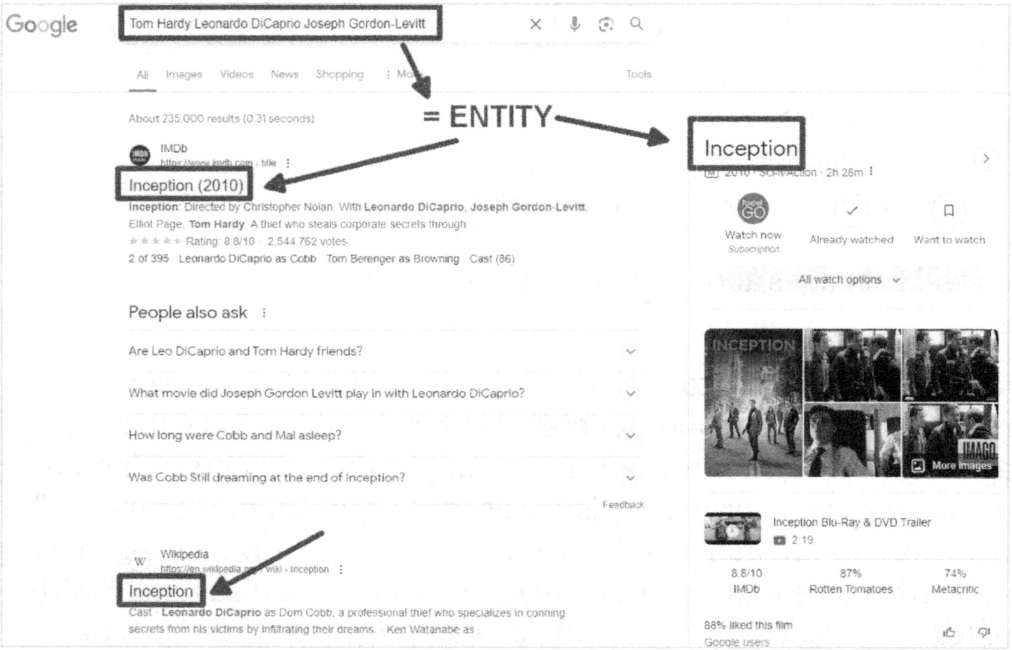

Figure 11 An example of Google finding an entity.

In the context of Google, an entity has an ID in the Knowledge Graph (covered later), so this is an exact meaning.

Keywords

Keywords are the words and phrases that (we think) searchers enter into a search system. Although the term "keyword" suggests a single word, in the search engine context, it can be several words; thus, some people use the term "keyphrase" to mean the same thing.

Although we have long talked about "keywords," nowadays, it makes more sense to think of the entities they represent rather than their literal interpretations. A "home insurance" entity could well consist of 20 to 100 individual keywords, but we might have just a handful of pages covering that entity. We can use a few of those keywords to populate those pages.

Another benefit of an entity is that it can help convey meaning across languages. As Google improves, it can provide more accurate answers based on entities, though results still vary by language, locale, and available sources.

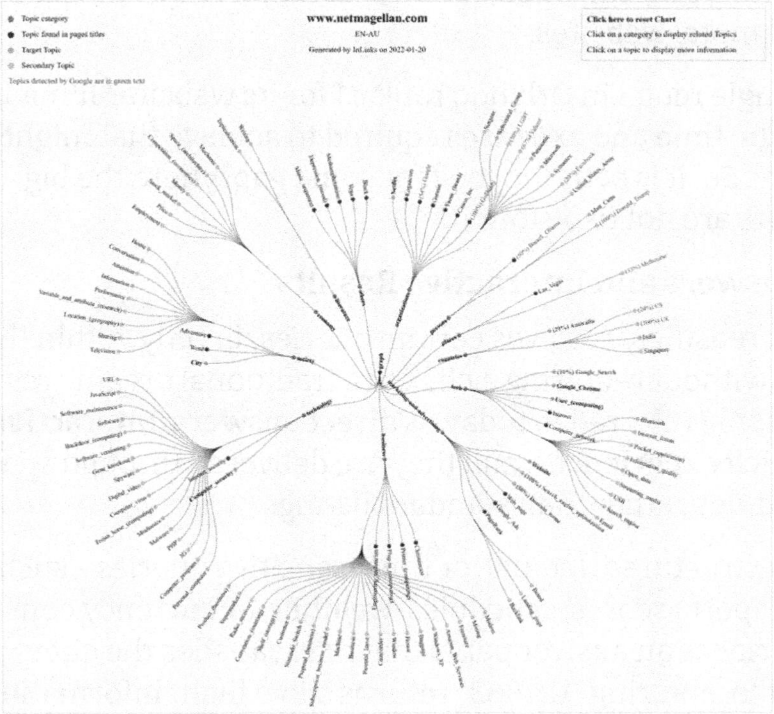

Figure 12 A topic wheel of my blog generated by Inlinks.

ANSWERING QUERIES

How a search engine analyzes a page needs to be understood by those who want their pages to be selected for display on "page 1." Perhaps there are a few hundred motels in a tourist city such as Orlando, Florida, and all of them would love to rank for "Orlando motels" on page 1, or even in position 1. That's not possible for a typical results layout, especially when large aggregators dominate the most visible placements. At the time of writing, not one of them is a motel website –

almost all are aggregator booking sites. That is because Google's algorithms process user intent – people want to find accommodation, usually at a reasonable price and close to attractions. Aggregator sites compare hundreds of hotels and motels and let users choose based on many criteria, offering information that might not be available on individual motel websites.

Could a single motel in Orlando rank #1 for its website? It might not be easy, but the time and expense required to achieve that might make it prohibitive. So, it is better to look for some gap where the big aggregators are not to be found.

Direct Answers and Interactive Results

Google increasingly resolves certain queries directly within the search interface, without requiring a click to a traditional organic result. These are commonly referred to today as **direct answers**, **interactive results**, or **zero-click experiences**, and they are delivered through specialized result modules rather than standard listings.

For highly structured, factual, or time-sensitive queries—such as flight numbers, sports scores, schedules, weather, or currency conversions—Google surfaces an answer panel that fully satisfies the query intent. For example, entering "UA863" returns a live flight information module that shows departure time, elapsed flight time, arrival status, and related details. In this case, the user's task is completed entirely on the results page, and no website visit is required.

Similarly, navigational and location-based queries often trigger **map-based results**. A search such as "Brentwood, Los Angeles, CA to Rosecrans Avenue, Manhattan Beach" produces an interactive map with driving directions, estimated travel time, and route options displayed prominently at the top of the page. If geographic ambiguity exists—such as multiple locations sharing the same name—Google resolves intent using contextual signals (or prompts for clarification) while still presenting the result as a map module rather than a list of links.

These experiences are not anomalies; they reflect Google's broader shift toward **task completion within the search interface**. For SEO managers, the implication is clear: visibility is no longer limited to ranking blue links. Search performance must be evaluated in terms of **eligibility for inclusion in answer-driven and interactive result formats**, many of which deliver value without generating a click.

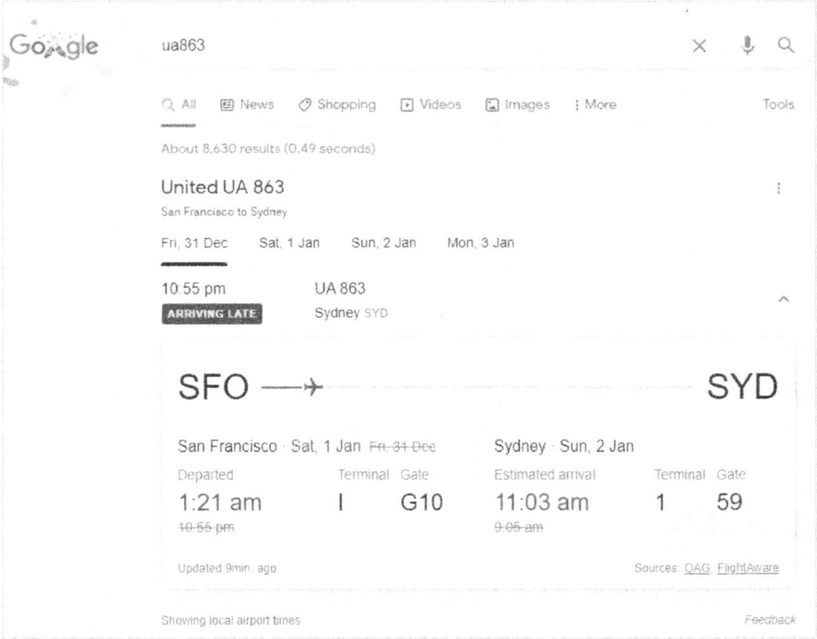

Figure 13 A direct result is shown for a flight number.

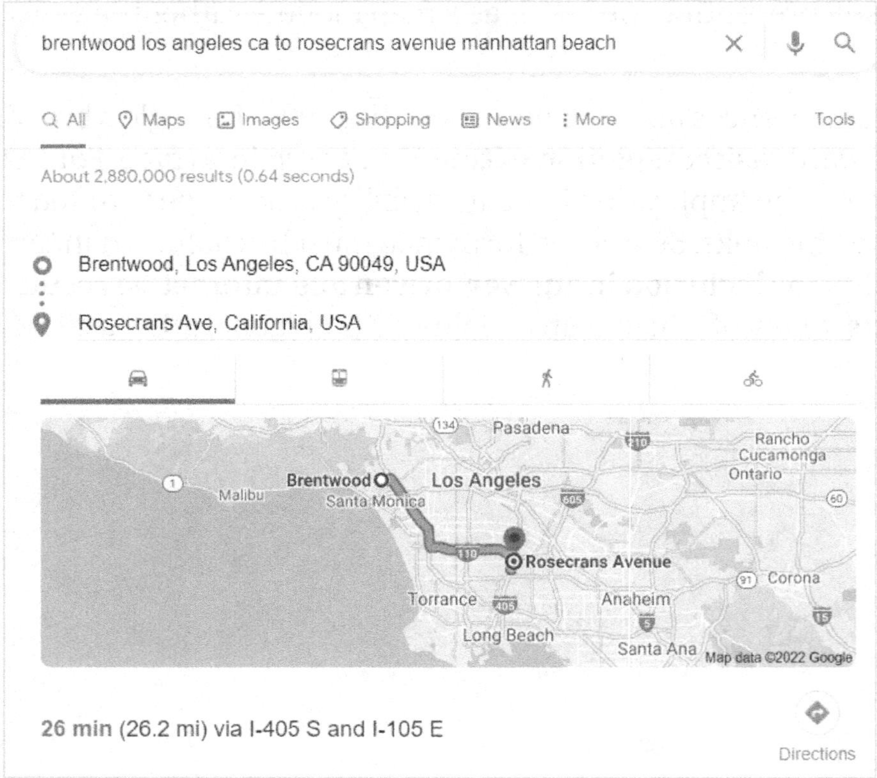

Figure 14 A map snippet is displayed when the query requests driving directions.

SEARCH INTENT

In simple words, search intent conveys to the search engine what the searcher might be looking to see in the search results and ultimately in the pages they visit. This drives search engines to fine-tune their understanding of the words searchers use, so the best webpages are presented on the first page of the SERP.

When a user types a search query, their choice of words can make all the difference between useful and useless results. The search engine algorithm needs to determine the user's "search intent." The verb in the query is important. Consider the following searches.

Query	**Typical Google Search Results**
Camera	• Camera manufacturers and retailers (100%) • Popular Products (sponsored) • Deals on Cameras (sponsored) • Videos • People Also Ask • People Also Search For • Ads
What is a camera?	• AI Mode • AI Overview • Wikipedia and other definition sites • No ads • People also ask (inset) • Videos • People Also Search For
What is a DSLR camera?	• AI Mode • AI Overview • What is a DSLR (100%) • Videos • People also ask (inset) • Research what a DSLR camera (inset) • People Also Search For

As you can see, some brands sell products that are vastly unrelated, so the search intent needs to be very precise. For optimal results, a web page needs content that matches a specific user intent.

TYPES OF SEARCH INTENT

Most people agree on four types of search intent, but there can be as many types as apply to a niche. Let us stick to four types:

- Navigational intent
- Informational intent
- Commercial (Investigation) intent
- Transactional intent

Navigational Searches

Many of us type a few words of an otherwise longer URL to save time, e.g., a partial company name, hoping that the search results will present a clickable link. This is a navigational search. It is eagerly counted as an organic search visit by people who monitor website traffic, but a branded visit is a triumph of the company's brand rather than the SEO's skill.

Many people search for "Google" on Google—often to avoid typing a full URL.

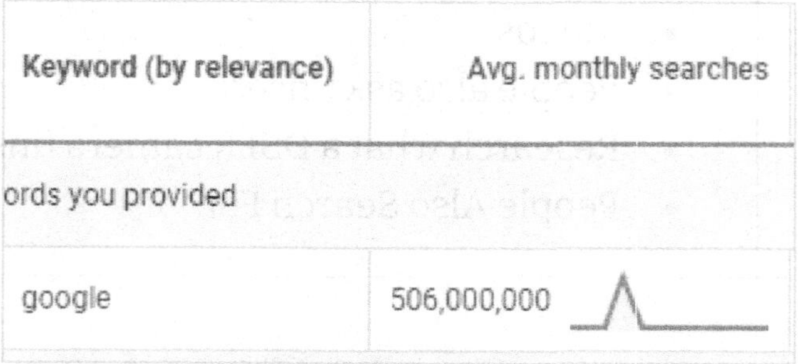

Keyword (by relevance)	Avg. monthly searches
ords you provided	
google	506,000,000

Figure 15 Google search for Google on Google.

Some searches are beyond the search engine's ability to guess, so it offers alternatives.

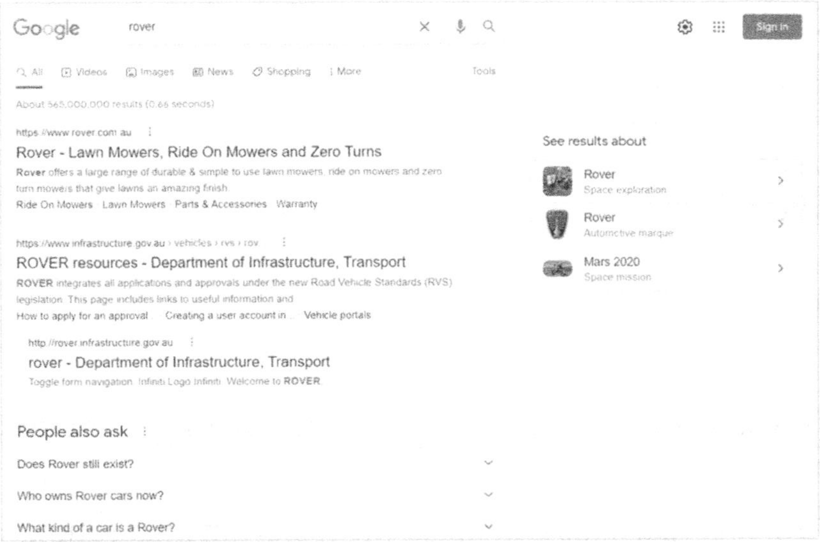

Figure 16 Example of an unfocused search – "rover".

Informational Searches

I once had a manager who warned me about time wasters (on the phone), whom he called "eager seekers of knowledge." Much later, Anthony Parinello, in his book *Selling to VITO*, warned us about the "Seymour" (who always wants to see more) in a prospect company who gathers information but is not a decision maker. Many casual information seekers conduct informational searches. These searches might lead to a transaction sometime in the future, or there might be no transaction at all. However, a website is perfect for the Seymours out there.

My sincere apologies to anyone named Seymour, because many potential buyers are also researching thoroughly before transacting. A website that provides detailed information signals trust. Omitting some details might add to the workload of customer service agents. Their search terms usually begin (or end) with:

- What
- Why
- Where
- When
- Who
- How
- Best
- Reviews

Many of these searches can be served with more than one type of content:

- How-tos – perhaps enhanced with relevant illustrations or videos
- Frequently asked questions (FAQs)
- Descriptive text of any kind
- Information about products or services
- Tabular text
- Essays
- Reviews
- Still images
- Videos

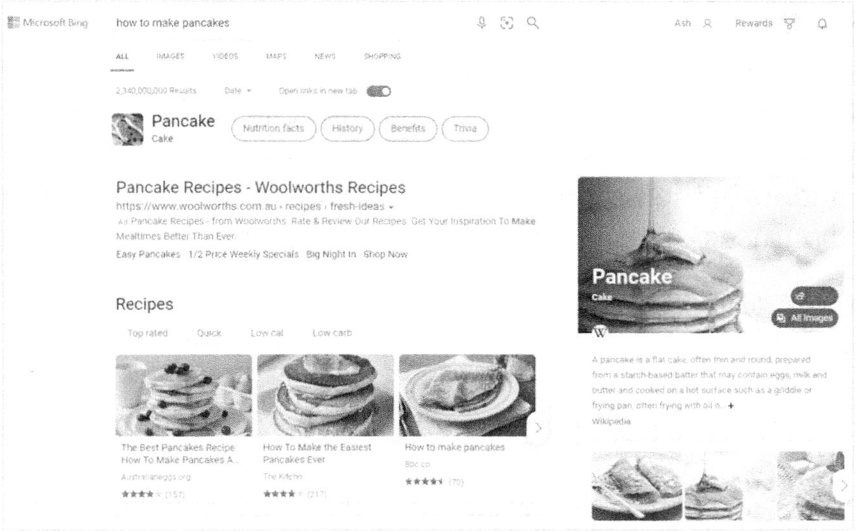

Figure 17 An informational query for a recipe.

Commercial/Investigation Searches

A searcher who started with broad queries might have narrowed it down to a few options and might look for comparisons, including price searches to ensure they are within budget.

Commercial searches can be served with detailed information about products and services, even if no transaction is anticipated.

Google compare gift cards

Discounted eGift Cards - OzBargain Wiki

Store	AGL Rewards	Blatchys Blues	Cash- rewards	Lumo Rewards
Accor Hotels	-	10%	3%#	-
Adrenaline	-	6%	-	14%
Amart	5%	-	-	-

View 174 more rows

Figure 18 A comparison table can help you appear at the top of search results.

Transactional Searches

Once the searcher is ready to transact (not necessarily monetary – it might only be the filling of a form), the searches will be transactional. These could be names of e-commerce portals in the query, perhaps retail outlets in their city or near them; they might include transaction-related phrases, such as "price," "near me," "application form," etc.

Such queries can be served by providing exactly the pages the seeker anticipates.

SEARCH INTENT OPTIMIZATION

We should also consider search intent from the website owner's perspective and optimize content to achieve the best outcome.

Search Intent Optimization (SIO) is the set of actions you take to ensure your content aligns with searchers' intent. For example, if you notice a low clicks-to-impressions ratio in your analytics dashboard, it might be worth looking deeper to check how many of those clicks result in a conversion. If they aren't converting sufficiently, your content might attract the wrong intent.

We can look at examples of words in search queries and the possible intent labels for each. Those words also give clues about the customer journey through the marketing funnel. If we are selling a product or service, we need to ensure that we have pages that address each step in the customer journey.

Sometimes there is mixed intent: a query might be informational but also transactional if the page satisfies their need. Such a page should be optimized for the transactional value.

Ambiguous intent cannot be addressed reliably. A user searching for "jaguar" might be looking for a radio software brand, a car brand, or an animal. Google is likely to show a sample from all possible interpretations.

WHAT HAPPENS AT THE SEARCH ENGINE?

As time goes on, speaking specifically about Google, we have to think less about specific keywords on our pages in large quantities and more about search intent. Google's systems are increasingly good at matching intent and meaning, not just keywords. " There are instances of a high-ranking page that does not contain the keyword at all.

Here are some well-known algorithms, otherwise known as "ranking systems":

RankBrain

RankBrain helped Google better interpret unfamiliar queries and match them to relevant results.

Neural Matching

Neural Matching is a 2018 ranking algorithm that Google uses. It tries to understand a query in context. Google says it is an "AI method to connect words to concepts better."

BERT

Bidirectional Encoder Representations from Transformers is more commonly known by its acronym, BERT. It (introduced in 2019) improved Google's ability to interpret the context of language in queries and content.

MUM

In 2021, Google introduced the Multitask Unified Model (MUM). It expanded Google's ability to work across languages and content formats for more complex tasks.

Helpful Content System

In 2022, Google introduced the Helpful Content system to reduce visibility for content that appears unhelpful or made primarily for search, and to reward content that better serves users.

By 2024, Google described the Helpful Content system as integrated into its broader core ranking systems.

Reviews System

In 2022, review pages were rewarded or demoted based on how helpful they were to readers, while thin, unoriginal, or untrustworthy reviews tended to lose visibility.

Personalization

Personalization is limited and inconsistent, but results can vary by location, language, settings, and prior activity—especially for ambiguous queries.

Chapter 3

TYPES OF SEO EXPERTISE

Although most Search Engine Optimization tactics are common, it is important to recognize specializations that may apply to your situation. Some of these have practitioners with many years of experience, so you should consider that when recruiting. In addition, the software used in these environments differs, as do the workflows.

There are overlaps; for example, a large multinational company will have elements of enterprise SEO, international SEO, news SEO, e-commerce SEO, and even some Local SEO.

ENTERPRISE SEO

The main feature of Enterprise SEO is that the working environment is multi-user, multi-team, multi-location, etc. Many teams might create and upload the content, but not all would have the SEO team in their workflows. The page count is in the thousands, if not millions.

Workflows in large companies are quite different from those in a small workplace, where a single webmaster does most of the SEO strategy and implementation. Large companies with large user bases often rely on complex architectures, such as distributed hosting, content delivery networks, and tightly managed deployment workflows. A team of several people might manage analytics tasks. Most activities need to be managed as individually numbered tasks with some tool such as Jira. This provides an audit trail, so walking up to a developer and asking for some "small task" is out of the question. Some SEO operatives will be permanent staff or contractors, and some will be from an outsourced agency.

Enterprises differ in their business focus, so an enterprise SEO working for a national TV network will encounter different challenges than one working for a global car manufacturer.

BRAND SERP SEO

Knowledge Panels can appear without notice. In some cases, you can request control via Google's verification pathways, and you can improve consistency with authoritative references and structured data. Google Business Profile primarily applies to local entities.

.

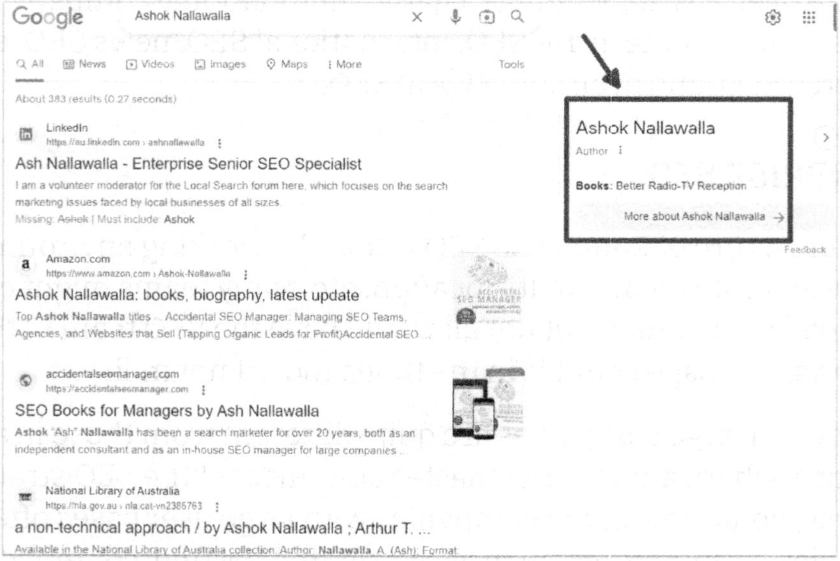

Figure 19 A partial Knowledge Panel.

People who are not public figures can get a knowledge panel, provided they have been featured on numerous websites. My friend Kristine has such a strong SERP without doing any specific tagging on her own site.

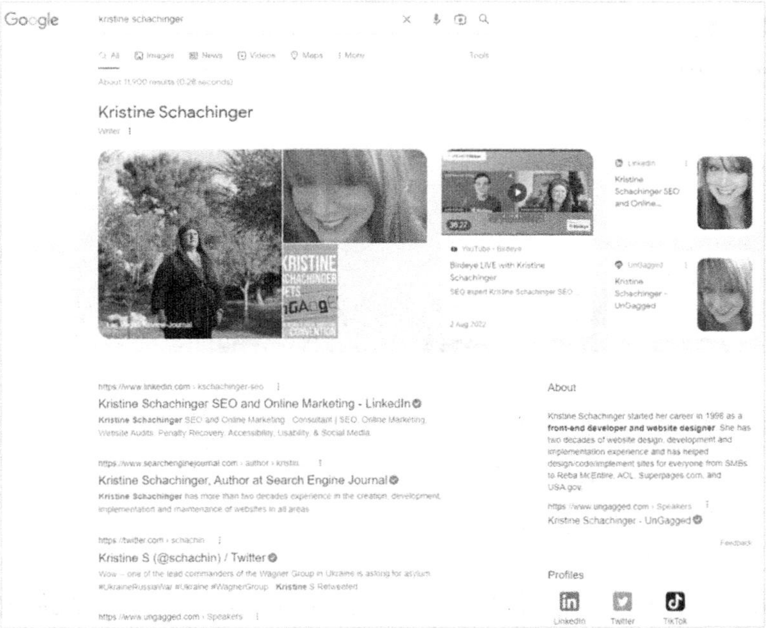

Figure 20 A richer example of a personal brand SERP.

PLATFORM/SAAS SEO

Most e-commerce sites use one or more specialized platforms to display product or service catalogs. Some of these use a software-as-a-service (SaaS) model. Some of those platforms are more amenable to SEO tweaks than others. For example, your SEO team might wish to use schema.org ItemAvailability type markup on products, which has the following values.

- BackOrder
- Discontinued
- InStock
- InStoreOnly
- LimitedAvailability
- OnlineOnly

- OutOfStock
- PreOrder
- PreSale
- SoldOut

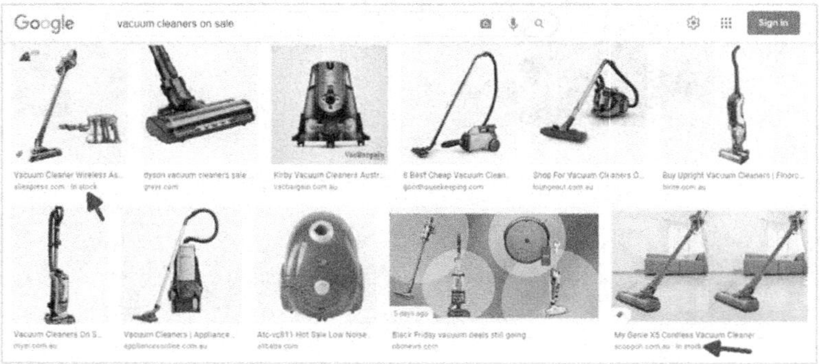

Figure 21 Google Image Search can display an "In Stock" label.

Structured data can improve eligibility for rich results and reduce ambiguity, but it does not guarantee visibility.

Social Media Optimization

Optimizing SaaS platforms can include Social Media Optimization (SMO). SMO occurs outside of search engines. Many social platforms limit indexing or restrict crawler access for policy and product reasons. Occasionally, such content does appear in search engines, but coverage varies by platform and format.

Social links usually pass limited direct value, but they can drive discovery, demand, and secondary links. SMO deserves a book of its own, but the purpose of mentioning it here is to be aware of it as a competitor to SEO.

Young people are turning to social media platforms such as TikTok and Instagram to search for consumer goods and services. That's a worthy challenge for your marketing team.

JAVASCRIPT SEO

Technical SEOs should have a basic understanding of JavaScript. We call this JavaScript SEO, but given that the language is on most websites, I wonder if it needs a special label. On modern sites, JavaScript is common; SEO risks arise from rendering dependencies and performance overhead.

JavaScript is a scripting language and works in the JavaScript "engine" of web browsers and in some web servers. If you switched off JavaScript in your browser and looked at your website, you might experience one of the following:

- A blank page
- A partially rendered page
- A fully rendered page that does not work when you try to use some interactive elements

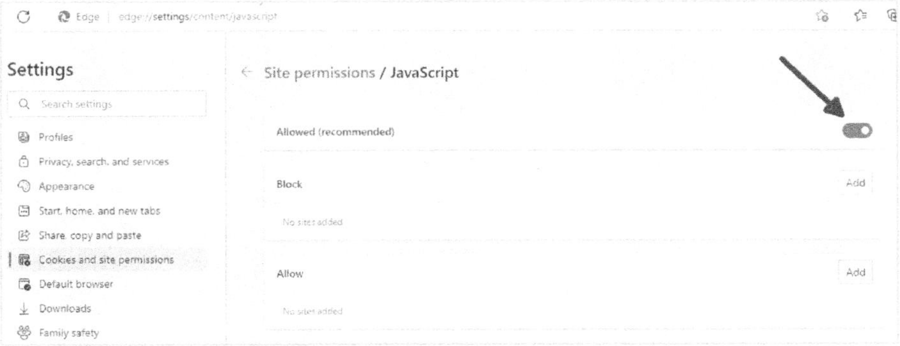

Figure 22 Turning off JavaScript in the Edge browser.

At this point, consider the possibility that a search engine cannot "see" the page as you intended. Google and Bing can execute JavaScript, but rendering can be delayed, incomplete, or inconsistent, especially on complex sites. So, it's worth turning off JavaScript in your browser temporarily to see how much of it is functional in that state.

Rendering

JavaScript enables interactivity on a webpage by running one or more scripts in the background. The scripts are files with the .js extension. Some are written for your site, and many are taken from pre-written "libraries. I doubt any of the scripts are written with SEO in mind, so that a technical SEO will be reminded of this during site audits.

Examples of JavaScript include:

- Refreshing news items at a busy newspaper website
- Search box
- Form submission
- Image carousel
- Collapsing or enlarging FAQs or product feature lists
- Playing media such as music or video
- Changing the font size to help with accessibility
- Navigation menus
- Calculators
- Continuously scrollable pages

Search engines need to execute your JavaScript and render your page as intended. A common error is constructing links in ways that are not exposed as crawlable <a href> URLs, for example, when routes, parameters, or IDs are assembled only at runtime. In those cases, crawlers may not reliably discover internal links, even if the pages work for users. The SEO still needs to audit the site and confirm that key navigation and internal links are crawlable and render correctly.

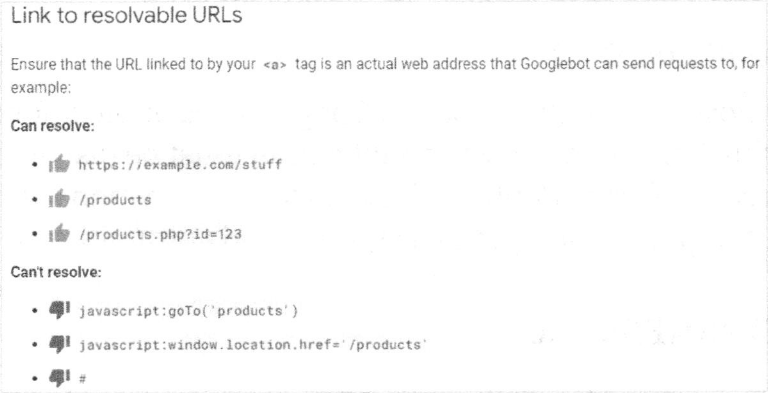

Figure 23 Examples of uncrawlable JavaScript links.

NEWS SEO

To appear in Google News, Google needs to recognize your site as a news source. You can no longer manually set up a publication in Publisher Center, so discovery and evaluation depend on Google's systems and the signals your site provides:

- Page Experience (Core Web Vitals)
- Fresh, high-quality content, compliant with Google News policies
- Structured data (schema) tags
- Original content should exceed syndicated content
- Ads must not overpower the news content
- Clear dates, bylines of authors, author pages
- Information about the publisher
- Contact information
- A separate News sitemap.xml file

A news listing can also appear across Google products such as Google Search, YouTube, and Discover, as well as in other Google assistant-style experiences, depending on device and market.

Google Publisher Center

Google removed the ability to set up Google News publications in the Google Publisher Center, so your publication must be discovered as a news source. Publisher Center still exists for certain management functions, but publication pages are generated automatically.

SMALL BUSINESS SEO

Small Business SEO shares the core SEO principles used in larger organizations. Still, the entire SEO responsibility usually falls on one or two people, whether in-house or outsourced. However, they will find it difficult to excel at everything – say, in technical skills and as a good content specialist; thus, they tend to use external agencies.

INTERNATIONAL SEO

In addition to core SEO principles, International SEO has the following characteristics:

- Multinational companies selling the same or similar products in many countries
- Multiple languages, scripts, and currencies
- Single SEO team in the headquarters or independent SEO teams in each country
- Common software environment or a mixture, owing to historical reasons

E-COMMERCE SEO

E-commerce SEO is a loose term used for businesses, large or small, that are primarily online and have few or no brick-and-mortar locations. The selling platform might be hosted in-house or in the cloud as a SaaS.

There are several selling platforms, and it might be challenging to recruit a specialist SEO who has worked with the one you have, but the principles and challenges are the same.

NICHE SEO

SEO agencies that specialize in a niche target business, such as:

- Law offices
- Gambling
- Adult

- Pharmaceuticals
- Travel
  - Booking sites
  - Comparison sites
  - Accommodation sites
  - Content sites
- Real estate
- Food and hospitality

Agencies specializing in a niche know the terminology and business models, so they can deliver better outcomes than those that do "everything." For example, they would have established connections with writers, bloggers, niche directories, and so on.

APP STORE SEO

App Store SEO or App Store Optimization (ASO) is a niche worthy of a separate mention. There are millions of apps in the Google and Apple app stores, and in the Microsoft Store, so individual apps compete to be found and downloaded. There are two challenges:

- Being found within the store
- Being found in a search engine

The tactics for optimizing in-store are similar to those for organic search – refreshing content, choosing the right keywords, titles, and descriptions, getting ratings and reviews, etc. In addition, the company website links to the app store pages, so it is optimized as usual.

App Store Search Engine

An app store has an internal search engine for users. As with regular search engines, the algorithm is not shared with us, so we have to do some guesswork and compare notes with others. The consensus is not surprising – possible factors for a high ranking in a search result might include:

- Effect of reviews and rating scores
- Choosing the right category
- Brand equity
- Age of the app and freshness of updates
- Number of downloads
- Links and mentions elsewhere

AFFILIATE MARKETING SEO

Many individuals, including SMBs, engage in affiliate marketing. This usually involves creating pages about products or services and tagging the links to a merchant's sales page with a personal ID. The merchant or an affiliate network intermediary keeps track of such clicks and, if they result in a sale, after a predetermined period (to allow for returns or cancellations), credits the affiliate's account. At some later point, the affiliate collects their commission.

Affiliates face a hurdle when optimizing their pages, as they may take shortcuts and copy the merchant's catalog word-for-word. This is sometimes permitted, but this creates thin content, and the search engine will not list the merchant's page or hundreds of affiliate pages that offer the same item. A solution is to create unique content that mentions the product and an affiliate link. For example, the affiliate will write a book review and link it to a book site with a "nofollow" link. However, this is slow work and cannot be done at scale.

The other SEO considerations of getting good links, good code, and fast-loading pages also apply. Affiliates, therefore, tend to pick a few niches and stick to them.

PROGRAMMATIC SEO

Programmatic SEO (pSEO) is an SEO-adjacent approach that involves generating thousands or millions of pages based on a program that pulls data and images from a data source.

There is what I call good pSEO and bad pSEO.

Good pSEO is simply the generation of unique pages that cover every data point in a database. For example, a travel site covering every known geographic location can generate millions of pages, gradually filled with reviews written by real travelers. TripAdvisor is an example of good pSEO.

Bad pSEO is a site built without adequate thought. This could be a product catalog or an amalgam of several data sources combined to create an illusion of uniqueness for search engines, but not fleshed out with human-generated content, such as reviews exclusive to this site and not copied from elsewhere. They are likely to create thin content and would struggle to be indexed.

AGENCY VS. IN-HOUSE SEO

Before engaging agencies or sole operators, ask whether the work includes diagnosis and implementation, or only diagnosis. The diagnosis is presented in an audit report and may include a list of recommendations. It would help if you also implemented these recommendations for the advice to be meaningful.

Budget-Priced Agencies

SEO agencies have several operating models. Some are high-volume, "one-size-fits-all" operators. They are looking for the budget-conscious customer, and all I can say is that there are a few high-visibility placements for valuable queries. The layout varies widely by query and device. The prospect of disappointing their customers is high. Their monthly pricing starts in the four-digit range but can go higher. Their model is to lock in the client for the duration of the contract, even when the client begins to complain. The main issue is not setting a realistic expectation for the client.

Sydney Today 20 °/ 28 °
news.com.au
Sign Up Log In
National World Lifestyle Travel Entertainment Technology Finance Sport Shopping
Finance › Small Business

'It's ridiculous': Tradie pays $20,000 to SEO firm, website gets four views per month and zero sales

A tradie who paid nearly $20,000 for a new website has slammed the "ridiculous" situation after getting just four views per month.

Frank Chung
@franks_chung 4 min read February 15, 2025 - 11:38AM news.com.au

Figure 24 Example of an unhappy client going to the news media.

Sole Operators and Mid-Priced Agencies

Then there are the agencies/individuals who offer customized services. They are the best kind, but convince yourself that they know their stuff. Their monthly pricing starts at four digits.

High-End Agencies

At the top end is what I call the glamour agencies. They are often subsidiaries of international advertising powerhouses. They build relationships with CEOs and top managers and might already have a leg in the door as a marketing contractor. They are literally "in the building" and can easily say, "We also do SEO." They are likely to bill in the five-digit range each month. Whether you will get value from a glamour SEO agency is a matter of luck. Despite what they say in their pitch about their size and expertise, do not assume they can "scale" easily. If they lose a staff member working on your account, they won't necessarily have a spare worker on hand – they will recruit from the outside pool.

In-House SEO

As the name implies, an in-house SEO presence is a dedicated employee or team who knows your organization inside and out (if they are allowed to). They focus on a single organization and its subsidiaries.

BLENDED MODEL

I have been in both in-house and agency-side SEO positions, so I think a blended model is best if the budget permits. The in-house SEO knows the company and products better than anyone outside the company. Therefore, it is cost-effective for them to attend routine internal meetings that may not have any SEO implications, such as the daily stand-up meetings I attended.

Conflicts

When a blended in-house and agency model is in play, there needs to be rules of engagement to avoid misunderstandings and deliver the best value to the enterprise. Here are some examples:

- Who is the SEO "director" (not by title but by role)?
- Who does what work (strategy, audits, reports, BAU), and how frequently?
- How is agency time to be recorded?

I have been in a situation where the agency was appointed without my participation in the selection. They would undertake tasks to maximize the billable hours, which were not shared with the in-house team. In another company, I was involved in shortlisting and choosing the agency. Their staff reported to me as though they were employees. They came to our office daily, so this model worked far better than one in which the agency reported directly to senior management.

Chapter 4

SEARCH CONSOLE AND WEBMASTER TOOLS

This book often mentions Google Search Console (GSC). Bing calls its equivalent Bing Webmaster Tools. These tools and their future iterations are your hotlines to the search engines – all critical communications take place on these platforms, at least in an automated, impersonal way. Commonly used SEO tools also need access to these tools so they can blend the data with their own.

If you market to China, South Korea, or Russia, their main search engines, Baidu, Naver, and Yandex, respectively, have similar interfaces in their languages.

REGISTRATION

Although registration in GSC is optional, please treat it as essential early in the website's existence. Don't delay verification and setup, especially sitemap submission and key diagnostics. I would include it in a site launch task list.

These search engine interfaces require you to register your website, which requires an authentication step, or else you will see very little information about your site. Please check that your web team has set up an account for all your domains on the major search engines of interest. You should do this before you launch the website.

Verification

A common verification method requires placing a unique, coded file in the root directory of your website. It's up to you, but I like the comfort of having only one such file per search engine.

Redacted example: google7b4216f44b0fe5ed.html

(Other verification methods are beyond the scope of this book.)

Multiple Accounts (Not Just Multiple Users)

Be aware that multiple accounts (with the search engines) can access your search consoles. They are email addresses registered with search engines, and their passwords are known only to those engines. You can register your work email address with the search engines, and that is how you will access the search console.

Here we are looking at a more significant issue – not external users of your official search console, but multiple search consoles, possibly unknown to you. Another way to say it is that a former employee or a former agency might still have access to your account. Google sees multiple "owners" of your data.

Since site owners in this context can issue commands to remove one or all pages from the index, it is a major concern.

Mature sites that have hired several external agencies over time are likely to have more than one verification file. If you cannot identify their provenance from their file names, investigate before deleting them, because removing a verification method can unintentionally remove legitimate access. If someone complains and has a valid case, add their email addresses to your search console user list and grant them the appropriate level of access.

Properties

You should add each website you own (a "property") to the master owner's account. The master owner grants individuals who need access to the specific websites. I would discourage requests for "everything" unless they work in the SEO or analytics team. If you grant access to all properties, you might find that users with only a casual interest in them will not use them.

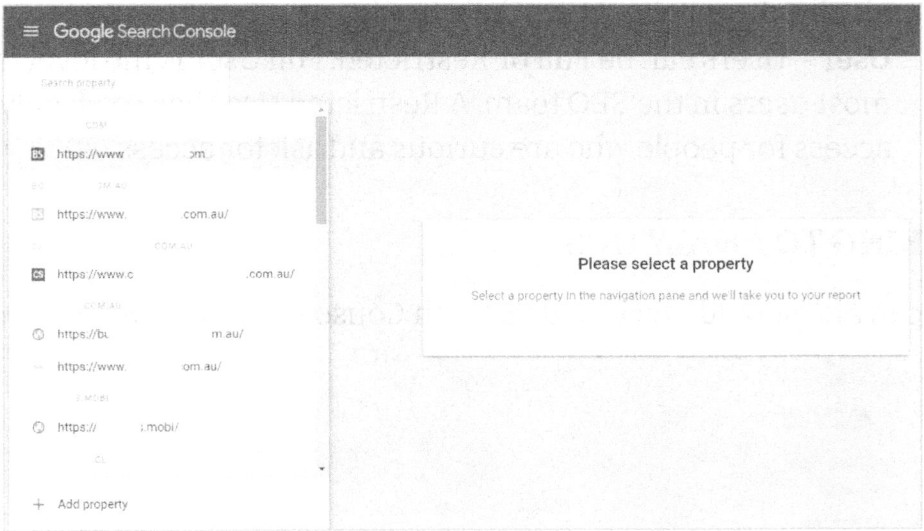

Figure 25 Google Search Console with multiple properties.

Pro Tip: You can add URL-prefix properties for subfolders when you need focused reporting for a section of a site. This can simplify analysis for large sites, but it does not reliably remove export and row limits. For deeper reporting, use the Search Console API or scheduled exports to a data store.

Users

Internal users will have (and should use) a corporate email address, not their personal one. External users should also use their corporate addresses so they are easy for their parent company to recognize. Keep checking these users periodically and remove those who no longer need access.

LEVELS OF SEARCH CONSOLE ACCESS

There are two main roles, with different permission levels for users:

- **Owner** – This is the full level of access. Grant with care, and ideally, do not allocate to daily users.
- **User** – Users can be Full or Restricted. Full User is the level for most users in the SEO team. A Restricted User has read-only access for people who are curious and ask for access.

LINKING TO ANALYTICS

You can and should link Google Search Console to GA4 if you use both.

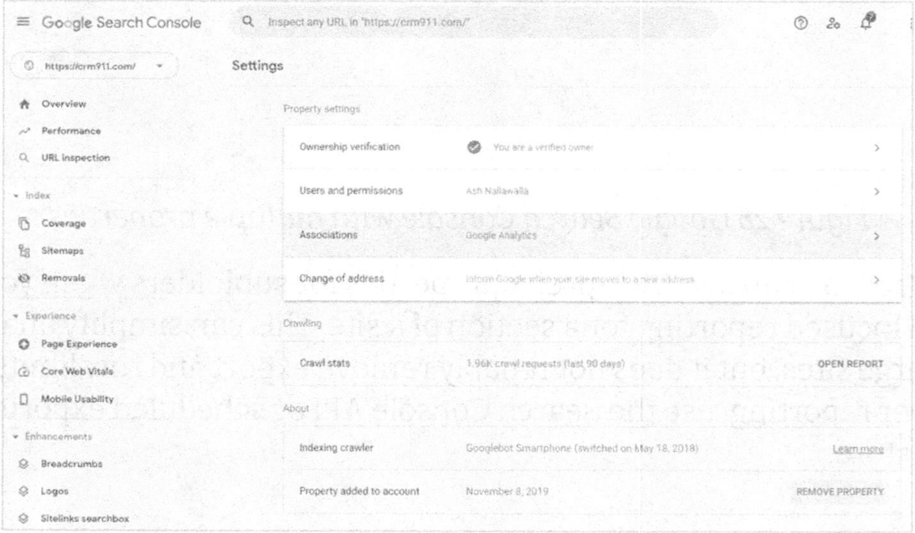

Figure 26 Linking with GA4.

GIVING ACCESS TO SEO TOOLS

Many popular SEO tools can be connected with Search Console and merge that data with the tool's discoveries.

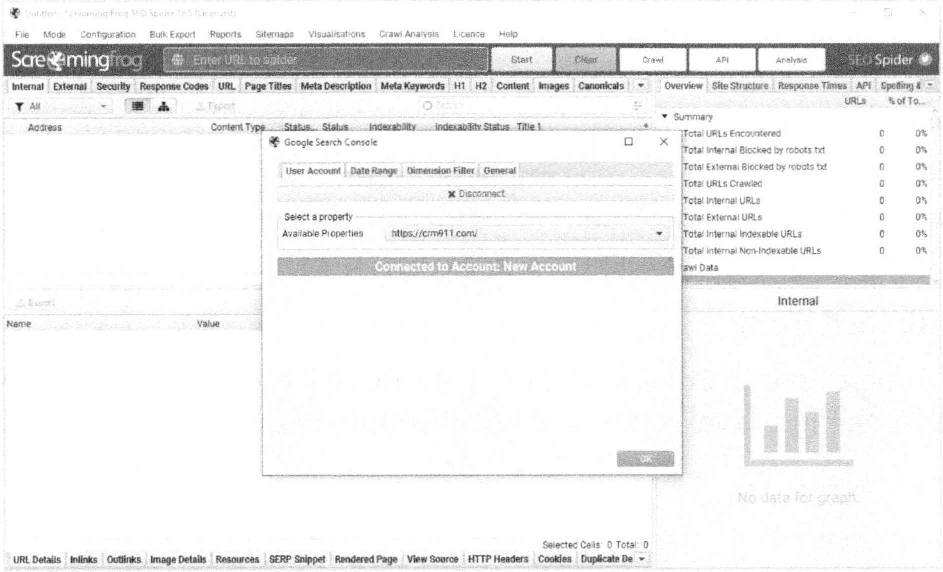

Figure 27 Connecting Screaming Frog to Google Search Console.

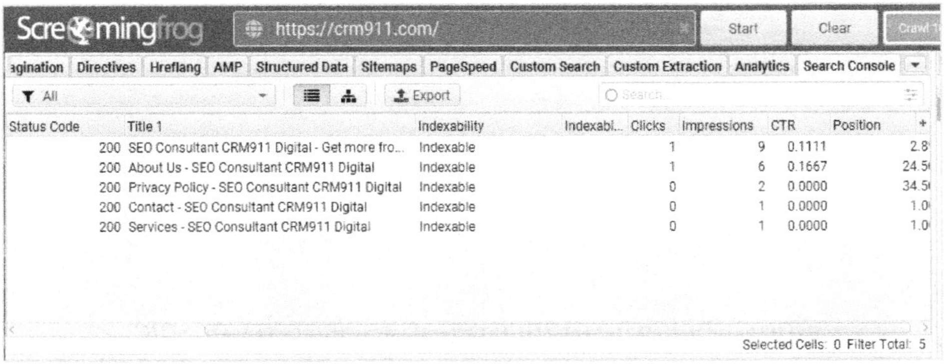

Figure 28 Google Search Console data seen in Screaming Frog.

DAILY CHECKS

Your SEO team will log in to Search Console every day, but if they cannot, they will receive emails from Google if there is an anomaly. Keep in mind that this data is delayed by a day or so, and the dates in the interface follow Google's reporting time zone (commonly aligned to US Pacific Time).

The daily routine check will show a few changes from the previous day. If there is a change, the cause might be something you or your competitors have done, a demand shift, a technical or indexing change, or a Google ranking change.

Dashboard View

The Google Search Console default view upon logging in is a dashboard with some high-level reports you can explore in greater detail.

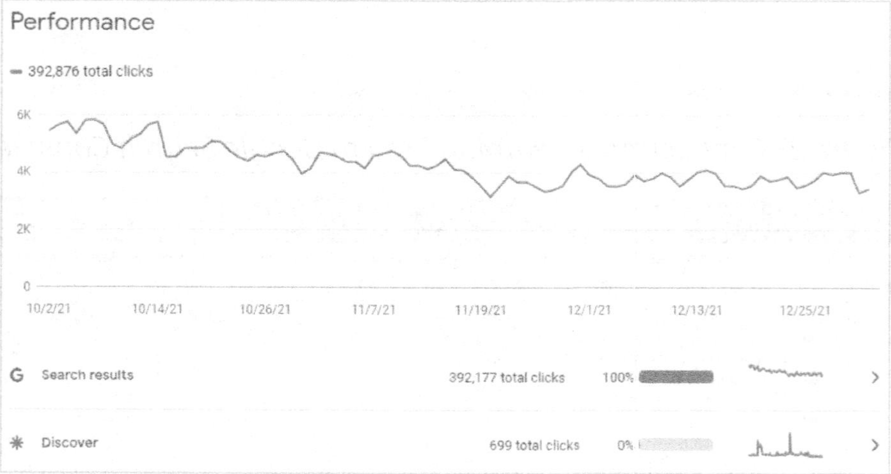

Figure 29 Performance report in Search Console.

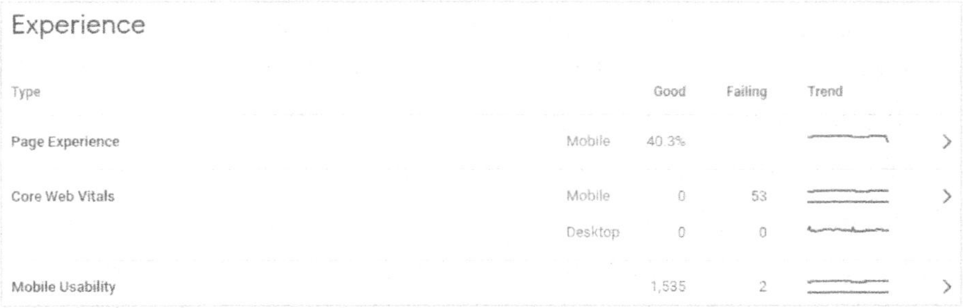

Figure: 30 Experience report in Search Console.

The detailed view of the Performance report is where most of the action is, at least in my experience. You can view up to 16 months through this interface, but you could get more data with some technical wizardry. I used to automatically query and store this data in a Google Sheet, so over time, a longer dataset could be built.

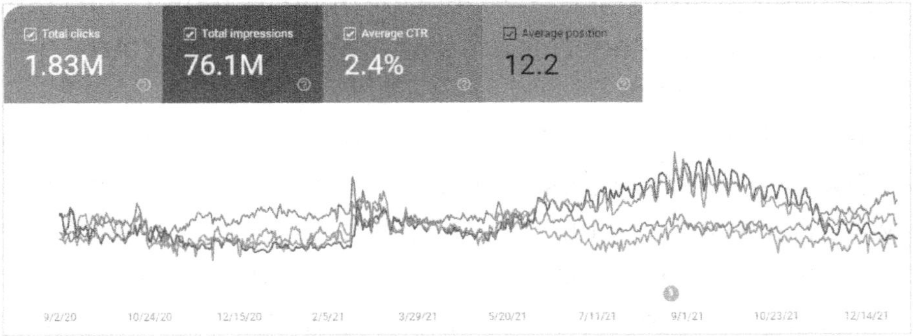

Figure 31 Performance report (detailed view).

Four key metrics are available:

- **Impressions** – If your webpage appears in a SERP for a searcher, it is counted here. This could be anywhere on the first page or a subsequent page.
- **Clicks** – If the searcher clicks your URL in the SERP, it is counted here. Not every impression will coincide with a click, so it is worth checking important pages and comparing them with

competitors'. For example, they might have more attractive messages in the SERP, which would get them more clicks. You will also lose clicks if the user clicks on an ad.

- **CTR** – The click-through rate is Clicks divided by Impressions.
- **Position** – Your URL's position (ranking) in the SERP is shown here, even if it is several pages deep. Your home page might rank for a long-tail keyword at a low position, resulting in an overall position lower than #1.

Six data views are available – up to 1,000 rows of data can be downloaded:

- **Queries** – Queries are conceptually similar to your preferred keywords, except that these are the strings typed by the searchers. This list is invaluable for understanding the language of searchers. The queries are sometimes in a staccato, shorthand format.
- **Pages** – Pages are the URLs with impressions, that is, the top 1,000 pages Google has chosen to show you. This is an excellent way to see your popular pages, particularly the ones that were clicked. These are organic search visits, whereas the data you will see in GA4 (or equivalent) will show all kinds of visits.
- **Countries** – The list of countries that generate searches might be of interest if your audience is more than a single country. Perhaps the visits from other countries might indicate an interest that your team could investigate further.
- **Devices** – You can see a breakdown of the three types of devices:
    - **Desktop** – The nature of the organization will determine whether most users prefer a desktop browser or a mobile phone. Some page content is better viewed on a large screen.

  - **Mobile** – Mobile phones are used by people on the move, even within their home or office. For example, they might look up a complex product, such as a home loan, on the phone but later go home and view it again on a large screen with their partner. I tend to find that people seldom go past the second page of the SERPs on a phone, while they go a page deeper on a desktop.
  - **Tablet** – For many years, across many industries, I have not seen much traffic from tablets, but the CTR tends to be a little higher than the other two types of devices.
- **Search Appearance** – Several types of search appearance data can be presented, depending on the website, for example:
  - **Page experience and speed signals** – Page experience is reflected through reports such as Core Web Vitals and HTTPS, and through your own performance monitoring.
  - **Videos** – You can click this row and then the Pages tab to see which pages showed up in a search for videos.
  - **Event listing** – You can see which event pages had the most visits through the Events rich results in the SERPs.
  - **Event details** – You can see which event detail pages had the most visits through the Events rich results in the SERPs.
- **Dates** – The Dates report breaks down the data by date.

Performance on Discover

A special report shows which of your pages were featured in Google Discover.

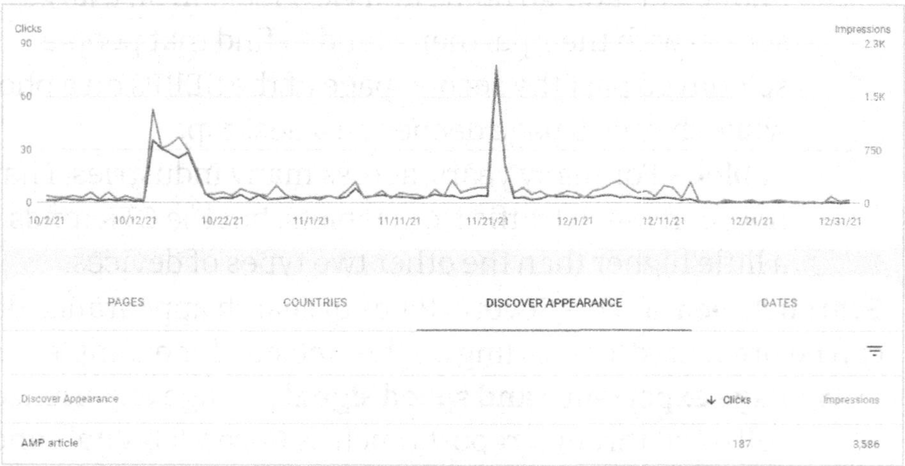

Figure 32 Google Discover data in Search Console.

Such content is shown to logged-in users of the Google Search app on phones and tablets based on their prior search interests and customizations when they start the app. Then, they can view these pages or perform a search.

Performance on Google News

If your website has been accepted as a valid news site, you will get a report on the pages in this report.

Figure 33 A newly accepted news site shows some traffic.

Coverage Reports

The index coverage reports convey a wealth of diagnostic information about the website's search health. Although it is reassuring to see the number of valid pages, your SEO team will be looking for the problems in the reports, such as:

- Server errors
- Pages not found
- Crawled, currently not indexed
- Duplicate content
- Blocked pages

Some of these errors are false positives or transient glitches that have since resolved.

Sitemaps

The Sitemaps interface is quite important, as it serves as both a submission form for new sitemaps and a report of submitted ones.

Figure 34 Sitemaps report in Search Console.

Removals

You will rarely need to remove a page from the index, but it usually happens when a serious error warrants removing the whole page rather than editing it. The removal tool in GSC only hides the page in search results, but does not actually deindex it.

This removal is temporary (about six months), but it will give you time to remove the page physically from the website. Google will take a long time to be convinced that the page is gone.

Page Experience

Google removed the Page Experience report from Search Console. Use the Core Web Vitals and HTTPS reports, along with your own monitoring, to evaluate page experience and technical quality.

Core Web Vitals

Core Web Vitals is covered in more detail in Book 4: *Is Our SEO Working?* But for now, think of it as a page-quality dashboard. For example, if your site receives an adequate number of visits from Google Chrome users, that data is part of the Chrome User Experience Report (CrUX).

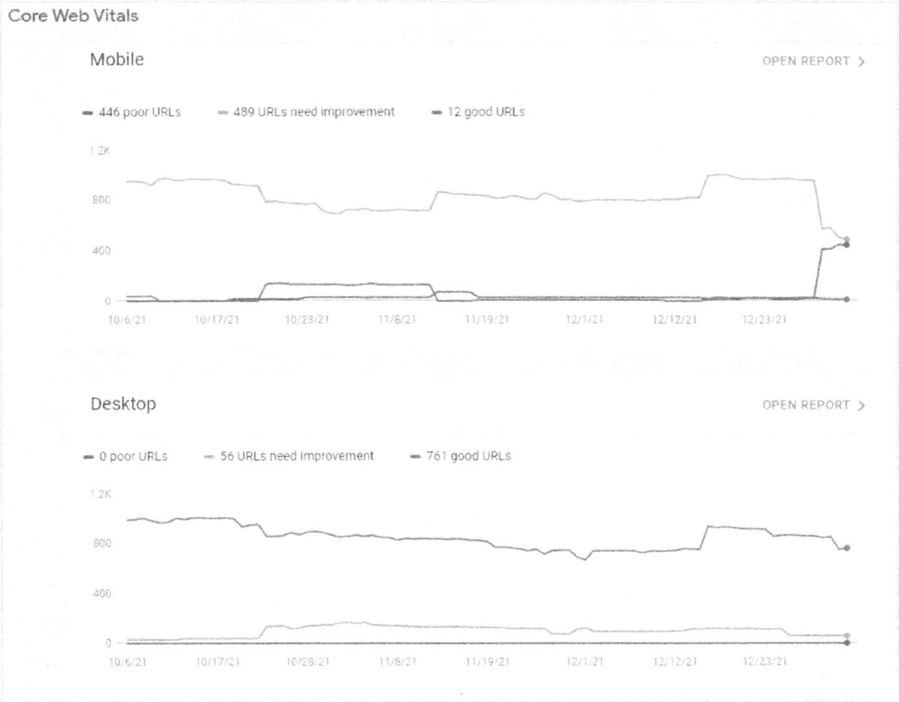

Figure 35 Core Web Vitals report in Search Console.

Breadcrumbs

Not all websites use "breadcrumbs" in their page design, so this report might not be populated for some sites. A breadcrumb is a secondary menu that shows the hierarchy of a given page relative to higher-level pages and the home page.

Figure 36 Breadcrumbs report in Search Console.

FAQs

As with other reports in GSC, the FAQs report will appear only if Google detects eligible FAQ markup and decides to surface it for reporting. In many cases, FAQ rich results are limited, so this report may not appear even when FAQs exist on the site.

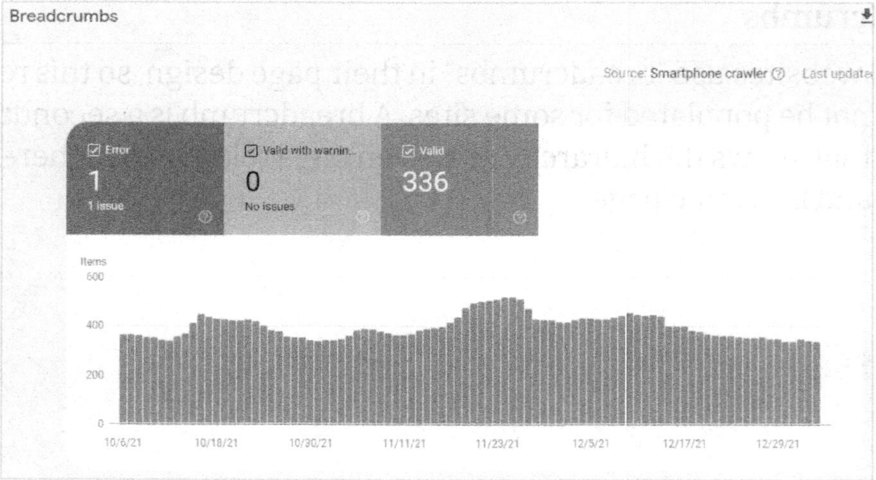

Figure 37 FAQs report in Search Console.

Logos

This report can surface issues with logo structured data and image eligibility where applicable.

Figure 38 Logos report in Search Console.

Products

The Products report shows how your product markup has turned out and the pages that need attention.

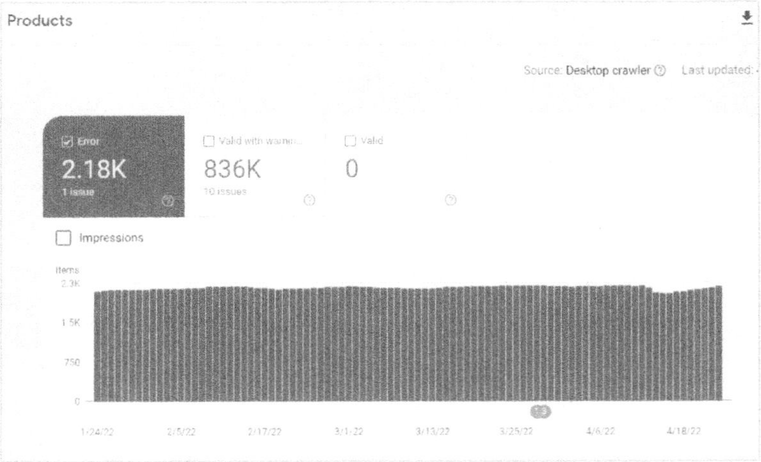

Figure 39 Search Console Products report.

Review Snippets

The Review Snippets report shows opportunities for fixing markup, if necessary.

Figure 40 Review Snippets report in Search Console.

Unparseable Structured Data

The Unparseable Structured Data report identifies opportunities to fix errors in your structured data markup.

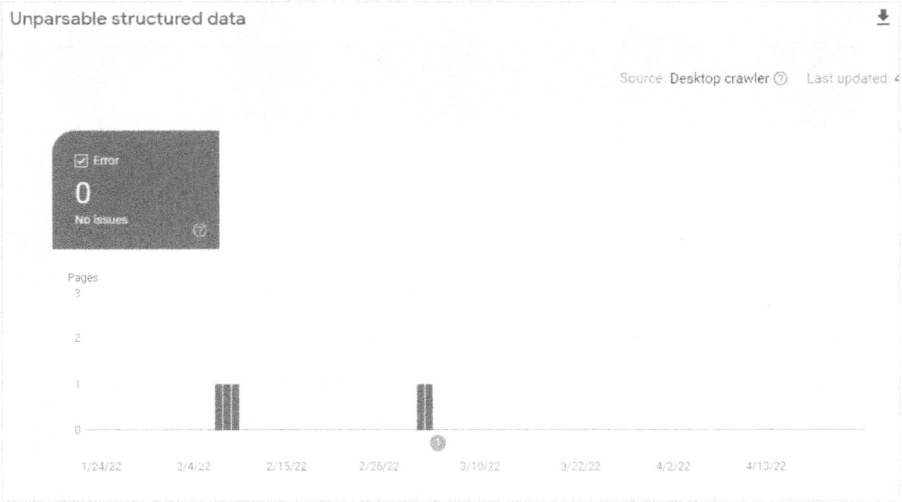

Figure 41 Unparseable Structured Data report in Search Console.

Videos

The Videos report shows opportunities to assess your structured data markup for videos.

Figure 42 Videos report in Search Console.

Manual Actions

You don't want to see any message from Google in the Manual Actions report, as it is terrible news about a manual penalty issued by a human checker. It is a big deal, depending on the penalty issued. In a serious case, the entire website might be removed from the index until you can make the necessary rectifications to Google's satisfaction.

Figure 43 Manual Actions report in Search Console.

Security Issues

The Security Issues report is another report you want to keep empty; otherwise, it will notify you if your server has been compromised and may be loading malware onto your visitors' computers.

International Targeting

The International Targeting report has been deprecated. Google still supports hreflang, so you should validate hreflang implementation through audits, testing, and Search Console signals where available.

Messages

A Messages panel on the side has replaced the old Messages report. You can view the messages by clicking the bell icon in the top-right corner. You will also receive these messages by email.

Links

The Links report shows you a sample of inbound and outbound links from your website.

Settings

The Settings report provides several administrative settings at a glance. The most commonly used feature here is the Users and

Permissions interface, which lets you grant additional users access to Search Console.

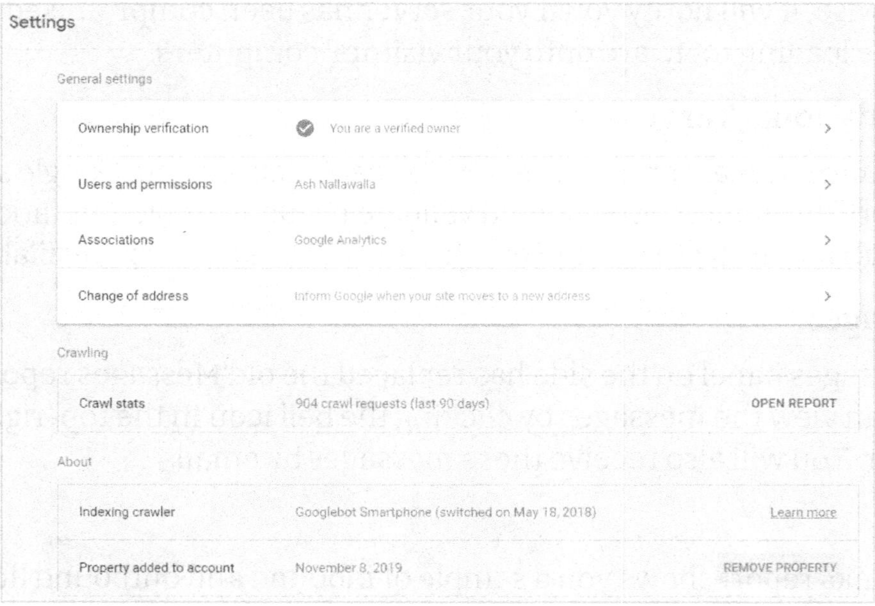

Figure 44 Settings in Google Search Console.

SECURITY OF THESE TOOLS

These interfaces are very important and should be well-secured, with access given on a strict need-to-access basis. This is not so much about confidentiality, but protection is important because you can remove your content from search engines almost immediately. Although the control is meant to let you remove single pages, you can also remove critical pages such as the homepage and product pages.

A disgruntled former employee whose access isn't revoked upon exit can cause significant damage, so your SEO team needs to check key dashboards daily.

Governance and Access Integrity

Search-console credentials represent operational control, not just reporting access. You should treat them with the same rigor as financial-system permissions. Governance policies should define:

- Who authorizes new accounts and property additions.
- How ownership changes are documented when agencies or employees leave.
- Which senior executive (usually the accountable SEO or digital head) is responsible for periodic access audits.

Every verified owner has the power to issue removals and site-wide changes. If those powers are not regularly reviewed, you risk accidental or malicious de-indexing. A formal quarterly review of access lists should be part of your digital-governance checklist.

Cross-Functional Oversight and Response Planning

No matter how mature your team is, oversight should not rely on a single person. When ownership and analytics rights span multiple departments, define how incidents will be detected and reversed quickly.

- Ensure IT, Marketing, and SEO each receive automated alerts for critical Search Console changes.
- Create an emergency contact list so that absences or role changes never delay access restoration.
- Record rollback procedures in your change-management system—treat them like disaster-recovery steps.

The best-run organizations simulate a removal or outage once a year. That rehearsal builds confidence that the business can restore visibility within hours instead of days.

ACCIDENTS HAPPEN

The good news is that you can reverse accidental removal very quickly, say if an entire site was removed, as happened to me once. Someone on my team was tidying up old accounts and suggested we remove the old "http" domains because we had been using secure "https" URLs for some years.

The removal took a few hours, and we went back to work. A few days later, traffic on our flagship website had plummeted! Our SEO agency found the issue – when you remove all your http URLs, you also remove your https URLs! We reversed the removal, and the site began to return to visibility quickly, though full recovery depends on recrawl and reprocessing. Phew.

Since those days, both Google and Bing have released a granulated set of removal options:

- **Temporary Removals** – the URLs are removed for about six months, then pop back in the index. Permanent removal requires you to delete the URLs physically from your website.
- **Outdated Content** – a new URL has superseded the page, but the old page is still showing up in the search results.

Chapter 5

MANAGING KEYWORDS

SHIFT FROM PERSONAS TO SITUATIONAL INTENT

Product management has traditionally relied on **personas**—detailed, static profiles used to frame language differences. For SEO, this meant assuming a "medical professional" would only search using precise clinical terms, while a "layperson" would stick to common language.

However, in modern search, fixed personas are less predictive than **contextual and situational intent**.

Language variation is no longer tied cleanly to a persona's identity; instead, it shifts based on the user's immediate environment. The same individual will search differently depending on:

- **Urgency:** A professional might use "clinical terminology" when researching at their desk, but switch to "shorthand/symptoms" during an emergency on a mobile device.
- **Device & Surface:** Queries vary significantly between a detailed desktop session and an ambient voice search or a quick mobile "surface" interaction.
- **Task Stage:** An evaluator moves from broad "awareness" language to highly specific "transactional" language as they progress through a research journey, regardless of their background.

Strategic Takeaway for Managers

Rather than building exhaustive keyword lists for "Business Traveler" vs. "Leisure Traveler," SEO teams must now optimize for **Situational Clusters**.

Success is no longer about matching a keyword to a specific person's profile; it is about ensuring your content is **context-resilient**—ready to be retrieved and synthesized whether the user is being brief, precise, or conversational.

KEYWORD GROUPS OR CLUSTERS (ENTITIES)

You can describe a single entity with a group of semantically related keywords. Some call this clustering. It's better to identify your keyword groups than single keywords because Google looks at a search query and can find a page that falls in the same cluster of keywords. Therefore, it is not always essential to have the exact keyword on your page, as long as the page clearly covers the entity and intent.

SEMANTIC SEO

Semantic SEO concerns how content is structured within a webpage and a website. It is the perfect marriage of user intent and entities. A page will bring the entity to life by using the best keywords, not just a single primary keyword. From the search engine's perspective, results include not only webpages but also rich content when relevant. If a video can also help to address a query, Google might serve a video carousel.

Google can understand intent even when users do not use precise language. For example, if I searched for "burger joints in Milpitas," Google knows I meant burger restaurants. The ranking pages might not have the word "joint" on them, but Google relies on the search intent and not the literal keywords.

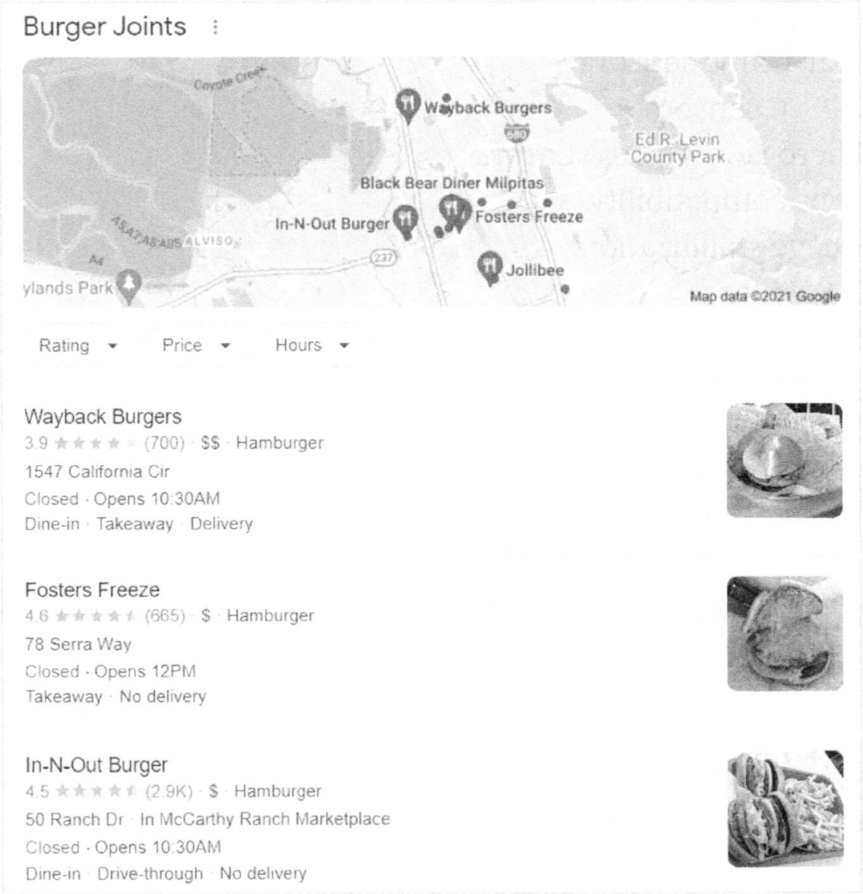

Figure 45 "Burger joints" is understood by Google.

Keyword Clusters the Old Way

For example, creating a keyword cluster can help Google better understand that a page is about mirrorless digital cameras. The following list is how we did it some years ago:

- Mirrorless cameras
- Digital cameras
- Interchangeable lens cameras
- EVF (Electronic Viewfinder)

- Autofocus
- Full-frame sensors
- APS-C sensors
- Micro Four Thirds sensors
- Lens compatibility
- Image stabilization
- RAW files
- ISO sensitivity
- Shutter speed
- Depth of field
- Bokeh

Entity Research: The New Way

Modern search intent for the mirrorless cameras example has shifted toward AI capabilities, hybrid creator workflows, and situational use cases.

1. The "AI & Computational" Evolution

Standard autofocus and ISO terms are being replaced in search queries by "Smart" variants.

- **AI-Powered Autofocus:** Replacing "Autofocus" for users seeking deep-learning subject tracking.
- **Subject Detection (Birds/Vehicles/Animals):** More specific than just "Autofocus."
- **Real-time Tracking:** The modern standard for "Focus."
- **In-camera AI Upscaling:** A major 2025 trend for high-res output from smaller sensors.
- **Computational HDR / Multi-frame Processing:** Moving beyond simple "ISO sensitivity" to "Low-light enhancement."

- **Depth-mapping assisted autofocus**: Emerging in some flagship bodies for faster subject acquisition.

2. The "Hybrid & Video" Revolution

As mirrorless cameras become "video-first," these terms now carry more weight than "RAW files" or "Shutter speed."

- **Open Gate Capture:** Crucial for creators who need to crop for both vertical (TikTok) and horizontal (YouTube) from one shot.
- **Log Video:** (C-Log 3, S-Log 3) and RAW video formats (such as ProRes RAW or N-RAW): High-intent terms for video searchers.
- **4K/120p & 8K/60p:** These specific resolution/frame rate combos have high commercial intent.
- **Active Cooling / Internal Fans:** A key search term for hybrid shooters worried about overheating.
- **Vertical Shooting Support:** Specific search intent for social media creators.

3. Situational Intent

Instead of searching for "Mirrorless cameras," users are now searching by **task and urgency**:

- **Best Hybrid Camera for Travel:** High-intent situational search.
- **Content Creator Camera / Vlogging Setup:** Replacing "Interchangeable lens camera."
- **Street Photography Compacts:** A massive niche trend (Ricoh GR IV, Fujifilm X-E5).
- **Zero-Edit Workflow / Film Simulations:** Users searching for "Post-ready" results straight from the camera.

GOOGLE TOOLS FOR FINDING KEYWORDS

When we think in terms of entities, we must remember that they consist of keywords. Google is a logical place to look for keyword inspiration.

Google Keyword Planner: Benchmarking the Firehose

Modern research must go beyond the "firehose" of the Google Keyword Planner (GKP).

If you enter a high-level entity like "mirrorless cameras," the tool's first response is often a list of specific camera models. This reflects Google's "commercial" bias—the tool is designed for advertisers **(to build ads)** who want to sell products, so it prioritizes transactional keywords over the nuanced, situational language used in the early stages of a search journey.

Why the Planner is Still Useful

Despite this bias, GKP remains an essential "sanity check" for managers. It serves two specific purposes that AI tools cannot yet replace:

- **Market Sizing (The Benchmarking Tool):** It provides a useful "monthly average" signal for search volume, though the numbers are modeled and often shown as ranges. While AI tools can tell you *what* people are talking about, GKP tells you *how many* people are looking for it. It is your primary tool for sorting the "popular" from the "obscure."
- **Seasonality and Geographic Trends:** Because the data is based on twelve months of historical averages, it reveals when demand peaks (e.g., Black Friday for digital cameras) and which countries or cities represent your strongest potential audience.

The Limitations of "Ad Logic"

You must remember that GKP often groups close variants such as plural/singular forms and similar phrases. Third-party tools may present these differently, but their counts are also modeled. Furthermore, GKP will not help with "Black Swan" events—discoveries, sudden trends, or viral news that haven't yet built up a 12-month average.

For SEO purposes, treat Keyword Planner as a Commercial Mapping Tool. It shows you the keywords that Google's advertising engine considers most valuable. Use it to find the high-volume "anchor" terms, but look elsewhere (to AI surfaces or situational research) to find the "connective tissue"—the intent-driven questions and phrases that bridge the gap between a user's problem and your product.

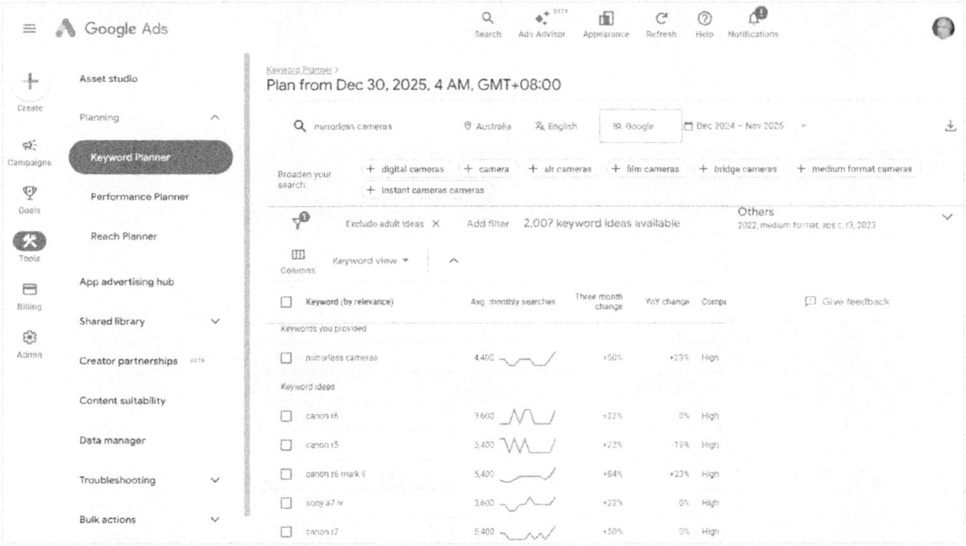

Figure 46 Google Keyword Planner.

Keyword (by relevance)	Avg. monthly searches
Keywords you provided	
cell phones	100K – 1M
mobile phones	10K – 100K
Keyword ideas	
iphone 12 mini	100K – 1M
iphone 11 pro	100K – 1M
find my phone	100K – 1M
iphone se 2020	100K – 1M
s21 ultra	10K – 100K
phone	100K – 1M
oneplus 9 pro	10K – 100K

Figure 47 Unfunded Google Keyword Planner shows a range of search volumes.

Iterative Keyword Research

I rarely take the first set of downloaded keywords as the final selection. For example, after sorting by search volume, I might notice a couple of interesting keywords that are different from the rest. Out of curiosity, I will supply them as seed keywords to see what the tool finds. I then merge these with the original collection and sort them by the search volume.

It might be worth using more than one tool for this exercise in case I find some long-tail gems. Rinse and repeat a few times, and the final collection is ready.

How Many Keywords?

For most entities, I find it reasonable to pick the top 20-30 keywords for visibility measurement. Sometimes, an entity cannot use so many different words on one page, and there is no point in including keywords that will never find a home on your website. You will get a misleadingly low visibility score. You can pick a few more if you are collecting the keywords to place in a keyword register for your writers.

Your seed keywords will include the phrases used on your website, as you are confident they are the language users use or are specific to your website. If they show a very low or zero search volume in a tool like Google Keyword Planner, do not discard them. Sometimes, you will find that the tools do not accurately capture search counts.

Google Trends: Identifying Velocity and "New" Intent

While Keyword Planner is a look-back tool based on averages, **Google Trends** is a look-forward tool that measures **velocity**.

Google Trends is essential for capturing those "Black Swan" events and discoveries—such as a sudden breakthrough in mirrorless sensor technology or a viral photography trend—that Keyword Planner misses because they haven't existed long enough to generate a monthly average.

How to Read the "Arbitrary" Scale

A common point of confusion for managers is the "Search Interest" scale. Google Trends does not show total search volume. Instead, it uses a normalized scale from **0 to 100**:

- **100** represents the peak popularity for that term in the chosen time and place.
- **0** means there was not enough data for the term.

Because the scale is arbitrary, you are looking for **trend lines and momentum**, not absolute numbers. For actual volume, you must still cross-reference with Google Keyword Planner. For a sanity check, search for the keywords in Google.

Strategic Use Cases

1. **Spotting Market Shifts:** A car designer or product owner can compare "Electric Vehicles" against "Hybrid Vehicles" to see which concept is gaining cultural momentum in real-time.
2. **Seasonality Audit:** It reveals exactly *when* intent spikes. For mirrorless cameras, you might see a spike in "travel camera" searches in early summer, whereas "camera deals" peak in November.
3. **Regional Nuance:** It shows where a topic is "heating up." This allows managers to allocate budget to specific states or cities before a trend goes national.

Once a product design decision is made, the SEO team can use Trends to validate the "freshness" of their keyword list. If you are only using Keyword Planner, you are optimizing for the past. By incorporating Google Trends, you are optimizing for where the market is moving.

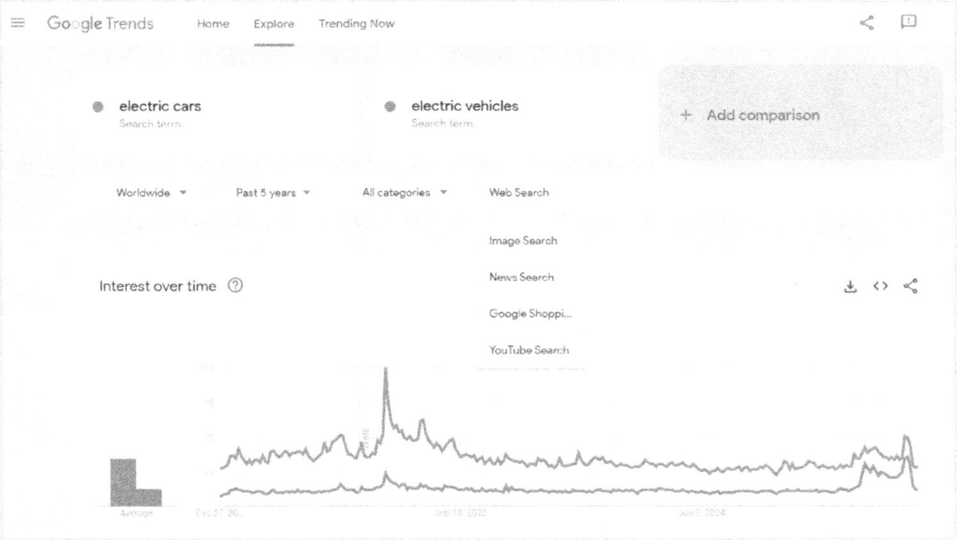

Figure 48 Comparing search terms in Google Trends

Further down in the Google Trends result page, you will notice two sections:

- Related Topics
- Related Queries

The related topics help you confirm that Google sees your seed keywords as part of a specific niche. If they are unrelated, then alarm bells should go off in your head in case you did not anticipate keyword competition from an unexpected quarter.

Related queries can serve as additional seed keywords or topic ideas for writers.

The map helps writers to research further why there is more interest in one state or country than in others.

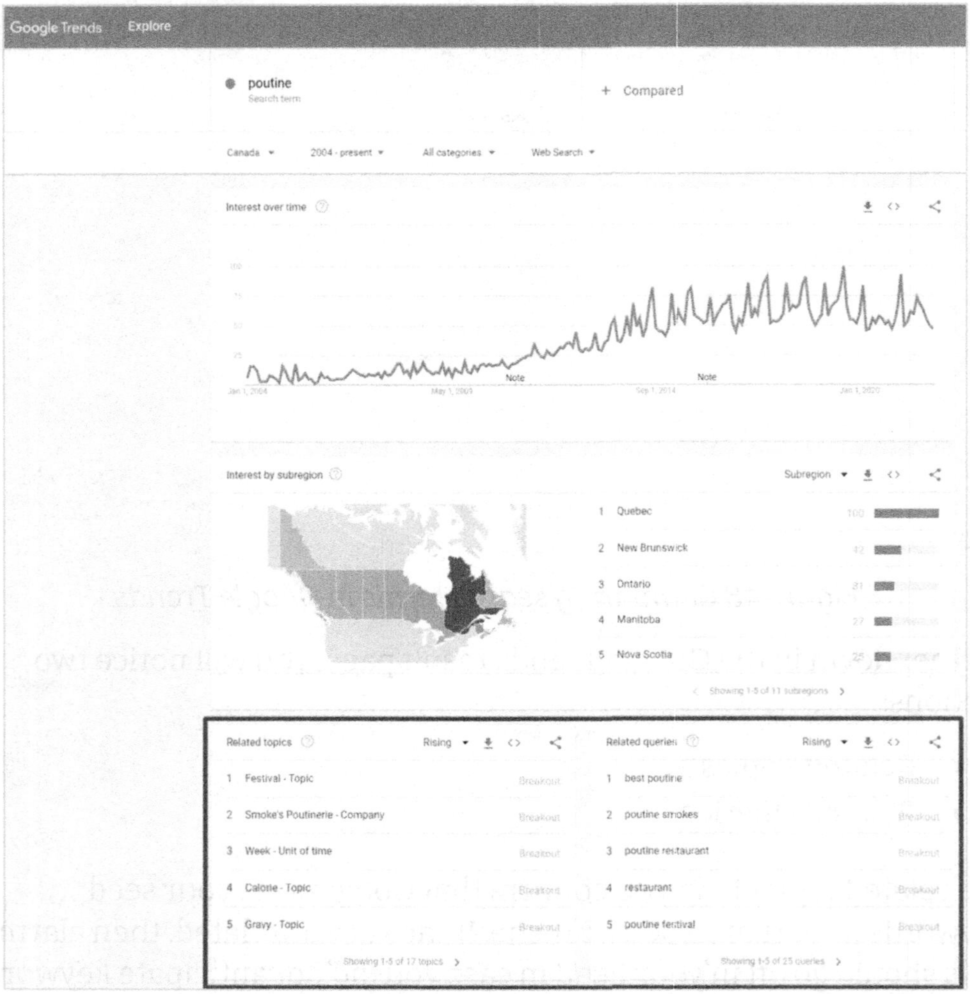

Figure 49 Google Trends helps to find related keywords.

Google Search Console

The Performance section in Google Search Console shows a list of queries visitors use to reach your site. This is another good source of validation because this data is yours. It reflects impressions and clicks for your site rather than market-wide search volume, which might raise some doubt about the rounded numbers in Google Keyword Planner.

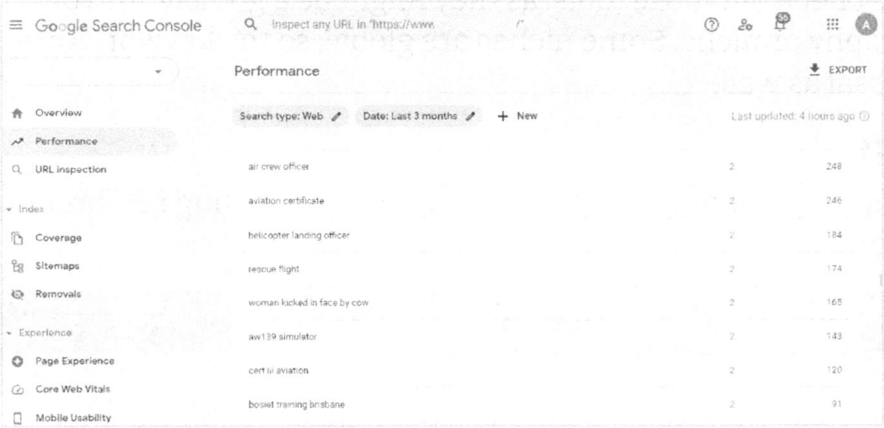

Figure 50 List of queries in Google Search Console.

There are two caveats:

- Google only shows 1,000 rows of data for any report. So, if the search volumes are high when you reach the 1,000th row, you will not see any more rows.
- You will only see queries for which Google recorded impressions for your site, and low-volume queries may be omitted or aggregated. If you don't rank for an otherwise relevant keyword, you will not see it.

NON-GOOGLE KEYWORD TOOLS

There are a few other keyword-finding tools, but I found they weren't as accurate for Australia as I'd like. This is because they would include, for example, keywords in high volumes that were clearly North American, such as names of US banks. That would make me question the search counts for the otherwise relevant keywords.

Please check out those tools, as they might be a good fit for your geography or niche. Some niches are global, so the keywords are universal as well.

Ahrefs

Ahrefs is a popular tool for many SEO tasks, including researching keywords.

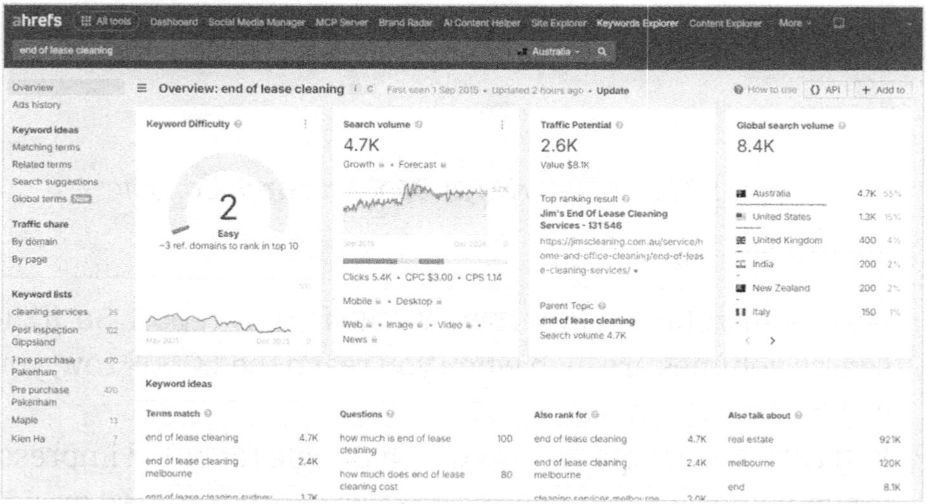

Figure 51 Keyword research in Ahrefs

AnswerThePublic

AnswerThePublic is an aggregator of Google Suggest results that helps users auto-complete their queries by showing similar search terms.

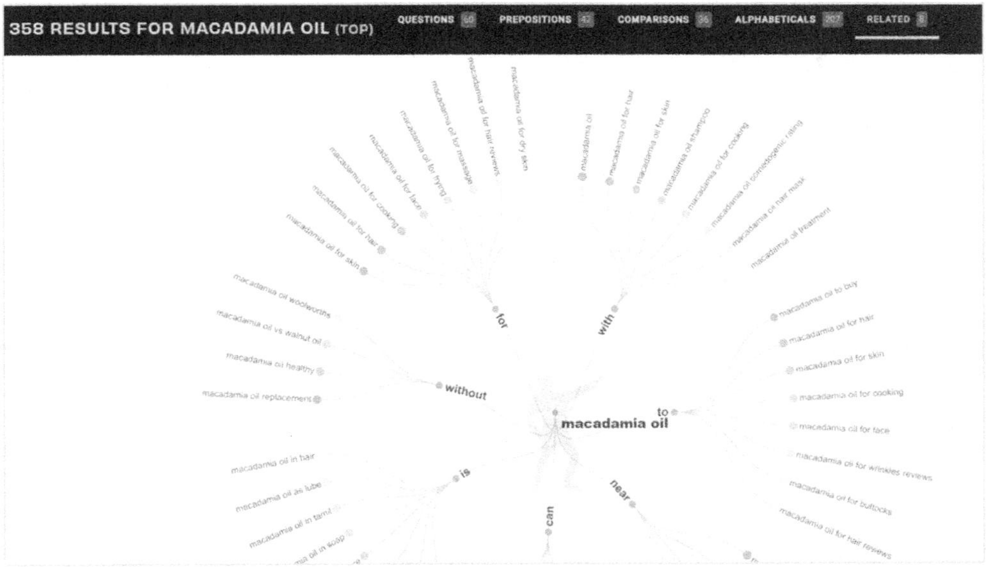

Figure 52 Questions relating to a keyword (AnswerThePublic).

AlsoAsked

AlsoAsked is a tool that aggregates "People Also Ask" (PAA) questions from Google Search results. You feed it a keyword, and it shows the related questions that searchers asked. These results can help you to find other keywords, or you might create pages that answer those questions.

Figure 53 People Also Asked questions in AlsoAsked.

B2C AND B2B KEYWORDS

Although the techniques for finding keywords are similar, the main difference in Business-to-Business (B2B) is that search volumes are typically lower than in Business-to-Consumer (B2C) keywords. This is because businesses need specialized products and services that are not relevant to home-based consumers.

I once met an SEO whose niche was floating heavy-lift cranes. These are special vessels that can lift a partially sunk ship; at that time, there were just three in the world. The daily lease fee is astronomical, so it costs millions for the vessel to reach the accident scene before it can begin the job. Competition for customers is intense because the ship might lie idle all year without a customer, but needs to be kept ready to sail at a moment's notice. He explained how difficult it is to find such a crane because numerous floating cranes regularly perform dockside work. He had to find the appropriate keywords and then create content for this obscure but lucrative niche. The keyword tools were utterly useless to him.

B2B SEOs will need to work hard to understand the market language in their niche and then look for generic language that overlaps. This would be a way to find new customers who might not have the right vocabulary but need the product.

Trust the Website

Some B2B keywords will show zero monthly searches. That means that the keyword tool has not registered such searches in its database. However, if the website offers these products or services, they are valid keywords and should be used on core and supplementary pages.

"Near Me" Keywords

Keywords that include the phrase "near me" are interesting. Consumers use it a lot, particularly on phones and in other voice searches. Yes, if you are hankering for a pizza, you would search for "pizza near me." Consequently, the keyword tools will show some of these keywords with a high search volume. For example, in the image below, I searched for keyword suggestions based on "pizza."

Keyword (by relevance)	Avg. monthly searches
pizza	301,000
Keyword ideas	
pizza near me	201,000
dominos near me	74,000
pizza hut near me	27,100
pizzeria	3,600
pizza delivery near me	12,100
pizza hut menu	12,100
pizza places near me	6,600
pepperoni	8,100
calzone	12,100
new york pizza	2,900

Figure 54 Google Ads Keyword Planner shows "near me" keywords.

Google Suggest is an "autocomplete" feature within Google Search that helps you find likely search phrases once you begin to type your query.

It’s fine for a quick check, and the same word entered a few days apart might show a slightly different list.

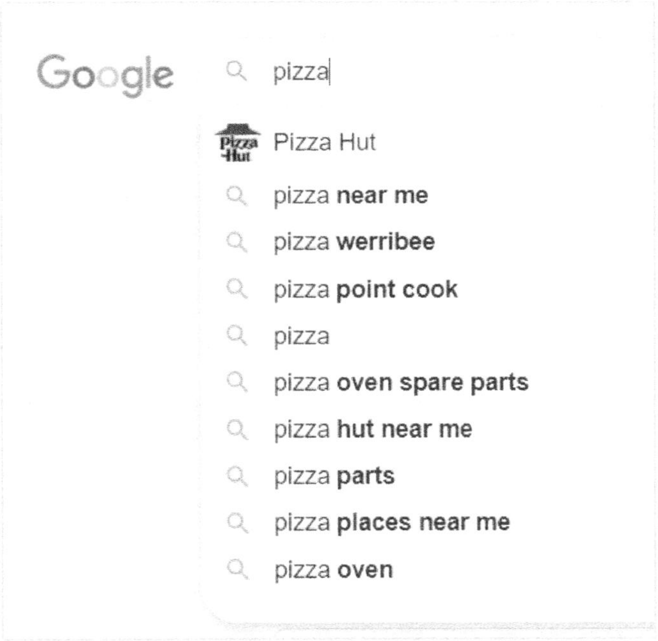

Figure 55 Google suggests “near me” as a likely phrase.

These “near me” keywords are a trap for novice SEOs. No, one does not fill pages with the literal phrase “near me.” Google will not show them to someone looking for a pizza near them in Orlando if the pizzeria is in San Francisco. Instead, the pages should be optimized for the business's actual location, with consistent address and location signals where appropriate. Next, let the search engine find pages from businesses near the searcher’s location.

Chapter 6

MANAGING CONTENT

If there were one area with the greatest leverage on visibility, it would be content—provided it is technically accessible, indexable, and trusted. Users are trying to satisfy a need—sometimes by reading content, sometimes by getting an immediate answer. They are looking for something and may encounter it via a result, summary, or linked page in the SERP.

In modern systems, content accuracy and maintenance are as important as initial creation.

TYPES OF CONTENT

Content does not imply text alone. The nature of a website will determine the mix of different types of content, which could be grouped as follows:

- Text
- Images and multimedia
- Structured and machine-readable content
- Third-party advertising elements (not content, but page elements that affect experience)

That is a simplification; search systems also evaluate purpose, prominence, and trust signals, but we shall pick them up in more detail later. Another useful distinction is between primary (core) content and supplementary content.

POSITIONING THE CONTENT TEAM

This book does not go deep into the writing profession other than to explore its overlap with SEO considerations. You will note that the Content team is in a similar predicament to the SEO team, as it is rarely in the same hierarchy across companies.

Here are some possibilities in a large organization.

Content in Product

In a robust, product-led organization, a Content Strategist oversees website content policy and governance. This person does this at a high level and does not manage the details.

One or more Content Managers have **Content Writers** reporting to them. They create the bulk of the content one sees on the website.

Content in UX

The User Experience (UX) Manager has UX Writers and Content Designers reporting to them. UX writing overlaps with Content Writers' work, so it needs to be monitored to avoid conflicts. For example, the product pages are maintained by the Content Writers, who are a part of the Product team. However, the UX Writers manage how they are translated into a mobile app. The latter team also looks after the "small text" on a website, such as error and alert messages, form design, and help text.

Content in Marketing

Marketing owns the organization's branding, tone-of-voice standards, graphics, and style guides, so all content must adhere to them. Their contribution to writing is **Copywriting**, usually found in marketing collateral and advertising. Some companies assign corporate blogs to content marketers because the writing style must differ from that on product pages.

Keep these role overlaps in mind when discussing SEO content, as all key players need to collaborate.

OUTSOURCING YOUR CONTENT CREATION

Small and large organizations might need to outsource content creation, which is not limited to text, but I shall use written content as an example. Outsourcing brings additional challenges.

AI-Generated Content

AI-generated content is allowed as long as it's high-quality and not spam.

Google focuses on value, accuracy, and originality, not whether a human or AI wrote it. What they *do* penalize is low-effort, mass-produced AI content that adds no user value.

Managing External Writers

The hiring Content Marketing Manager is the thought leader who works with the external agency's Content Manager. They convey expectations and the desired outcome.

The agency should provide a Content Strategist who obtains client sign-offs and manages the details. They source images and text and deliver them in accordance with the contract.

Knowledge Transfer

External writers are unlikely to know your products and services and your employees, even if they have worked with similar clients before. Treat the writers as you would a new team member. Please provide them with all existing information and training materials.

If you sell niche or complex physical products, such as farm machinery or electronics components, you might need internal experts to write the key points and leave the rest to the writer. Allow time to check their work before it is ready for the website. If you sell common household items, the writer will need minimal information from you.

Many companies have content style guides and a defined tone of voice for each product line. Make sure the writers have this information.

Location of Writers

In larger companies, I have seen contract writers working on-site full-time. That is an ideal location for contract writers, but most writers work remotely.

Content Brief

A content brief is a standardized form that suits many types of content. It contains fields that depend on the company and its workflow. You will see fields such as:

- Product family
- Intended location in the website hierarchy
- Word count
- SEO requirements

There is no need to repeat information you have already provided, such as company writing standards, style guides, etc. At one workplace, the in-house content leads would task internal and external writers and fill in the SEO field. The SEO team would always review the document before sending it to the writers. If the workplace has implemented a keyword register, there is no need to list the relevant keywords in the content brief.

NATURAL LANGUAGE

It's important to appreciate that search engines now use Artificial Intelligence (AI) and machine learning to comprehend human speech or text. In addition, you will hear of Natural Language Processing (NLP) and related language-understanding systems.

The key message here is that we should not write for search engines but for human comprehension, in a style they will enjoy reading.

An earlier tool I used was the Google Keyword Planner, which, in addition to taking seed keywords to recommend similar keywords, will also take a website URL. If this second method showed a high number of unrelated keywords, I would look more closely to see what was causing Google to misinterpret the page.

Book 4: *Is Our SEO Working?* covers this in depth.

SEARCH QUALITY RATER GUIDELINES

You should know about the "quality evaluators" or "quality raters" (the terms are used interchangeably), who Google contracts, and the guidebook they are given. They are chosen to represent the people in their country. Additionally, their site ratings are used to fine-tune algorithms, making them a "second opinion" resource. They primarily evaluate pages from a mobile perspective, though evaluation is not limited to a single device type.

Bing has a similar concept, and their raters are called Web Content Assessors.

It's important to note that the Search Quality Rater Guidelines do not address the algorithms that govern search quality and are not written for an SEO audience. We can, however, use this document to understand Google's concept of quality content, which can be summarized by the initialism E-E-A-T, which stands for:

- Experience
- Expertise
- Authoritativeness

- Trustworthiness

Google's Hyung-Jin Kim, VP of Google Search, confirmed at a search industry conference that every search query is evaluated with E-E-A-T considerations in mind, and that these concepts inform Google's core quality systems. (Note that he did not say it is a ranking factor.)

Experience

Experience is a relatively recent addition to this set of factors. If your content demonstrates experience in the subject matter, it can improve search visibility. This is easier for some websites than others.

A restaurant that posts recipes of its menu items and supplements them with videos and photos taken on the premises demonstrates more credible experience than a recipe site that uses stock images or videos. A product reviewer who posts their own photos and videos demonstrates personal experience.

An online discussion forum with good moderation can demonstrate experience through its users' posts. You might notice that search results for certain consumer products will include a couple of forum threads.

Sometimes, it's not possible to demonstrate personal experience. A tropical disease such as Ebola can have expert, authoritative articles written by medical researchers in another country. Many articles about types of cancer that rank high, for example, are not written by cancer patients or oncologists. They could be written by pharmaceutical researchers who have conducted trials with the help of other experts.

Articles by survivors of diseases, such as Long COVID sufferers, would have low levels of Expertise and Authority, but a high level of Experience.

Expertise

Google describes "expertise" as follows:

- The facts are easily verifiable.
- The author seems to know the topic well and could be described as an expert.
- The content demonstrates subject-matter knowledge appropriate to topics that affect money or life decisions.

Authoritativeness

Google does not have an explicit definition of authoritativeness. Still, the document uses the commonly understood meaning of a site or page that appears to be an authority on the subject matter. The author's credentials should be easy to check – ideally, linked from the article. The content should reflect this air of authority. Think about some authoritative person you see on TV and why they seem to be an authority. They might hold a senior position in an organization in that field; they often speak publicly on that topic; and they might have published many articles on the topic, some of which reach the mainstream news media. Eventually, the public accepts them as experts on the subject without questioning it.

Author-level metrics have long been used in academia to allocate research funding. We don't know whether Google uses these or other metrics, but a study of author-level metrics will help you understand how authoritativeness can be demonstrated. For example, the i10 metric is used in academic publishing to recognize authors with 10 or more citations.

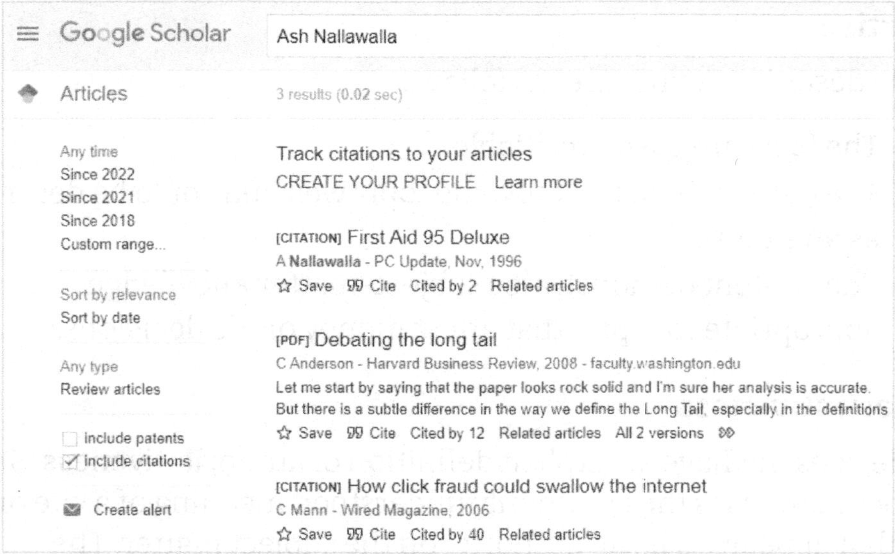

Figure 56 My name is cited in some articles.

Over time, most of your website content might display these signs of authority and be in a position to confer authority to another linked website. Once your brand or website is mentioned on several authoritative websites, it will exhibit authoritativeness of its own.

Trustworthiness

The content should make the reader trust it to the extent that they might make a significant financial decision or life choice based on it. Google says little about trustworthiness, so we need to use the dictionary definition. In a webpage context, its appearance and content should not show any features that would make the reader uneasy.

It's reasonable to assume that Google can interpret words to determine trustworthiness. If, for example, a page presents medical claims framed around conspiracy narratives rather than established evidence, it is unlikely to rank well for informational queries about vaccines.

As a more familiar example, an e-commerce site that provides no customer service contact point is likely to be perceived as less trustworthy than one that does. Displaying returns and refunds policies conveys trust.

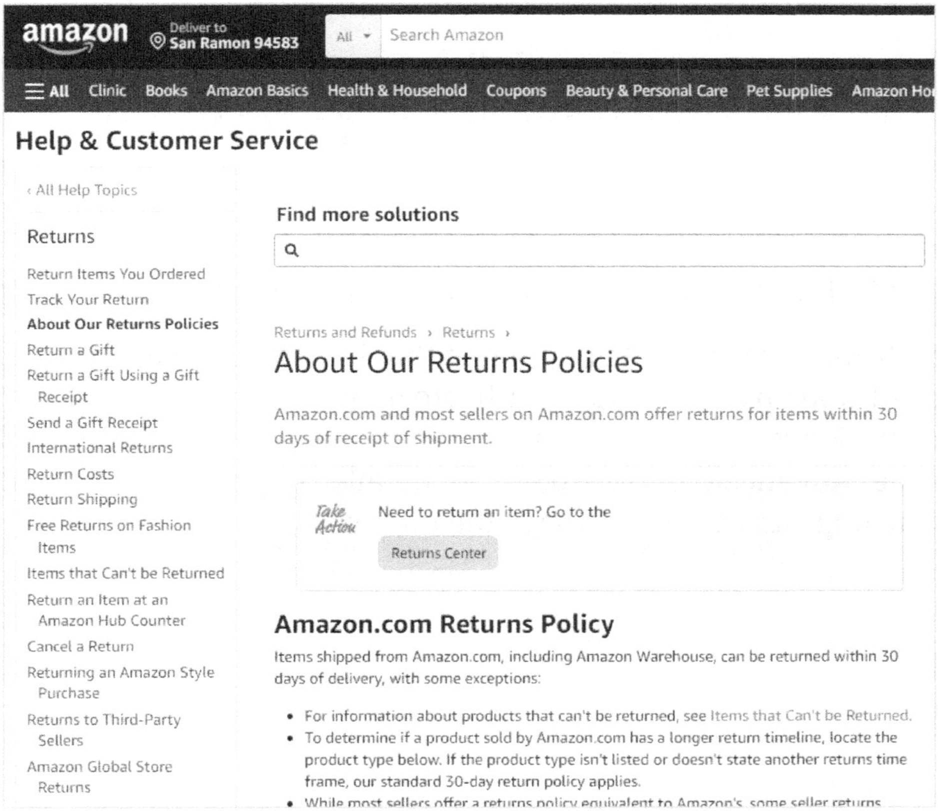

Figure 57 Amazon's returns policies.

Likewise, a website that does not use secure HTTPS connections and a valid SSL certificate will be treated as less trustworthy than one that does. Google Chrome and Microsoft Edge actively discourage users from interacting with such pages by displaying a 'Not Secure' label next to the address bar.

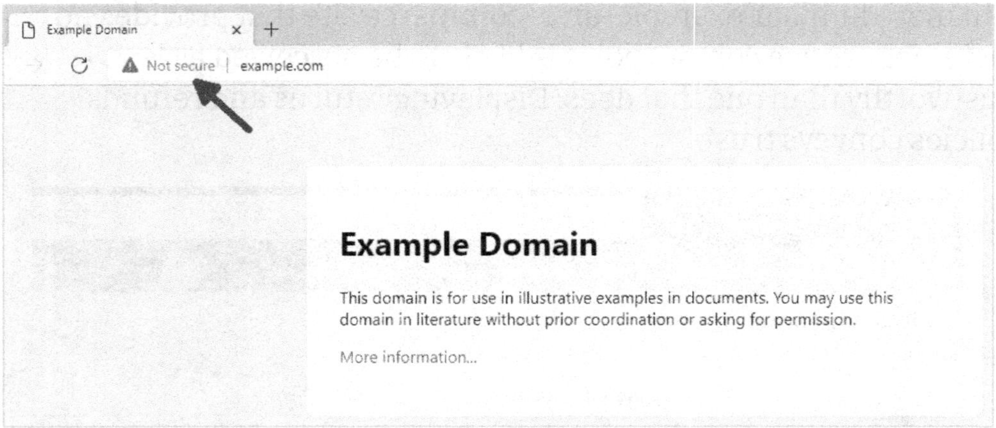

Figure 58 The Microsoft Edge browser warns a user about an HTTP URL.

A poorly managed website might find that its organic search traffic has dropped, and an expired SSL certificate may be the cause. Most users would back out of such an error message (shown below). They could click the "Advanced" button to see the detailed explanation and ignore the warning, but they would be in the minority.

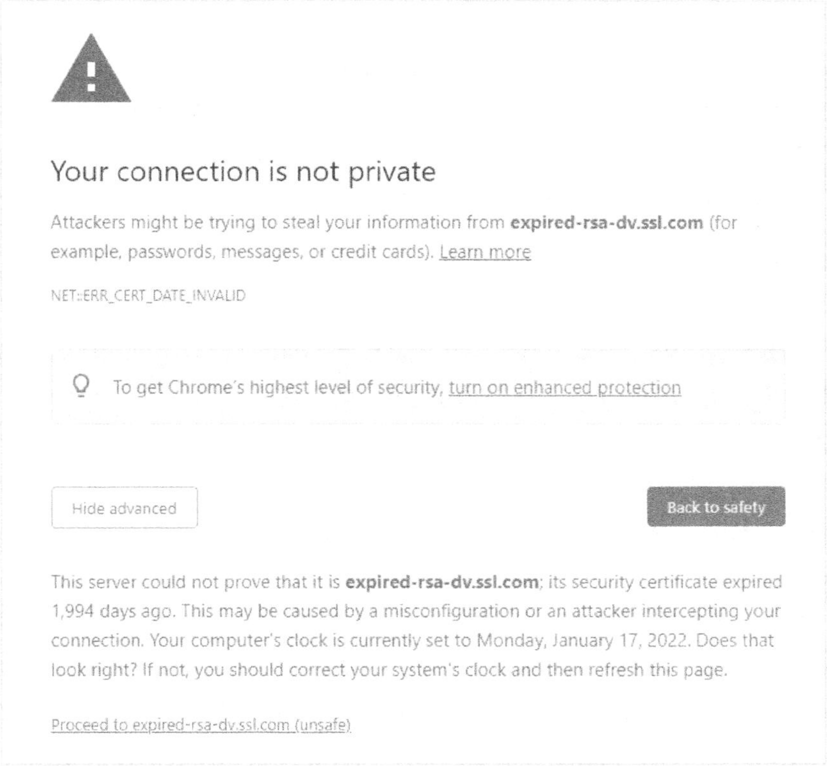

Figure 59 The Chrome browser warns about an expired security certificate.

Specific antivirus browser add-ons might also warn against downloading and running a file if the tool has little history of being downloaded by others.

Some third-party companies display 'trust seals' intended to reassure visitors. This might show that a financial transaction on the site can be trusted or that the business belongs to a reputable membership organization. Examples include:

- Better Business Bureau (BBB) seal
- PayPal Verified seal
- Partner seals

Your Money, Your Life (YMYL)

Google places importance on content that concerns your money or your life. "Money" refers to all kinds of activities where money changes hands, while "life" covers all aspects of physical and mental well-being, particularly medical advice. Here are some examples of YMYL:

- **Finance** – Banks, insurance companies, financial planners, money lenders, etc.
- **News** – News media that feature essential subjects that can affect your life or well-being, but not entertainment or sports.
- **Healthcare** – Pharmaceuticals, health insurance, hospitals, nursing homes, etc.
- **Shopping** – All kinds of buying or selling sites are in this category.
- **Government** – Most government websites can affect your life.
- **Education** – Websites that offer online learning or represent bricks-and-mortar educational institutions and the like.
- **Categories of People** – Websites that cover groups, such as religions, sexual orientation, victims of crime, refugees, etc.

If your activities cover those two topics (EEAT and YMYL), the algorithms will pay particular attention to your material.

Grading of YMYL

There is an undefined grading of YMYL that might affect some businesses. If your products are low-priced, would Google be as critical as it would be for products that most people need a loan for? We don't know the answer, but EEAT is likely to affect unknown websites compared to leading businesses. For example, if you are a home builder and your blog runs an article on home loans, you might think this is a reasonable topic because home buyers usually need a loan. From Google's perspective, would a home builder have more authoritativeness than a bank on this topic? The reverse scenario also occurs: a bank blog might publish an article about home renovations to support its loan products. Since the bank is not an expert in renovations, the article should focus on the financial angle.

The takeaway here is to recognize your area of expertise and capitalize on it.

What Is "Quality Content"?

According to Google, "quality content" has the following characteristics:

- It satisfies the searcher's query.
- It provides original information, reporting, research, or analysis.
- It is a substantial, complete, or comprehensive description of the topic.
- It provides insightful analysis or interesting information that is beyond obvious.
- If it draws on other sources, it provides substantial additional value and originality.
- The headline and page title are a descriptive, helpful summary of the content without exaggeration or shock value.
- It is a page you would gladly bookmark or recommend to a friend.
- A print publication or encyclopedia would gladly print or reference such a page.

Essentially, these evaluators are given definitions of the concepts and examples of websites that might or might not exhibit those properties, and then asked to evaluate several pages for those attributes. The results are then compared with Google's algorithmic assessments. The algorithms are adjusted as needed, so those evaluators play a relatively indirect role in ranking keywords (entities).

Google makes this document available publicly and updates it regularly, so you can find its current location with a simple search if it is no longer at the link below.

How to Use EEAT

I have often pointed writers and editors to the above book, and I am unsure if they have looked at it beyond a quick skim. Although we can make guesses about what EEAT means, it's better to cross-check it with Google's definitions. After all, our own opinion of our expertise is biased and lacks a complete understanding of competing experts. We might think we are an authority on some topic; how would a computer algorithm make that judgment? Why should anyone trust us? Can an algorithm make that call reliably?

I urge everyone to read this booklet or skim through its pages if they cannot make the time. Large publishing houses and e-commerce shopping sites will generate millions of pages. Unless content guidelines are in place, you will rapidly lose the EEAT advantage to a competitor who has taken the time to implement them.

Key Takeaways

I use these points to explain the concept of quality content, which some writers tend to use carelessly, as if it were self-explanatory. In the context of SEO, content is one of the main ranking factors that we can control.

1. **Relevance.** The information (textual, video, app, or audio) must be relevant to the searcher, thus helpful to them. If they are searching for a pizza, the best content might not be in their city or country, so Google finds the content closest to them. If they are searching for a car to buy, the results might be from their metropolitan region, rather than their suburb. Sometimes, Google might present more than one kind of content, such as video and news, in addition to web pages.

2. **Context.** Google tries to find content that best matches the search intent. Searchers often type vague search terms that don't convey why they are searching. If your jewelry business buys more than it sells, the content must send "buy" signals when a customer is looking to sell their jewelry.
3. **Quantity.** There is no perfect quantity of content. If a single word, figure, or sentence satisfies the query, then that is sufficient content. Numeric queries, such as currency conversion or the current time in a given country, are a good example of minimal content.
4. **Website.** The characteristics of the web page and the website come into the equation of quality. Is the information presented helpfully? Does the page load fast? Is it accessible?
5. **EEAT.** The content should meet the quality rating guidelines.

CUSTOMER JOURNEY MAPPING

Marketers follow one of several customer-journey models, such as "AIDA":

- Attention
- Interest
- Desire
- Action

Some might go for a simpler model of three stages:

- Awareness
- Consideration
- Decision

They can guide the content-creation process for online and offline channels. Sometimes an offline channel can prompt a later online search, so a customer's journey can take many routes. Depending on each stage of the buyer's journey, online content can be created to be found in a search engine.

For example, in the early stages, the potential buyer must be made aware that the product or service can meet their needs. Sometimes, they might not know they have a need, so the journey can begin with introductory content that seeds new words and phrases in buyers' minds. If digital cameras were just invented, then film camera magazines or websites would be seeded with news about the digital camera.

Users are now ready to research digital cameras. Such content can address the What, Where, When, Why, How to, and How Much questions. They are now convinced that they need a digital camera. They can be fed new information to keep that desire alive, such as news and reviews about digital cameras.

When they are ready to buy, the user performs intentional searches for comparative reviews, single reviews, specifications, and, of course, prices. You know they are about to convert when they look for shipping options. All this content needs to be on your website.

KAIZEN FOR SEO CONTENT QUALITY

The Japanese concept of *Kaizen* means continuous, incremental improvement rather than big-bang change.

SEO performance improves the same way — one refinement at a time. Encourage teams to build Kaizen into weekly routines:

- improving internal links
- refreshing outdated statements
- compressing images for faster load times
- rewriting FAQs

- adding missing schema markup

Small improvements compound into sustained gains.
Kaizen turns content optimization into a habit — not a scramble when traffic drops.

SOURCING FRESH CONTENT

A website that sees no change in its content will likely stop ranking for searches in competitive niches, so the rule of thumb is to keep it fresh, depending on your resources. These might be in-house or reliable individuals you can trust to write the material for you. Unfortunately, only large businesses can afford in-house writers.

Refreshing Content Superficially

Some people change the dates in old articles and try to pass them off as fresh content. Google considers this tactic spammy. It seems to work for some, but I would not do it. Sometimes there are legitimate reasons to do it. For example, a public service agency might have a single page for fire alerts and needs to ensure it is up to date. Many people would have linked to it or bookmarked it.

At the other end of the spectrum, small sites change the date and have no other content changed on the page. They should consider using a new URL, deleting the old one, and redirecting the old URL to the new one.

Using AI to Create Content

Google no longer treats all AI-assisted content as inherently problematic. Instead, its current guidance focuses on **how content is produced and governed**, not whether an artificial intelligence system was involved. Content generated or assisted by large language models—such as OpenAI's GPT-class models—is evaluated using the same quality standards applied to human-written material.

The risk arises when AI is used to produce content **at scale, without editorial oversight, original insight, or accountability**. In those cases, the output may fall under Google's definition of **scaled or low-value auto-generated content**, which can still trigger algorithmic demotion and, in extreme cases, manual action. The issue is not automation itself, but the absence of purpose, accuracy, and human judgment.

Modern AI systems are substantially more capable than earlier tools, and their output can appear fluent, coherent, and superficially authoritative. However, this fluency can mask factual errors, vague generalities, or unverified claims. From a governance perspective, this creates a new class of risk: content that looks credible enough to pass casual review but fails under closer scrutiny by evaluators, regulators, or search quality systems.

Large organizations should therefore approach AI-assisted content with caution. Uncontrolled use—especially for explanatory, advisory, or reputation-sensitive material—introduces legal, brand, and visibility risk. Search systems increasingly assess **experience, expertise, accuracy, and source integrity**, and AI-generated text that lacks clear ownership or validation can undermine trust signals rather than strengthen them.

The historical parallel remains instructive. Earlier generations of automated content—such as synonym-based article "spinners" applied to scraped or plagiarized material—briefly exploited algorithmic blind spots but were ultimately neutralized as search systems improved. The same pattern applies today: tactics that prioritize volume and speed over clarity, originality, and review may work temporarily, but they do not survive sustained evaluation.

For SEO managers, the practical rule is straightforward: **AI should assist creation, not replace accountability**. Content produced with AI support must still be reviewed, edited, and owned by subject-matter experts, aligned with a clear page purpose, and governed by the same standards applied to human-authored work. When those controls are in place, AI can improve efficiency. When they are absent, it becomes a liability rather than an advantage.

Copyright Date

Editing the copyright year on a website or webpage to show the current year can attract a lawsuit from someone else with the same material that shows an earlier year. The earliest demonstrable copyright claimant may have a legal advantage unless you can produce other evidence, such as a copy kept in archive.org. By all means, show a range of years, with the start year hard-coded and the end year generated by a programming call.

Example: Copyright © 2011 – 2026 (the latter being the current year)

MAIN CONTENT AND SUPPLEMENTARY CONTENT

Google uses the term Main Content to refer to the main body of a page, while Supplementary Content is used to describe everything else that is on the page, whose presence does not affect the objective of the MC.

Main Content (MC)

In addition to the main body of the page, the MC also extends to the text that might bring people to this page, such as the article Title (which might repeat as a Title attribute), URL, and Meta Description, which may appear in a SERP (unless Google has substituted them algorithmically).

Supplementary Content (SC)

Usually, the navigation elements at the top, sides, and bottom of pages are SC.

CORE CONTENT

The core content on the website is everything you need to make it a viable destination for the audience. It includes the following main groups of pages:

- Home page
- Pages for products and services
- Pages with helpful content, such as Frequently Asked Questions
- About Us
- Contact Us

Core content is owned by the "product" side of the organization, while Marketing owns ancillary content. Therefore, the two silos must be in sync.

ANCILLARY CONTENT

Marketing Content, or Content Marketing, is ancillary or supplementary content, often time-sensitive. Such content can be placed on your primary website or on another.

Landing Pages

A Landing Page is the page visitors are directed to when entering the website through organic search, paid search, or direct mail. In the context of PPC search, a core content page can serve double duty as a landing page, though it is more common to build dedicated landing pages that are free of typical navigation cues or distractions.

Keep the SEO team informed about all core content targeted by marketing initiatives so they are not caught off guard by a surge in traffic. Proper tagging will ensure correct attribution. Temporary campaign pages are usually hidden from search engines to prevent them from being indexed and competing with the core content. When the campaign is over, there are no disappointments for organic searchers because the pages are not in the index.

Blog

Many companies have a blog on their website. Some are reluctant to label it a blog, so they might call it "News," "Articles," "Reports," etc. A blog offers many SEO benefits, in addition to the intrinsic branding and marketing value:

- **Fresh Content** – Search engines like to feature fresh content, and a blog post serves this purpose, particularly if done frequently.
- **Links** – If the blog is on a different website, such as Medium, links to your website are welcome for discovery and referral value, even though direct ranking impact is limited.
- **Larger Vocabulary** – Blog articles provide the opportunity to use a larger vocabulary, including words that you might not want in the primary content. For example, the word "cheap" makes brand managers nervous, but you might fit it into a blog post.

Infographics

Infographics are meant to convey information through graphics. I am skeptical of their SEO benefit because they were overused when Pinterest came on the scene, and links from it are "nofollowed." Pinterest enables other Pinterest users to "pin" such content to their own virtual pinboards, which does not help you with SEO but will bring more traffic to the original infographic on your website.

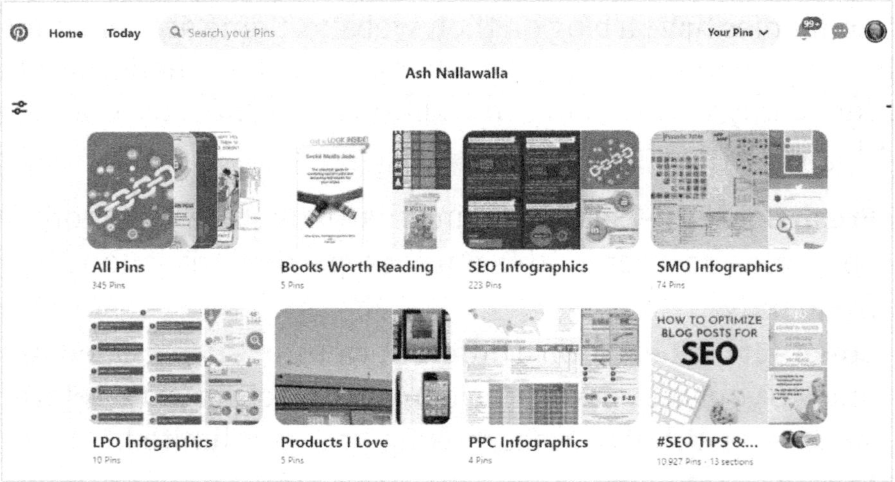

Figure 60 My long-forgotten Pinterest pinboard.

Figure 61 You can link an infographic to your website.

TITLE ATTRIBUTE AND META DESCRIPTION

Two important code elements are worth mentioning: they are usually filled out by content team members when creating a new page. Still, they may also be created by a developer when creating a data-driven page. So, what goes in those two fields is quite important for SEO. Google uses it to understand the page's content.

Title Attribute (Title Tag, Title Element, or Title Link)

The Title attribute is usually a copy of the article title (marked up as H1), but can be customized to be something else. You can see what is in the Title attribute of a given page in two places:

- The browser tab
- In the HTML code of the page

SEOs call it a Title Tag informally, but Google refers to it as a Title Element in HTML code and a Title Link in SERPs. Sometimes, Google rewrites the Title Element that you wrote and shows a different Title Link in the SERP. Tags longer than 60 characters run the risk of being rewritten by Google.

Figure 62 The Title attribute appears in a browser tab.

Some companies experiment with placing their site name before the title, though most place it at the end. Amazon has the luxury of testing across several countries, so we get examples like the one below.

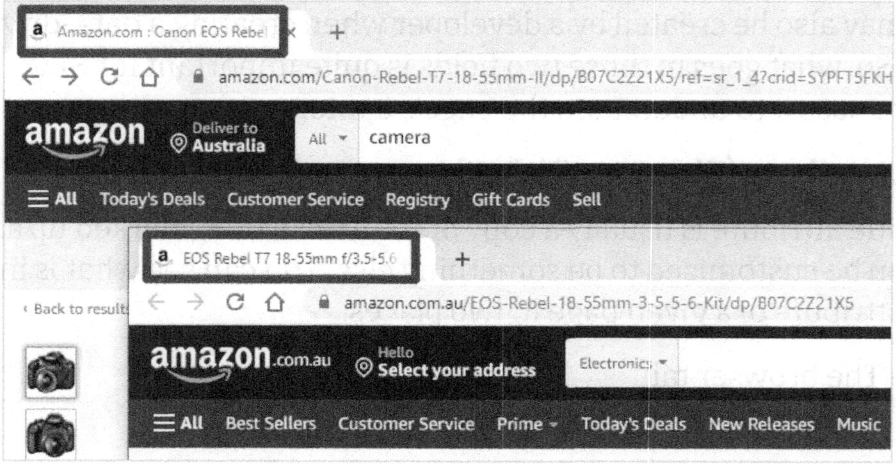

Figure 63 Trying different placements of the site name in the title tag.

If the Title Element is too long, Google replaces the truncated part of it with an ellipsis.

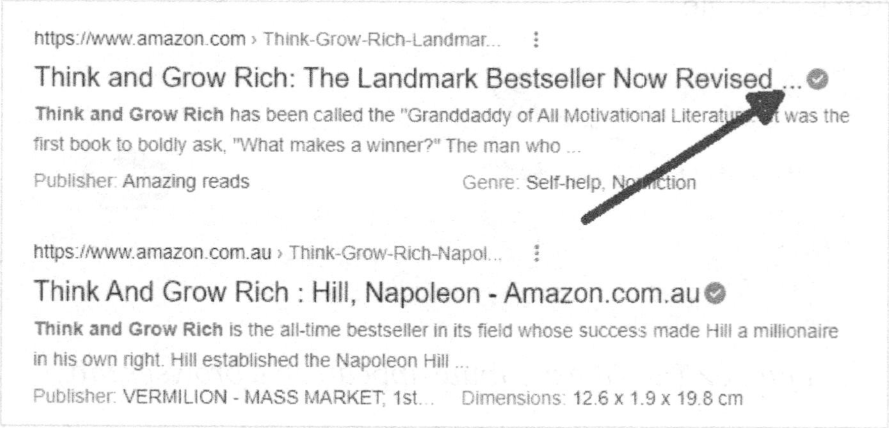

Figure 64 Long titles can be truncated in a SERP.

Meta Description

The text in the Meta Description HTML element is not visible on the page but is present in the page's HTML code. Usually, it appears in a

SERP, where it serves as an advertisement to entice the searcher to click this result rather than others.

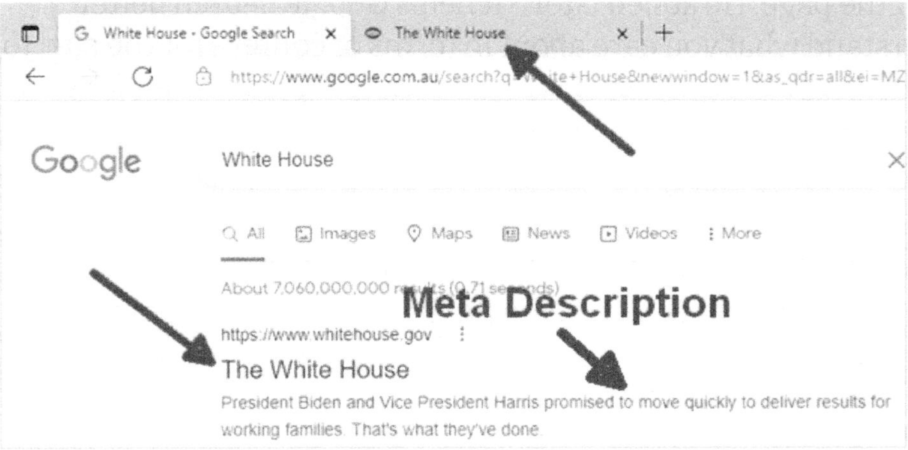

Figure 65 The Title attribute and Meta Description as seen in a SERP.

The Code

By way of illustration, the code for the Title attribute and the Meta Description looks like this:

```
<meta name="description" content="President Biden and Vice
President Harris promised to move quickly to deliver results for
working families. That's what they've done." />
```

Why They Are Important

The Title attribute and Meta Description are important for two reasons:

- Ranking
- To attract a click

The Title attribute has long been considered an important ingredient in the ranking algorithm. Please ensure that the most relevant keyword for a given page is placed there.

Google's Martin Splitt explained the importance by saying that the two elements give Google a summary of what you consider important about the page. He added later, "It helps Google Search better understand what you care about in terms of content for the site, too."

Figure 66 Google explains the importance of the Meta Description.

Google's John Mueller added that the ranking algorithm does not use the Meta Description. The SEO community is skeptical of this element, but I treat it as an ad to drive a click.

When Google Decides Otherwise

Google does not always show the Meta Description text in the SERP. Suppose a searcher's query contains words that match the page content exactly; then that snippet of the page is shown with the matching words in bold. This provides the searcher with confidence that the result is relevant to their query.

The actual Meta Description of the sample page below reads, "Google understands both page-level meta-tags and inline directives. Explore a list of the special tags that Google Search can support." Yet, you will see that it was not shown in the SERP because it does not contain words that closely match my query text. Instead, it showed the nearest words from the body of the page.

Interestingly, the Title attribute of this page reads, "Meta and Inline Tags that Google Understands | Google Search Central | Google Developers." A slightly shorter text replaced it.

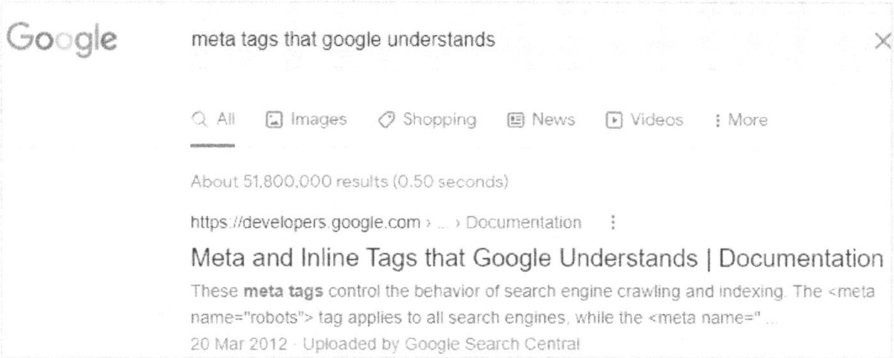

Figure 67 An example of a snippet that is shown instead of the Meta Description.

Google understood my vague search query and found a suitable page, but the algorithm had to tweak its SERP appearance to ensure I would click it. Furthermore, it interpreted my search intent: I was not using Google to make a statement but to ask a question.

There are ways to persuade Google to use your Title attribute and Meta Description element, but your SEO team can explore the following URL for details.

Very short and very long (over 70 characters) Title attributes will likely be replaced by Google. Do not spend too much time on Meta Descriptions if there are bigger issues to fix.

FEATURED IMAGES

Where pages contain non-decorative images, one of them should be marked as a "featured image". This thumbnail appears when the page is shared on social media or when it appears in Google AI Overview results. It should pique interest and help to get a click.

Many CMSs and shopping platforms offer a handy option to designate a featured image.

RATINGS AND REVIEWS

Reviews are written by customers, usually on third-party websites such as Google Business Profiles. Ratings are usually on a "star" scale of 1 – 5, but other ranges exist. Reviews might be written by your company, such as an online magazine covering certain products. The review must mention something not in the manufacturer's literature.

Positive reviews contribute to prominence and trust signals when other relevance factors are satisfied. Positive reviews enhance a page's reputation, so you should encourage them.

For example, a search for a Thai restaurant near you will very likely show you some results with these characteristics:

- **Relevance** – the restaurant offers Thai cuisine.
- **Distance** – the restaurant is near you.
- **Prominence** – positive reviews and ratings are part of the secret algorithm.

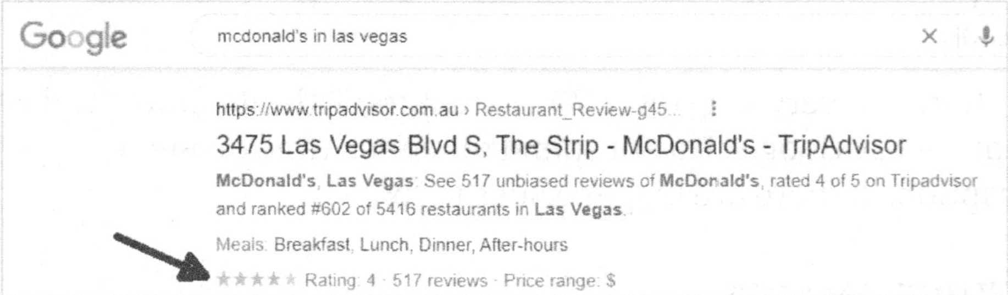

Figure 68 Reviews and Ratings in a Google SERP.

Ratings and reviews appear in both regular search results and map results, so it is worth encouraging customers to leave honest reviews, preferably with photos. Reviews with photos tend to remain visible longer than those without. If you don't, only the complaints will be posted. Higher average ratings improve prominence, though there is no fixed threshold required for SERP eligibility.

Many review sites encourage users to upload photographs. Travel sites are a great example of that. Positive reviews accompanied by many photos are likely to be shared and attract visits. Almost all such sites use "nofollow" links, so the links work as Citations.

If you manage a site that publishes ratings and reviews, you will get user-generated content and only need someone to moderate it before it is displayed.

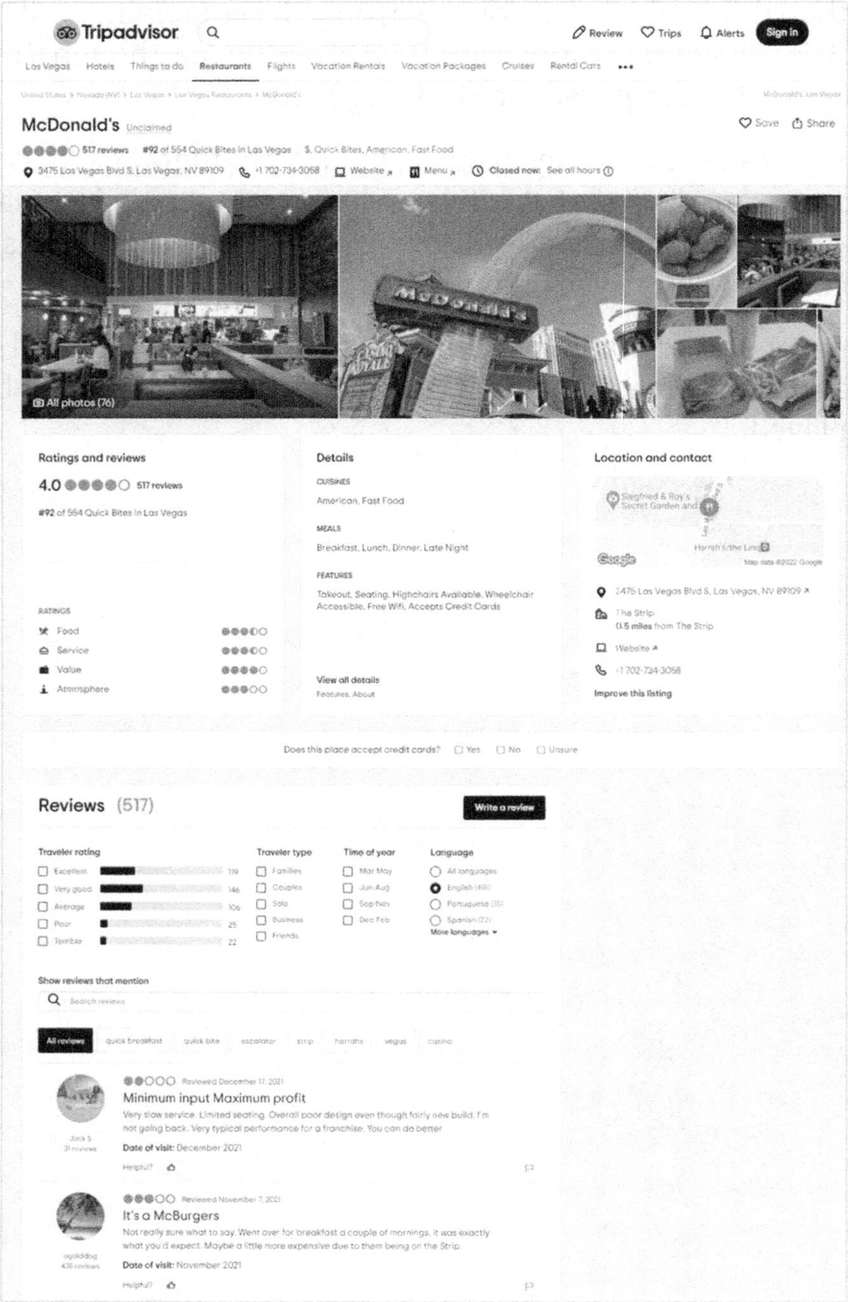

Figure 69 Reviews and Ratings are a significant feature on TripAdvisor.

OPTIMIZED VIDEO

Video content is an excellent way to achieve a page #1 ranking because many queries yield SERP results with video.

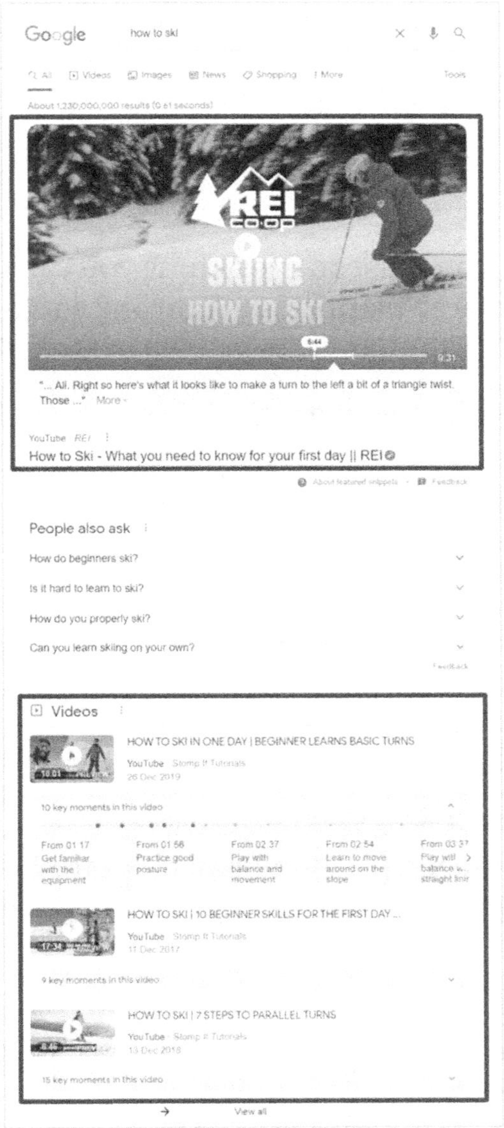

Figure 70 Videos seen on page #1 of a SERP.

You might notice that YouTube-hosted videos rank high, but they can also be on other platforms, such as Vimeo, DailyMotion, and others. Of course, you can also host them on your own website, provided that it can handle the load, such as using a suitable content delivery network (CDN).

There is a small catch here – except for videos on your site, the rest are hosted elsewhere, so you're optimizing someone else's platform. Yet, it is worth it.

What's Involved

As with all content, you must do everything you can to optimize video. Then it's up to the search platforms to find and serve your high rankings. Your SEO team should be looking at the following topics:

- **Targeted entities (keywords)** – What aspect of your offerings are capable of being featured in a video, and what are the likely search terms?
- **Competition** – Are there a few or many videos competing for the targeted keywords?
- **Metadata** – Each video benefits from well-chosen metadata, such as:
    - **Title –** something descriptive
    - **Description –** something descriptive
    - **Hashtags –** tags
- **Thumbnail images –** A thumbnail helps to show a compelling image rather than let the platform grab something less impactful.
- **Cards** – A card is a jump-off point, usually at the end of the video, that can serve as a call-to-action (CTA) on your website or link to another video.
- **Channel** – You can set up a branded presence known as a Channel, where all your videos are listed.

- **Playlist** – A playlist helps show your videos in some desired sequence, for example, steps toward purchasing a house. You can play it as a continuous piece, which suits viewers who have the time to see the content.
- **Transcript** – Providing a transcript serves a dual purpose. Automated captioning displays hilarious text if the speaker's accent is unclear. You can synchronize an uploaded transcript file with each scene. Search engines understand the intent of each scene and the video clip as a whole.
- **Audio bonus** – Certain videos, such as interviews, might lend themselves to having their audio extracted and turned into a podcast.

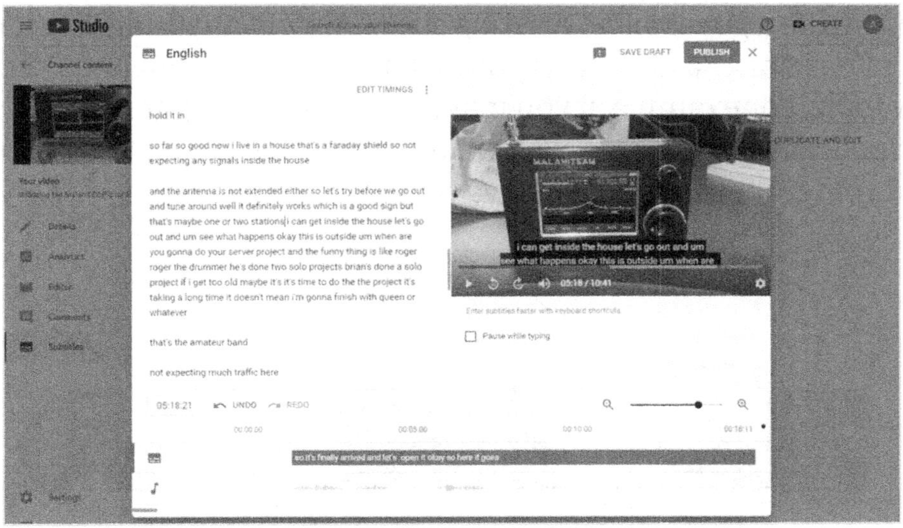

Figure 71 YouTube enables you to edit the auto-generated captions.

Optimizing videos is a specialty, and you might want to work with a professional with an excellent track record. Your SEO team can also learn to do it.

OPTIMIZED AUDIO

If you have audio files on your website, such as webinars, podcasts, or music, Audio SEO is important. Ideally, such files should have a landing page with the appropriate keywords and relevant images. A transcript file serves the same purpose as a video transcript. In addition, Google surfaces podcast content through Google Search and YouTube Music–related experiences.

Podcasting

Podcasting is a growing content marketing strategy. Many surveys show how many adults listen to podcasts, but you will need to look up the figures for your niche. If you want to build a new audience and have a solid plan, you could pleasantly surprise yourself. Test the waters by offering to be a guest on an existing show. Almost anything you can think of has either a dedicated podcast or one near enough to welcome a new topic. For example, if you make earthmoving equipment, you'll find a podcast covering excavation in mining, building construction, landscaping, or even archaeology.

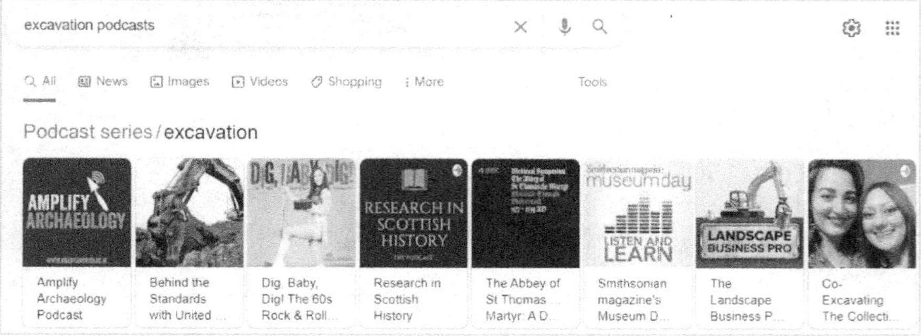

Figure 72 Even excavators have a podcast or two.

If you create a podcast series, get it listed in podcast directories and apps such as Spotify, Google Podcasts, TuneIn, Apple Podcasts, and many more. Browsing through lists of episodes will give ideas for creating episodes. Be sure to develop edited transcripts and publish them for SEO purposes and to avoid lawsuits from organizations representing individuals with difficulties.

KEYWORD REGISTER

The Keyword Register mentioned in the Managing Keywords chapter is a go-to resource for content writers. You choose the best keywords and use them to measure ranking visibility. The same keywords need to be used on your pages. Otherwise, you are analyzing pages that don't even have some of these keywords. This method works well on a new website and with new pages. On a long-established site with thousands of pages, you're unlikely to touch up old copy to fit these keywords.

The tabs in the spreadsheet correspond to the different entities (keyword groups), and the rows contain the selected keywords, sorted by search volume from highest to lowest. Each subsequent column header contains the URL of each page covering this entity. Generally, these will be product pages and some supplementary content pages. The cells below show a count of keywords used on a given page.

This is a low-tech way to ensure your writers use well-chosen keywords. If they do not cooperate, your SEO strategy will meet an uncertain fate. I have used this method at a few workplaces and with clients, and it works very well. The SEO team may need to populate the initial URL columns with the primary content keyword usage as part of an audit and initial launch of this keyword register.

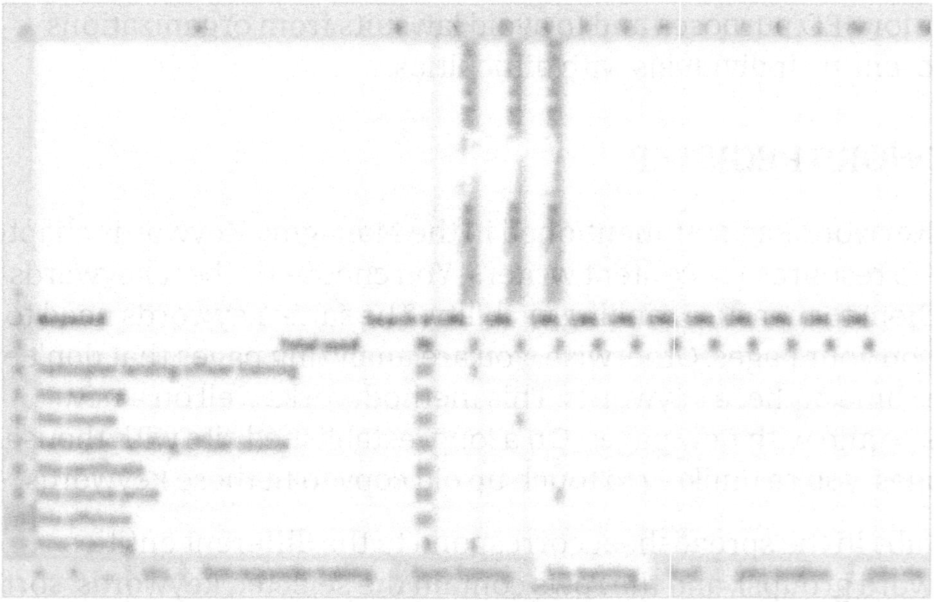

Figure 73 Example of a keyword register (intentionally blurred).

I have seen variations of this layout where tabs are not used, but a single worksheet, called a Keywords Matrix, has many columns of entities.

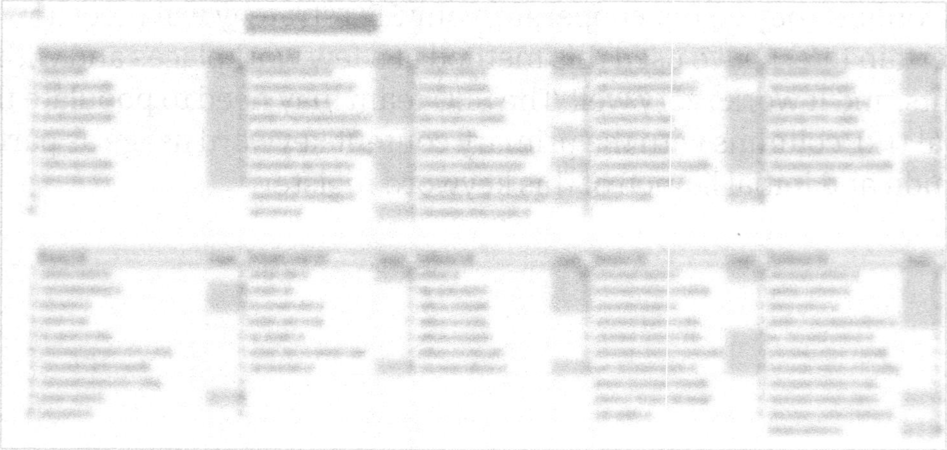

Figure 74 A keywords matrix (intentionally blurred).

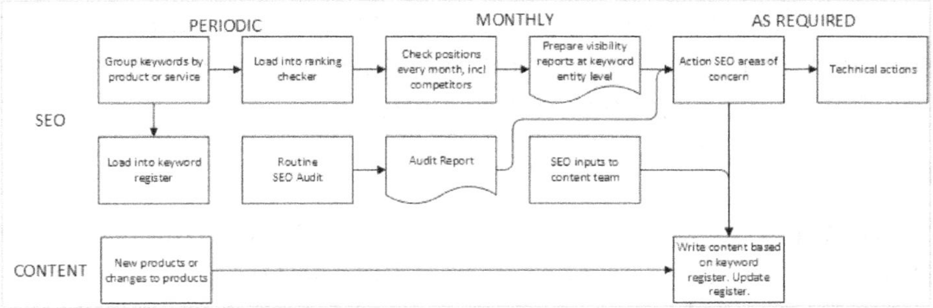

Figure 75 SEO and Content teams' workflow.

ADVERTISEMENTS IN CONTENT

Some websites are happy to show third-party advertisements that are not competing with them. For example, a car review site can display ads from car makers and car accessory vendors. The guidelines for ads primarily concern your commercial relationships with the ad platforms and legal obligations, but we are only looking at the SEO impact here.

Do Ads Hurt Your SEO?

An SEO's usual answer also applies here – it depends. The impact is more significant on phones than on desktops because it's easier to accidentally click an ad on a phone than on a desktop, where the user often has a mouse for precise control. So, if the ad harms user experience (UX), it is more likely to break SEO.

Degree of User Control

Can the user dismiss the ad if it obscures the screen, or do they have to wait for a timer to finish counting down? Does it appear before the user sees anything else?

Code

You enable third-party ads by inserting code provided by the intermediary entity. Unfortunately, this code can potentially affect your site performance, as reported by a performance-checking tool. For example, it might contain "unused JavaScript," and you will have no hope of getting the ad platform to remove it.

Banners

Banners usually occupy a strip across the screen, leaving the rest of the screen visible. So, they don't affect SEO, but they might push your content below the fold.

Pop-ups

A pop-up could be a generic term for anything that displays unexpectedly in front of the page you are trying to reach. It might be an ad or a part of the site operation. It might be a pop-under, meaning it appears in a separate window behind the main content, so you see the ad after you close the main content window. You see very few of these nowadays, perhaps because sites were penalized for it. Many browsers block them by default, or via plugins and extensions.

Modals

A modal is usually part of the site navigation or operation, for example, a refinement filter that narrows your search on the site. Check that it does not block a search engine crawler from proceeding deeper.

Interstitials

An interstitial is a transient page element that takes up most of the screen and cannot be closed until a timer removes it. This usage might hurt SEO.

Overlays

An overlay is an element that does not cover the whole screen. That has greater significance for small, mobile screens than for desktops. For example, when used for ads, they could serve as a sign-up form.

Declaring Interest

Search engines and affiliate marketing networks usually require websites that display ads to clearly mark them, so visitors do not click ads by mistake. Sometimes, the ad broker has a similar expectation.

Cookie Policies and Consents

A pop-up or interstitial that requires the user to consent to cookies or to declare their minimum age might be a legal requirement in your country, so it would not run afoul of a search engine's guidelines.

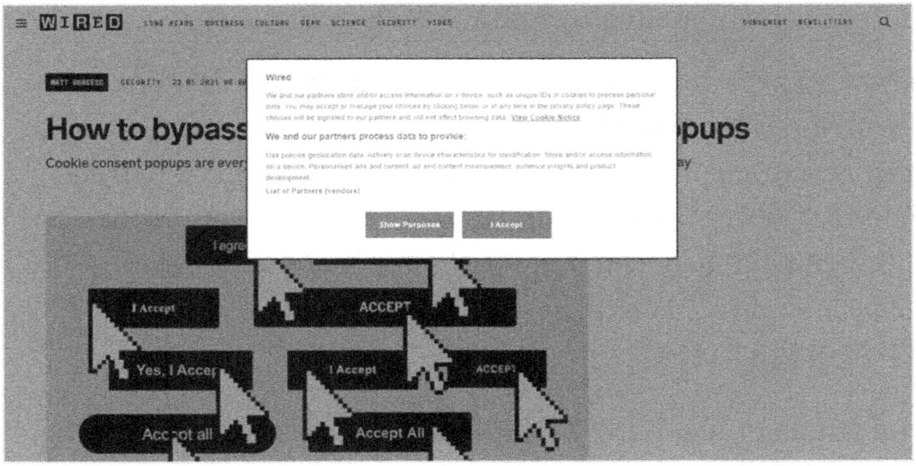

Figure 76 A cookie-consent pop-up.

FORCING A LOGIN / PAYWALLS

Some sites will show nothing or very little before a user logs in. For example, Facebook users choose their own privacy settings, which also block search engines, while the *Wall Street Journal* uses a paywall.

Subscriber-only news content needs the appropriate structured data tag inserted into the code to avoid being ignored by search engines. However, some publishers, such as Facebook, know that search engines cannot see everything their users post.

Paywalled Content

If you are a News publisher, you might have considered implementing a paid subscription model to supplement existing revenue streams. However, your SEO team will need to use the appropriate structured data tags to ensure that Google or Bing can see all the blocked content and index the page. Consequently, the page code will display the full content to paid subscribers or prompt them to subscribe if they are not.

Restricting what content is visible to Google will negatively impact ranking, but many large publishers are happy to take this risk. There are two approaches to "flexible sampling":

- **Lead-In** – This approach might show a paragraph or two of the content and is followed by a call-to-action to subscribe.
- **Metering** – Such sites give the visitor a small number of free articles to read in full each month before the paywall comes up. They can switch to a lead-in model after that point.

CONTENT FORMATTING

Your SEO team can guide CMS operators on SEO-friendly formatting. For example, Google has confirmed that judiciously bolding some words can help with ranking. However, bolding entire paragraphs and pages will not work. I have covered elsewhere how the content needs to follow a semantic HTML hierarchy, namely, heading levels that don't skip levels.

What if your site does not use HTML heading levels? Google has said in the past that it can look at text marked up with large fonts, particularly when bolded, and deduce that it must be a heading.

FEATURED SNIPPETS

Writing content to appear in a Featured Snippet is a winning move, particularly if you cannot seem to get a top-ranking spot for your desired keywords. A Featured Snippet, also known as a Position #0 ranking, sits at the top of the page. There are a few tricks to planning such content, as it depends partly on the website's nature.

For example, if you can set up some pages that answer a "What is x?" or "How to" question, your SEO team can work with your writers to prepare them. Such pages do well if they do not carry brand names – let the visitor explore your product pages after reading the landing page.

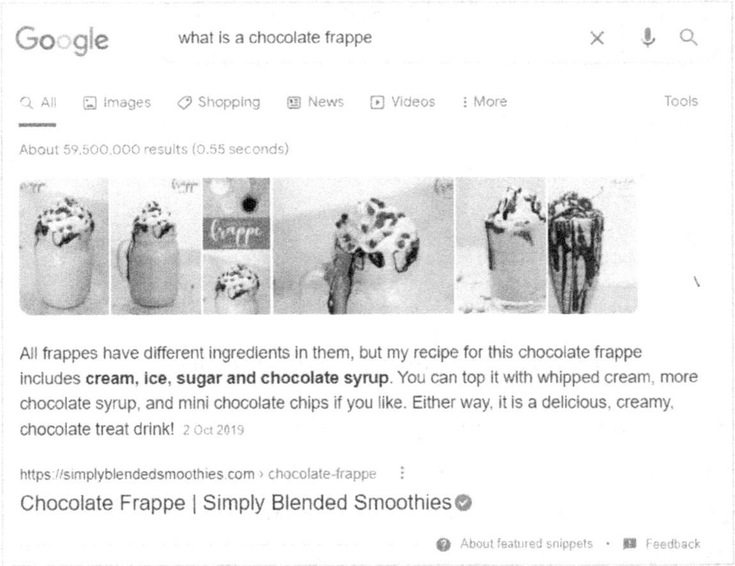

Figure 77 A recipe could get your site into a featured snippet.

VOICE SEARCH

Voice searches continue to occur, particularly in mobile and hands-free situations where speaking is faster than typing. Users also perform voice searches, say, while walking. My example is walking on the noisy Las Vegas Strip and asking my phone to find the closest Mexican restaurant or a drugstore. This example shows that the searches are likely for pages that provide the answer without requiring choices to be selected on the page.

So, if I am hankering for a *chile relleno*, I say "Nearest Chile Relleno restaurant" or, to be sure, "Chile Relleno on Las Vegas Boulevard." Most restaurants put their menus on a couple of pages in an Adobe Acrobat PDF format. Then, Google shows me a SERP with a map so that I can check the results closest to my physical location. Although Google can find a chile relleno on a menu page, in addition to a regular menu, I would like restaurants to create a page per dish, perhaps with a recipe, to stand out from other results for such a search.

Figure 78 Voice search in Google.

Usually, Google narrates the Featured Snippet in a voice search result. Creating content for such searches means anticipating likely voice search queries and creating pages with corresponding titles. Google warns against overdoing this; otherwise, it may be treated as spam.

Bing also supports voice searches, so your content has a good chance of being featured on this search engine.

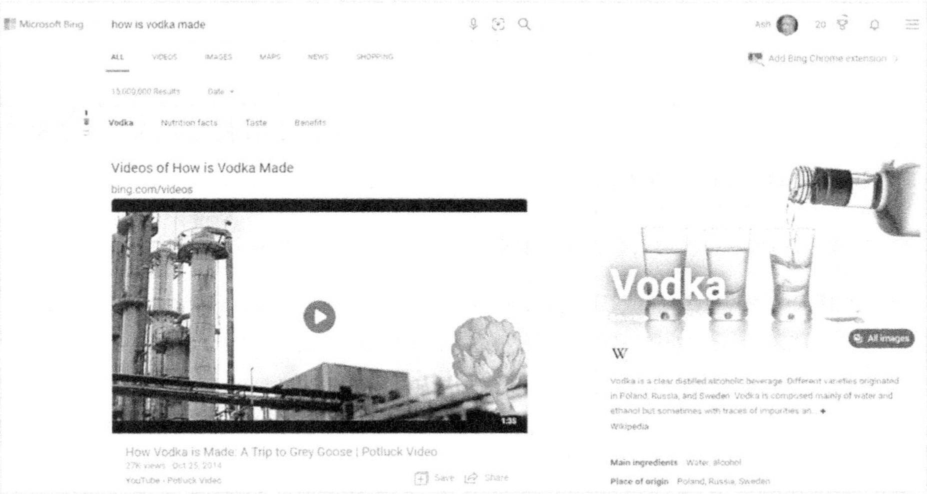

Figure 79 Bing reads out a voice search.

People use Google and Amazon voice-based smart devices to perform voice searches. Google Assistant and Alexa are the respective apps used in voice searches. Therefore, the same Featured Snippet you see in Google Search is likely to be used on a voice device.

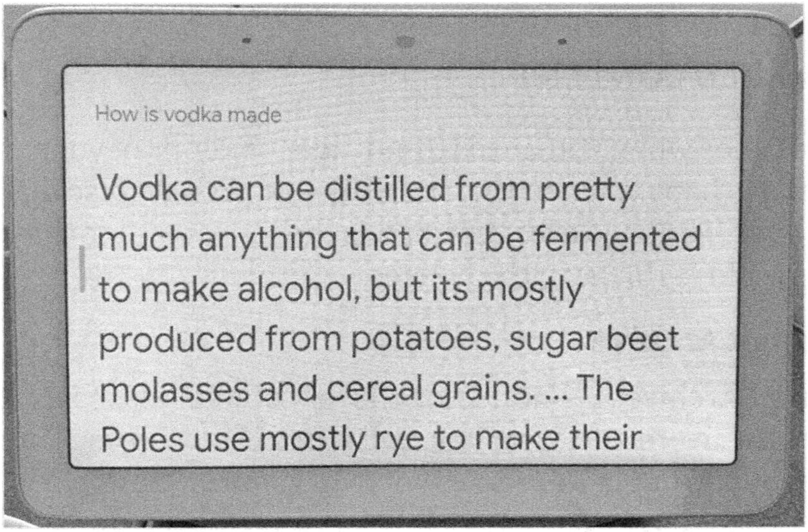

Figure 80 An answer displayed (and read out) on a Google Nest Hub.

If you write content in the language customers use, it should appear in voice search results (provided you follow other good SEO practices). Try searching by voice on your phone or voice display for a page that ranks well on a computer, and see if the same page comes up. If a competitor shows up, thoroughly review their SEO tactics.

Optimizing for Voice Searches

Think about how you might type a search query in Google – it is likely to be in a shorthand format, such as "vodka made" or "vodka ingredients." However, in a voice search, you are more likely to ask a grammatically structured sentence, "How is vodka made?" or "What are the ingredients of vodka?"

GOOGLE WEB STORIES

Google Web Stories are a web version of the short videos you might have noticed on social media platforms. These can be a series of clickable or tappable screens with their own URLs, though their visibility is limited to specific Google surfaces.

FINDING OLD CONTENT

There are times when you need to find older versions of your webpages. Perhaps you need to look up an old product disclaimer if a customer has launched a lawsuit, or it is the more common need to reuse some old verbiage with changes.

The Internet Archive

The Internet Archive is "a non-profit library of millions of free books, movies, software, music, websites, and more." You can use it as a search resource, but in the context of this chapter, its "Wayback Machine" might have taken snapshots of your website over a long period. Sometimes, you are buying a used domain and want to see what it contained – nasty, spammy content might have earned it a Google ban, so you would need to rethink that purchase.

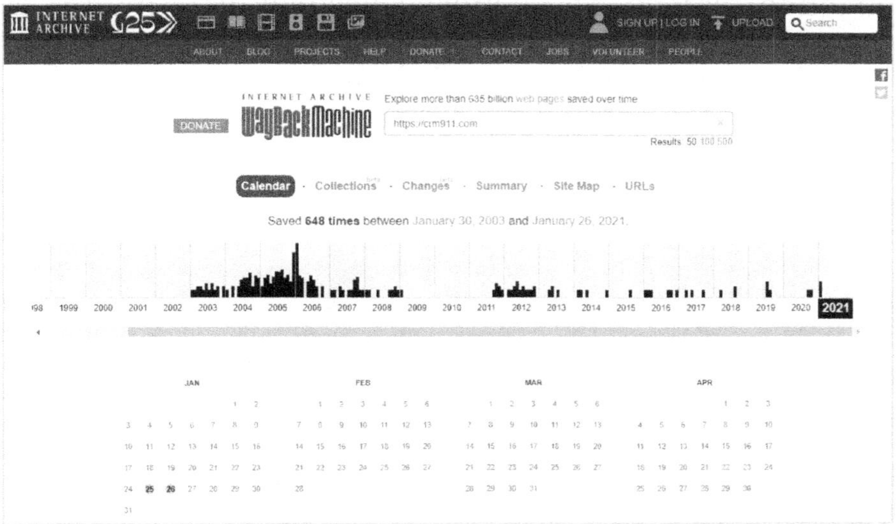

Figure 81 Archive.org might have old copies of your website.

The Wayback Machine does its best to capture your pages, but it will sometimes do so only partially – it does not replace internal backups, but the latter might be textual and not show the rendered version on the website template. Sometimes the CMS changes, so you cannot view pages built on earlier platforms.

Small sites might not get discovered by this handy resource, so you can help it by entering one or more pages in its search box. It will prompt you to save it, and after it takes a look, you will be asked to confirm the save. Check it from time to time, and be sure to look at obscure parts of your website, not just the home page.

GOOGLE DISCOVER

Google Discover is a mobile- and tablet-only experience through the existing Google Search app for either Android or iOS. Google will show content that is likely to interest the logged-in user. Articles with an image at least 1200 pixels wide have a good chance of being featured. You can refine this feed to get better suggestions in the future.

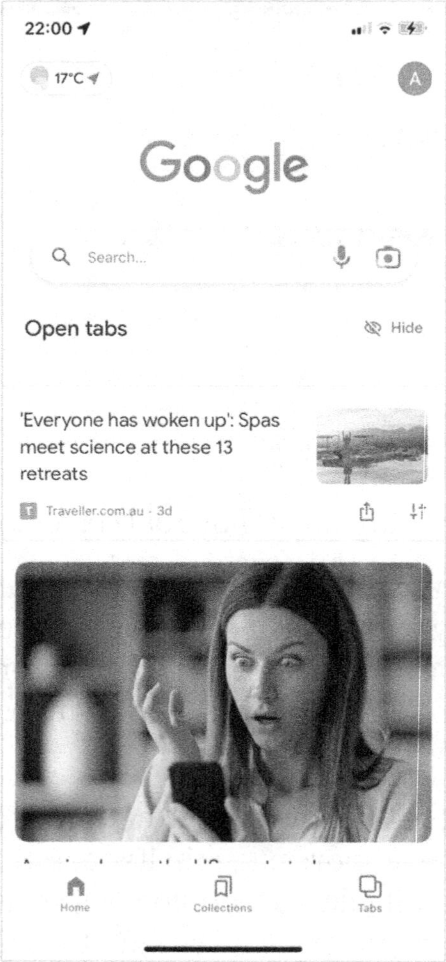

Figure 82 Google Discover on my iPhone.

ORGANIZING CONTENT

Having covered the types of content, let's see how they can be organized on the website for the best user and SEO value. First, I say that the SEO literature and conference/webinar content use this terminology, but I have not seen content managers use these terms. Usually, the product owners commission the content team to create the website pages. In a few years, the original creators have moved on, and the incumbents touch it up if necessary. Now, let's look at some theoretical models, and perhaps you might get to design a content architecture from scratch.

Hub-and-Spoke Model

We need our product or service pages to rank high; that means they should be the most relevant, authoritative pages for the most applicable, valuable keywords. This keyword would be transactional, such as "<product name> <price>." The supporting pages would contain related keywords, such as "<product features>," "<compare products>", etc. They would link to the hub page; hence, we use the wheel analogy of a hub and its spokes. A hub and its spokes are also known collectively as a Cluster.

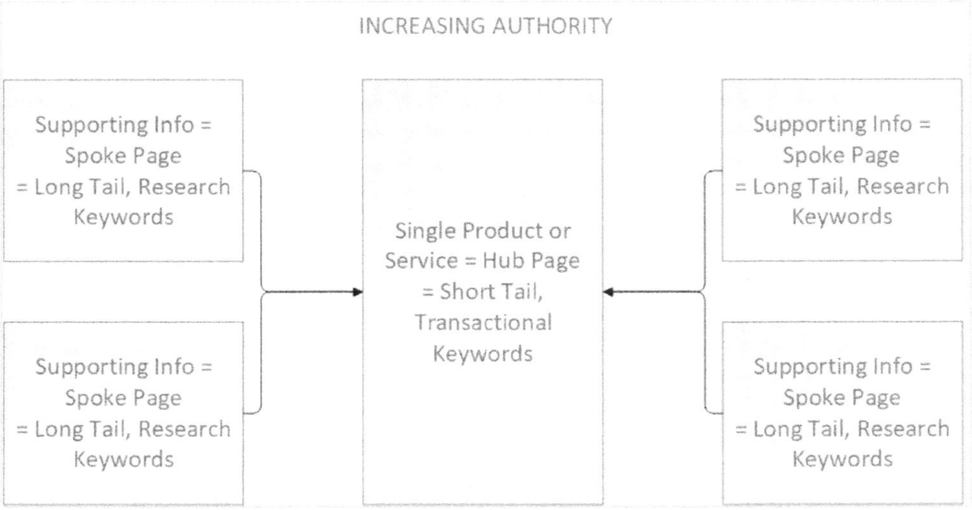

Figure 83 Hub-and-spoke content model.

It's very likely that your website already has such linkages between related content and the core content, between topics and sub-topics, and vice versa. Keep that thought in mind for later, when we look at pages that link to every other page on the website via the navigation panel.

Pillar Pages

The pillar approach is to have very long pages covering the entire topic on a single page. Wikipedia is a good example of a pillar page that could optionally link to other pages, such as clusters (hub-and-spoke).

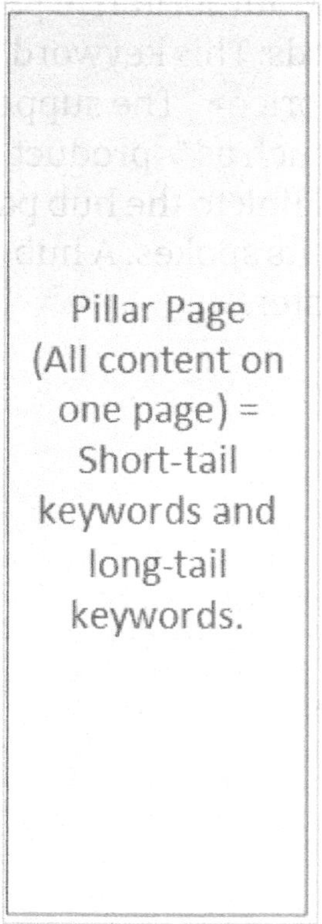

Figure 84 Pillar Page.

Content and Site Architecture

While organizing pages and topics, you also create a website's information architecture as you go along. Once you have determined how much content is essential to launch a website, you can also plan for future content growth. A well-planned navigation system also helps focus topical "link juice" where needed, while keeping it out of pages that would waste it.

THEFT OF YOUR CONTENT

Sooner or later, good content gets copied. Sometimes, the entire website is copied. The thieves are often insignificant individuals whose only intention is to place ads and make money through them. They need text and images, so plagiarism seems to be their cheapest and fastest option. Many are in foreign jurisdictions and sometimes untraceable personally. Anticipate such a day and prepare for it.

Discovering Theft of Content

It is rare for a stolen copy to rank higher than the original page, but it can happen. You might find such a page in a web search. You can always pick an unusual sentence and search for it (enclosed in quotes). If a few search results appear, check if you have been copied. Some unprofessional "content writers" working for competitors steal smaller chunks and flesh them out. It is not worth worrying about minor instances. Tools such as Grammarly or Copyscape have free and paid options for finding copies. The paid option will enable it to monitor and alert you to suspected plagiarism.

Actioning Copyright Infringement

I see two options for dealing with copyright theft, and I am only talking about the most severe cases where you have made a business decision to take action. Your legal team must be on board. In both cases, you should try to contact the infringer if possible. Contact their web host, if necessary. Sometimes that will suffice.

The first option is cheap and, from the SEO angle, will hurt the plagiarist immediately. Often, that is sufficient. It is covered below under "Digital Millennium Copyright Act." There is also a "gotcha."

The second option is the formal, legal route that legal counsel advises. That is beyond the scope of this book.

Digital Millennium Copyright Act

The United States Congress passed the Digital Millennium Copyright Act (DMCA) in 1998, and it is relevant to copyright owners everywhere because the major search engines of interest to SEO are also based in the United States. It targets copyright violators.

Takedown Notice at Google

Google will remove copyright infringement and other undesirable content reported to it, such as cracked software and malware. You file a DMCA Takedown Notification, but it is not a confidential process. Your complaint will be displayed in the Lumen database for anyone to see. Google will not contact you unless necessary, so you will need to check the dashboard for updates.

The infringing page will disappear from search results if your complaint is upheld. You have to submit one complaint per infringing page, so you could hire a third party to handle it if the infringement is significant.

Sometimes this tool is wielded maliciously by a competitor or someone with a sick sense of humor. Sometimes a URL might contain a typo, affecting an innocent party.

In May 2022, the well-known SEO tool website Moz had its home page and seven others taken down.

Unfortunately, this tool is open to abuse and innocent mistakes. That can be costly when the accused site does not connect a drop in visits and sales with plagiarism. In the Moz example, the SEO community reached out to Google, and the error was resolved within a day.

DMCA Counter Notification

As for the "gotcha," the infringer can challenge your complaint and file a Counter Notification. This option is offered when Google contacts the infringer. Should this counter-notification be filed, Google will reinstate the page and ask both parties to pursue litigation. Why might this happen? Sometimes, the other party is an innocent victim of an unprofessional contracted writer or a former employee who is no longer with them, so they might think the content originated with them. Sometimes, the other party knows the process and feels they are untouchable because they are in a foreign jurisdiction. This is another reason to ensure the Wayback Machine captures your content regularly. However, some of these battles might not be worth the extra time, and good SEO practices will keep your pages higher in the SERPs than the copies.

SYNDICATING YOUR CONTENT

If your business publishes great content, others may approach you about republishing it. Although that's flattering, and more so if you are being paid for the rights, there are cautions.

Generally, the first publisher (you) is the one whose content ranks highest on Google. Occasionally, the republishing site with a better brand image, in Google's estimation, might grab the higher ranks that are truly yours. To reduce that risk, I would require the following:

- All your pages should have self-referenced canonicals – these are HTML tags that look like this:

```
<link rel=“canonical” href=“https://ash.nallawalla.com/about-ash-
```

`nallawalla/">` Their purpose is to notify search engines that this is the only official URL for the page, but the common use case is something else we can read about later. In this syndication situation, the republisher must use your canonical tag and not theirs. This ensures that the search engine is left in no doubt about the original author.

- The republished page should be marked "noindex", which looks like this:
  `<meta name="robots" content="noindex">` - this confirms to the search engine that the copy of the page must not be indexed. Google caches your robots.txt file, so you should tell Search Console to re-fetch it.
- The copy must not be published until the original can be seen in the index. This ensures that the copy is not seen as the first publisher.

INTERNATIONAL SEO CONTENT

Multinational companies and manufacturers with international distributors often sell identical or near-identical products in those countries. Retailer websites list such products. The products cannot have different descriptions. The minor differences might relate to national safety certifications or electrical voltage. The product might be available in different colors or minor variants. Each country might not sell the full suite of products made by the manufacturer. This creates a thin-content risk – hold that thought.

I suspect the head office will delegate such content decisions to each country office or distributor. The SEO team at each website in the chain will want their own pages to be indexed and ranked high. Sadly, this does not always happen.

Country Switchers

Some multinational manufacturer websites use a single domain for the whole world with two possible paths:

- Subdomain, e.g., uk.example.com
- Sub-folder (directory), e.g., example.com/uk

Additionally, some companies force the user to view the version intended for their location. What if the viewer is a tourist visiting another country and needs to transact with the company in their home country? Please let the user choose the country.

Language Switchers

The manufacturer typically presents pages in the viewer's native language. Avoid the temptation to use an online translation tool, for the results might be embarrassing at best. Always use a professional translation service, as they employ native speakers. Although the differences between English and American English are well-known, there are smaller differences between, say, Australian and New Zealand English. The differences might relate to local usage, such as the increasing acceptance of Māori words in New Zealand English.

Google's Response

A Twitter user asked Google why their international pages were not all indexed. The website had a flag icon for almost every country, and a second language if any.

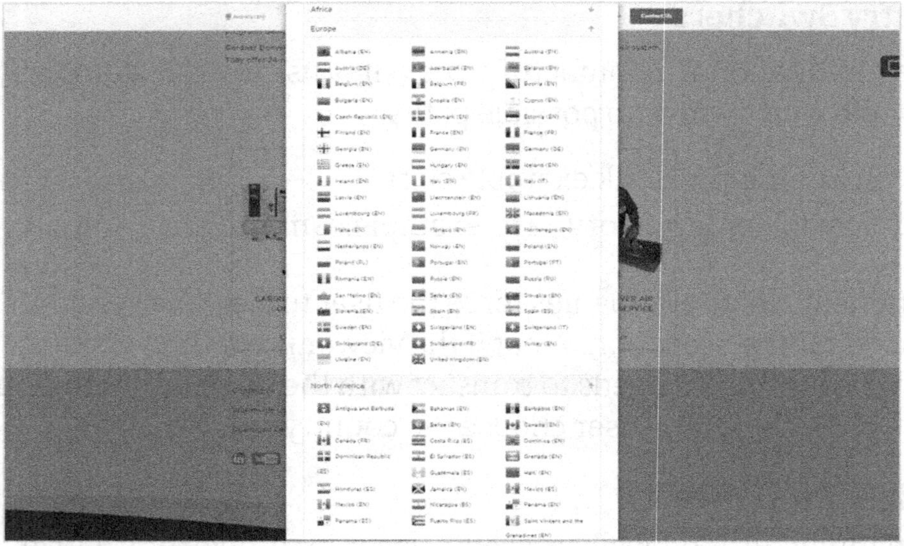

Figure 85 Google might not index a page for every country.

A closer examination of their pages shows that they don't have a page for each country; for example, many share the same English-language page. Google will not index every page substantially similar to another, regardless of the company's intention. Google treats substantially similar pages without meaningful differentiation as thin or redundant content.

Google suggests that users who see content for the "wrong" country should be shown a way to access the "right" information.

Chapter 7

MANAGING LINKS

The World Wide Web (WWW) consists of interconnected pages and resources, linked together and discovered in multiple ways. The web was invented before search engines, and links were designed to let people navigate and reference related information. Therefore, you should make it easy for audiences and platforms to reference your site.

Links generally fall into three primary categories:

- External (inbound) links
- Outbound links
- Internal links

Search systems also evaluate link purpose and context, not just link type. In modern systems, many links are discounted, and only a subset meaningfully influences visibility.

TYPES OF EXTERNAL LINKS

Understanding how search engines view links between websites (external links) is important, as misunderstandings can hurt your website's rankings. For example, when I worked in-house with an agency staffer who obtained links every month, I would ask for a list of proposed sites he was going to approach. Once I was confident that he would only seek high-quality links, I let him do that task without oversight.

Unprofessional agencies might have a loose interpretation of "quality links," so you need to be very clear about this topic in your mind. External links are also known as Inbound Links.

Natural Links

A natural link is one that no one can deem inappropriate in the context of search engine rankings. For example, if a medical practice links to a peak medical body from, say, a membership badge on its website, that's a natural link.

A natural link could be contextually relevant or irrelevant. The link's relevance is debatable if a large company sponsors a sports team or a sports stadium. At the other end of the link, the sponsored entity is proud of the association and will appreciate the link. Such a link is unlikely to improve its ranking for a sports-related search. On the other hand, the medical practice linked to a relevant peak body is a relevant link, giving both sites greater credibility in a search engine algorithm.

Unnatural Links

An unnatural link is one contrived for perceived search engine ranking advantage. If search engines did not exist, then the website owners would not look for such links. The major search engines react to unnatural links in these ways, although today many such links are algorithmically devalued or ignored, and only clearer cases may trigger a manual action:

- Issue you a manual penalty, usually if it looks like an obvious case of purchased links
- Disregard such links because the tactic is deprecated, such as most manipulative directory-style links
- Do nothing, probably because your links have not yet been detected as unnatural by the search engines.

Google documents link spam under its Search spam policies.

Here is a redacted example of a notification in the Manual Actions section of Google Search Console:

Unnatural outbound links from https://example.com/ violate Google Search Essentials

To the owner of https://example.com/,

Google has detected a pattern of links from your site to other sites that might be either unnatural or irrelevant. This pattern attempts to artificially boost the rankings of other sites in Google Search results. Such unnatural ranking would cause search results to favor results that are not relevant to users' actual queries, violating the Google Search Essentials. We are therefore discounting the trustworthiness of links on your website. The manual spam action has been specifically applied to example.com/.

To resolve the issue, please fix the links as described below, then file a reconsideration request in Search Console. We will remove the manual action applied to the website once our Search Quality team determines the issue has been resolved.

Find an example of a bad link on the page https://example.com/is-keyword-the-next-big-thing/, and search for the link text "investing money in keyword".

Here's how to fix this problem:

1. Identify any unnatural links on your site.
   Look for links added to your site in exchange for compensation, such as money, goods, or services, or for reciprocal links.
2. Remove or use <nofollow> on these links. The rel attribute values "nofollow", "sponsored", and "ugc" indicate the link's intent. In modern systems, Google treats these as signals about the relationship and

context of the link, rather than a guarantee of crawling behavior.

3 Submit a reconsideration request.
Please include any details or documentation that can help us understand the changes made to your site.

Redacted example of an approved Reconsideration Request:

> **Reconsideration request approved for https://example.com/**
>
> To: Webmaster of https://example.com/,
>
> Good news! Your reconsideration request has been approved, and Google has removed any manual action on your site. Keep in mind that removal of a manual action doesn't guarantee that your site's ranking will increase.
>
> Here's how to confirm your status:
>
> 1 Check the Manual Action Viewer.
> It can take some time before the status of your site is updated in the Manual Actions Viewer and our crawling and indexing systems. You can confirm that your site does not have any Manual Actions by looking in the Manual Action Viewer.
>
> 2 Check Security Issues.
> If your site was hacked, other vulnerabilities not mentioned in the Manual Actions Viewer could be affecting your site. Check the Security Issues section of Search Console for any issues that need to be fixed.

If you don't fix all the issues you believe have been flagged, Google will give you a single example of the issue, so you have another chance to fix them.

Deep Links

A deep link is not a special kind of link but is simply an inbound link to a deeper page relative to the home page. Getting a link to a specific product page or blog page is highly desirable, particularly from a topically related page on another website. That carries the most potent "link juice" or PageRank.

You can go even deeper than just going to an inner page URL. You can go to a specific paragraph on an inner page. That requires giving that heading or paragraph a "name," and you need to notify the linking site of that name so they can link to it. You are unlikely to receive an unsolicited link from a third party, but you can use this method to link from your other websites.

Cracked Links

Once in a while, you might hear of links inserted into an innocent website by crackers (some call them hackers). This might be because of a compromised administrator password or another technique you might not discover until you audit your pages.

Rebirthed Domain Links

Some entrepreneurs make a nice living by renting links for a monthly fee. I saved a client $15,000 each month from such a supplier. The link provider had been buying expired domains with excellent pedigree. One was a state government site built for a competition open to the general public. After the event ended, the government did not renew the domain, but it still had excellent backlinks from several government webpages. This enabled the link provider to charge a premium. I was disappointed that the linking page included boilerplate text about a specific phone brand, and the sidebar featured random, nonsensical links to prominent brands, presumably also their clients.

When my client ended the contract, the provider removed the links. Did my client's page #1 rankings drop? Nothing happened. Do not buy links, but if you do, look at the sites that offer them and avoid monthly rental fees.

Citations

A Citation is a textual mention of your product, brand, or URL without an underlying, clickable link. If you cannot earn a link but can get a citation, grab it. Most news outlets do not link to the company or brand in stories.

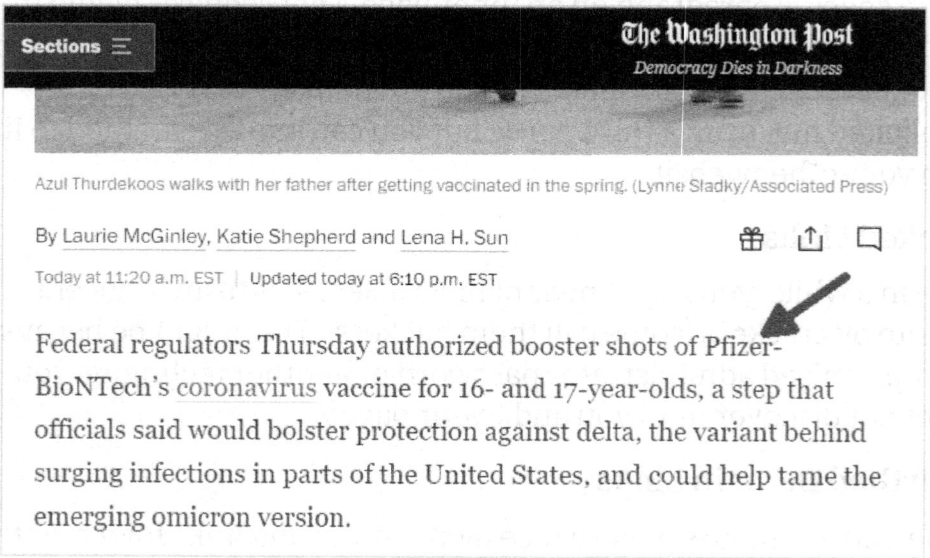
Sections

The Washington Post

Democracy Dies in Darkness

Azul Thurdekoos walks with her father after getting vaccinated in the spring. (Lynne Sladky/Associated Press)

By Laurie McGinley, Katie Shepherd and Lena H. Sun

Today at 11:20 a.m. EST | Updated today at 6:10 p.m. EST

Federal regulators Thursday authorized booster shots of Pfizer-BioNTech's coronavirus vaccine for 16- and 17-year-olds, a step that officials said would bolster protection against delta, the variant behind surging infections in parts of the United States, and could help tame the emerging omicron version.

Figure 86 Example of a citation (to Pfizer-BionTech) in The Washington Post.

Individually, citations do not help directly with ranking. There is speculation about that in the SEO community, but at best, an unknown brand will find that a mention in the news leads to a surge in visits because people will type the brand name into a search engine. Each such visit can lead to a link at some later stage.

A large number of citations on authoritative websites can help build authority over time.

Google has used the phrase "implied link" in a patent, so it's reasonable for us to speculate that brand mentions not surrounded by negative language are a vote of confidence and might send a positive signal to the ranking algorithm. In addition, links in social media are usually "nofollowed," so they would serve as citations.

Clean versus Nofollowed Links

A normal HTML-coded link looks like this:

```
<a href="https://www.example.com">Example site</a>
```

It is a standard HTML link. The term "dofollow" is industry slang used to distinguish it from links qualified with rel values such as "nofollow", "sponsored", or "ugc". Links are intended to be followed by search engine crawlers unless told otherwise.

A qualified link can look like this:

```
• <a href="https://www.example.com" rel="nofollow">Example site</a>
• <a href="https://www.example.com" rel="sponsored">Example site</a>
• <a href="https://www.example.com" rel="ugc">Example site</a>
```

A website user will not see any difference between the two, as they will only see the anchor text "Example site" in the page body. A nofollowed link might qualify as a citation if the product or brand name is mentioned.

Clickbait for Links

You can find clickbait content on any platform – websites or social media, but it serves as a source of links unless they are nofollowed. Clickbait content in this context is not about misleading visitors; genuinely useful content, when shared, can bring both links and citations.

App Links

App links are links on your web pages that can open an app on a mobile phone or prompt installation if it is not already installed. Such links help to increase app installation uptake if that is an objective.

App links are sometimes called "deep links," but that term can mislead because it suggests a regular web page link that goes deep into another site. For example, some sites offer a PDF for free download after a visitor completes a lead qualification form. However, if another webpage linked directly to the PDF, the website would lose a lead, so it might take steps to prevent this with a technical solution.

Directories

In our context, a web directory is a list of website links with appropriate descriptions. Unfortunately, many directories exist primarily to manufacture links, so search systems typically devalue them and treat them as a weak basis for earning authority.

For some years, a handful of genuine online directories pre-dated search engines. Users went to them to find businesses. The better-known ones were Yahoo and Yellow Pages (in many countries). Then there was the Open Directory Project (dmoz.org), a volunteer-managed site popular with SEOs. Still, it shut down after it became clear that humans did not actually browse directories and that using search engines was far more productive.

A few specialist directories still exist for their audiences, but avoid using them as a significant part of a link-seeking strategy.

Local Search Links

When you need customers who like to buy locally, say, appliances, food, anything where they prefer to see the product in person, you would need a Local SEO strategy (covered in depth later). This strategy includes getting local links and citations. This tactic is relevant for a small business with a local customer base or for a national enterprise with numerous locally branded outlets.

Getting a local link requires the other website to exhibit local characteristics as well. Many cities (local governments) have a directory of local businesses, which are legitimate sources of local links. Look for one using one of the following search terms:

- City business directory
- <city name> business directory
- <city name> local directory
- Business listings <city name>

Simply being active in the local community will generate local citations and the occasional link without asking, which is good for business. The company's nature will determine how this is possible, but most companies can offer one-day "work experience" opportunities for students or more formal traineeships, internships, or apprenticeships. An application form on the website will lead to many local links without asking.

Certain service businesses that rely on in-person contact can look for annual fairs and put up a stand with an unrelated offering – say, offering free barbecue food that would keep the prospects standing nearby and hearing a soft sell – such fairs often leave their participant lists alive for the whole year to attract sponsors the following year. In contrast, some of these pages might be kept alive indefinitely.

When looking for local links, don't be tempted to check sites for artificial metrics generated by tools like Domain Authority or Page Authority, as these numbers will be unreliable from a search engine's perspective. Search engines will recognize the local nature of the link and give it more weight than some contrived metric. For example, if a grocer donates unsold vegetables and fruit to some local charities and earns some links, you can expect those charity websites to show very low numbers in those tools. It's all about local signals.

Guest Blogging

Guest blogging involves asking (paying) others to write blog posts on someone's blog – yours or a third party's blog. The theory is that your blog gets new content, but the hidden angle is that the content includes links. When you publish the guest-written content on your site, it's the same as hiring a contract writer, just as you would ask an employee to write content. However, this isn't true guest blogging.

Now flip that scenario on its head, and you will see how guest blogging manifests itself. Spammers offer to write guest posts on other people's blogs with a link to your site – hence, this is a link-selling service. I have a few sites of my own, and I get pitches like this all the time.

If you feel your site could use more links, you might be tempted to guest blog. As with any other service, some providers are more diligent than others. A good operator will look for blogs complementary to your core offerings. Contacting such blogs is known as blogger outreach.

A finance blog might be a good fit for an insurance provider's website. However, a guest post in an African or Australian blog would probably not pass the sniff test if your company operates in North America. Even if search engines do not give you a manual penalty for such an arrangement, the link is unlikely to pass a signal of relevance to your page.

Advertorials

An advertorial article is clearly marked as advertising, so it will not attract a search engine penalty. However, links therein are likely to be "nofollowed." Thus, no link equity will be passed to your site. If you buy advertorials, do so for anticipated human visitors, since such providers tend to be well-known online publications. Some of them might give you a clean link ("dofollowed" by default), but don't count on it being any better than a nofollowed link.

Private Blog Networks

Private blog networks (PBNs) are websites that are not necessarily blogs in the truest sense. Their primary purpose is to give (sell or rent) links to other websites that cannot find a better way to earn natural links. They might, but do not necessarily link to one another. What they all have in common is staying under the radar of search engines.

Such PBNs are populated with carefully selected topical content and earned authority. Some websites in the network might have been pre-owned, so they don't all look as if they were started simultaneously. Their hosting is usually spread across multiple locations to obfuscate their purpose further. Many use WordPress, but some might use other content management platforms.

Many multinational corporate websites resemble PBNs because they link to one another. Sometimes, non-commercial sites link to each other in "rings," such as special interest groups. However, they do not run afoul of webmaster guidelines because they do not sell links or link to unrelated websites for no apparent reason.

Yet, PBNs commonly fall under link spam patterns described in search spam policies. They are not illegal or unethical, but they are risky because your website might receive a manual penalty and be unable to recover from it. Modern link-spam detection increasingly relies on pattern-based systems that evaluate networks, ownership footprints, publishing behavior, and content quality signals at scale. Avoid assuming any single detection method is decisive.

The other risk you face is that your SEO agency might outsource its link acquisition, which might continue ad infinitum. Such a practice might contain questionable links from PBNs. Your own appetite for risk will determine whether to seek PBN links.

ARE LINKS NECESSARY?

You might see Googlers say you don't need links to rank. Ignore that. Such replies are often honest, literal answers that allow no exceptions.

Figure 87 Are backlinks not mandatory for ranking?

Yes, there are anecdotes where a page that completely satisfies a user's query could be ranked #1, but in practice, most common queries have millions of competing pages that want to be ranked on page #1. If two pages have content that completely satisfies a query, the page with one or more backlinks implies some endorsement.

OBTAINING LINKS

Now that we have covered what good or bad quality links look like, let's examine the process of getting links.

Natural, Unsolicited Links

Simply being a successful or newsworthy entity is the first and possibly last step to gaining links and citations without asking for them. Household name brands and government entities don't need to worry about asking for links, but I'll encourage them to do so appropriately.

Lesser-known companies cannot get unsolicited links if nobody has heard of them. So, they need a PR and marketing budget.

Blogger and Influencer Outreach

Blogger outreach is the process of obtaining links from websites operated as blogs or information resources. Some of these are owned by "influencers." For example, if you are a home lending institution, a blog that features home loans is a likely place to ask for a link, usually for money.

There are two kinds of links seen in such schemes:

- The entire article features your product, so it comes across as a genuine review or news item. Often, your content team writes the review and looks for a suitable website to publish it. The article would have links to your product pages. Would it pass the sniff test? That would depend on the way the site was planned. If very little thought went into it, each article would be of varying quality, and Google would recognize it as a link farm. Such a penalty might already be in place when you seek a link from it. Nevertheless, many organizations use this method of seeking links.
- An existing article about home loans adds a link to your product. This is a lazy way to get a link. It could be picked up algorithmically, say, by comparing the page checksum computed during one spider visit with that from an earlier visit. Google can see the Main Content of a page and judge it differently from changes in the Supplementary content, which could frequently change, such as ads or lists of other pages. Such a link would not pass the sniff test.

Faked Link Authority

Some link providers go to great lengths to fake metrics that Google or Bing doesn't use, but are entrenched in some parts of the SEO world. Several websites have created metrics to show the relative strength of websites or webpages, but they do not equate to PageRank, the Google metric that is now hidden from us.

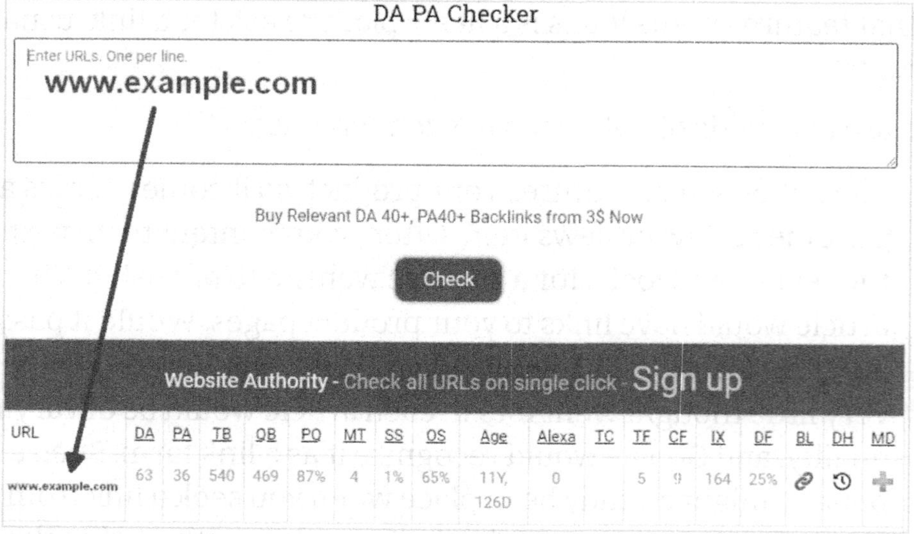

Figure 88 A tool for checking some of the dubious link metrics.

While some uninformed customers continue to pay for links from pages with high scores in those tools, scammers have entered the field. Unfortunately, uninformed businesses include some SEO agencies that are unaware of the fake metrics and buy them for their customers.

Example of a faked link source:
https://maps.google.co.jp/url?q=https://example.com

As this isn't a how-to book, I will omit the details of this trick, but it fools some of those checking tools more than it does others.

Dallas-based SEO consultant Joe Youngblood has written a detailed article on this technique, showing another way the link source is created. Your SEO team should know of such tactics.

Press Releases

I mention press releases in two contexts – the good and the bad.

The correct way to use a media release is to reach news media members and inform them about a genuine, newsworthy item. Established, known companies will find that some news outlets will cover the story, perhaps interview an executive for a quote. There is no expectation from the organization to get a link.

The "bad" way to look at press releases is to treat them as templated, mass-sent releases to dozens of so-called press release sites. The press release is intended to become the vehicle for links from the so-called press release repositories. Many questionable websites popped up, accepting submissions for a small fee, while a few were free. However, genuine news media do not go to such sites to get their story ideas.

Help a Reporter Out

Business journalists get a lot of legitimate news assignments, so they rarely need to scour press releases that may well land straight into their junk email folder. There are exceptions. Specific topics need timely comments from specialists, as was seen during the COVID-19 pandemic. Obscure people in the health industry became unwitting media celebrities and sometimes had to turn away pesky reporters.

Help a Reporter Out (HARO) began as a service connecting journalists with sources. In April 2025, Cision announced the sale of HARO to Featured.com, and the HARO brand and workflow have since been evolving under new ownership.

Qwoted

Qwoted is a service for three groups:

- Subject-matter experts – Subject-matter experts with no PR representation looking to secure press coverage for themselves or their business.
- Public relations professionals – Communication professionals looking to promote their clients or internal thought leaders.
- Journalists – Reporters, writers, podcasters, bookers/producers, event organizers, etc., looking for expert commentary.

The SEO angle for using Qwoted is to get a mention in relevant publications, possibly with a bonus link.

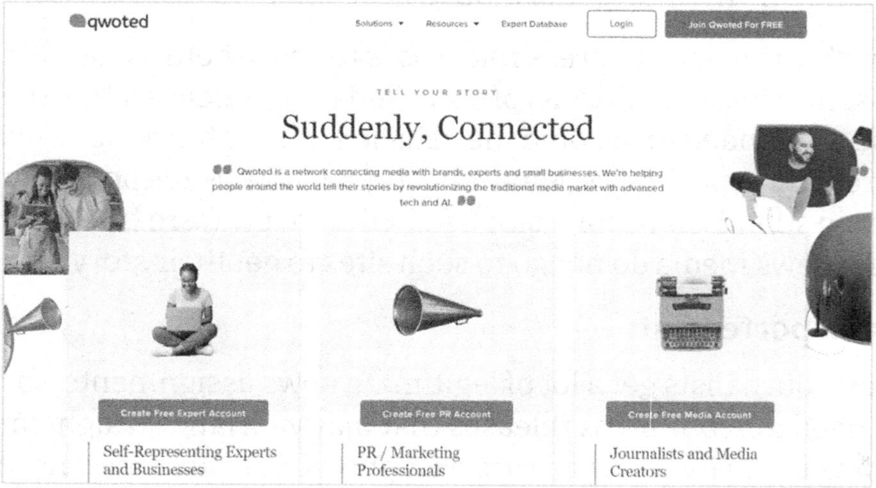

Figure 89 Qwoted.

Contrived Scholarships

Some years ago, some SEOs found a way to get legitimate links from educational institutions. But, of course, these links had the full blessing of the institutions, and this is how it was done.

The SEO client would establish a scholarship for top students, using criteria agreed upon by the institution. In return, the client would be mentioned on the.edu domain with a clean link.

Long before this method was widespread, one of my clients invented a variation of this technique. He was visiting his old high school and was the keynote speaker at a graduation ceremony. He announced a scholarship for the student whose article was judged the best by the teachers. He was not looking for links but content. He hosted the competition entries on his website, as they were about his niche topic.

Win-win? Perhaps for a short while, but SEOs like to talk about such tactics, and Google decided to devalue them. I would not go down this path today if the main objective were .edu links.

GIVING LINKS

Linking to third-party sites is entirely up to the organization and its purposes. What kind of links should you give? Do you need to reciprocate? Should links be followed or nofollowed? You can link from the primary pages or the supplementary pages.

Links to Business Partners

By "business partners," I mean related websites on any domain owned by a parent organization or a third party. For example, a multiple-brand company will certainly link to its other brand websites, and they will link back. Must they be linked from every page footer? I don't think so, but many sites do this.

Some linking is essential because it makes business sense. For example, a bank might link to all the independent mortgage brokers who sell its home loans. A supermarket giant will link to all its stores, but perhaps to a few of its major suppliers. If it sponsors sports teams or sports venues or supports a charity, it might link to them too.

Should such links be followed or nofollowed? Links to your own brands should be clean, that is, "followed." This is because you are demonstrating complete trust and full endorsement. The same applies to your major trading partners, as it shows that you are part of the same ecosystem - a larger entity. On the other hand, there may be cases where you might nofollow a link to your own brand if it makes no business sense. Or you might give it a single, clean link from an inner page, rather than a site-wide plethora of links.

Goodwill Links

A "goodwill" link is optional. The organization's operations are not affected if they do not give such a link. Such links are likely to be found on your supplementary pages, such as blog posts. You might want to consider making all links to third parties "nofollow" unless you need to make an exception.

Linking without Permission

In the early days of the web, some websites displayed a message threatening legal action against any other website that linked to them without prior written permission. Much of this was ignorance, while some were concerned about the linking intention.

You can show a page or image from another website inside a "frame," which is a legitimate coding method. A visitor cannot tell if this is legitimate or intended to deceive. If this has been done to pass off the framed page as one's content, then the other website is justified in taking legal action. The thief might claim that they copied nothing but inserted a link to "help" the visitor to fetch the page or image directly from the third-party website. However, the courts might not see it that way.

Another type of false attribution is to show well-known websites as business partners or clients when that is untrue. For example, they will not appreciate a link from such a site or the use of their logos without permission.

CHECKING BACKLINKS

It's good practice to regularly check your backlinks (inbound links). Of course, it's always a pleasure to see new, unsolicited links from relevant websites. Still, occasionally, you might see links from what seem to be dodgy or, at best, irrelevant-sounding websites. If you can work out why relevant websites are linked to you, then see if you can encourage more of this kind of recognition.

There are free and paid backlink-checking tools, and, usually, the paid options are, understandably, more informative than the free ones. Keep in mind that no tool can provide a complete list of backlinks, but some are more comprehensive than others.

Both Google Search Console and Bing Webmaster Tools show a sample of your backlinks. At best, these samples are interesting, but I prefer to use independent tools.

The Google "link:" search operator no longer works as it once did. Google hobbled this functionality, and it now provides non-backlink results and links. It is treated as a regular search and isn't very helpful.

A popular, paid backlink tool is Majestic. I have used it in the past for many audits. The screenshot below is from their demo.

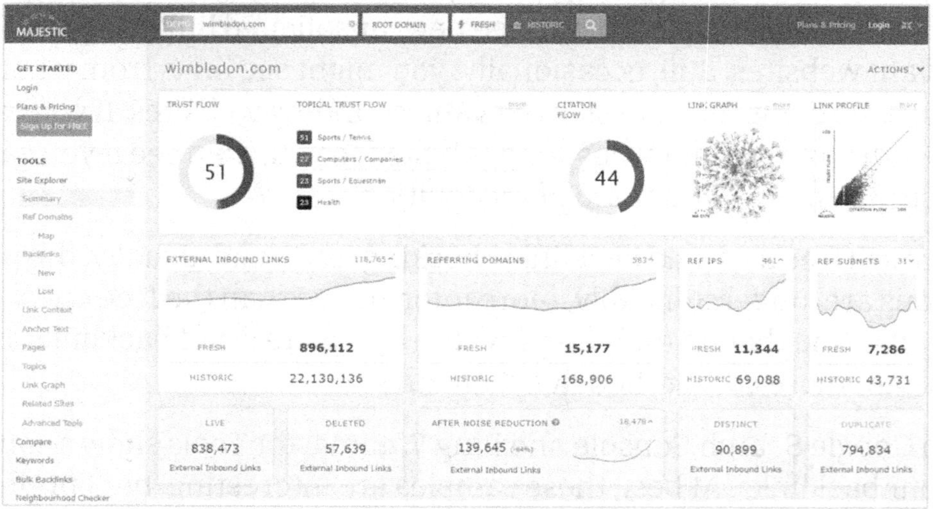

Figure 90 Dashboard view of a demo site in Majestic.

PARASITE SEO

This pattern is now more commonly discussed in terms of Google's spam policy against "site reputation abuse," where third-party pages are published on a host site's domain primarily to exploit the host's ranking signals rather than to serve the host's audience. Often, this requires payment or some other quid pro quo. In other words, it is a paid link and violates Google guidelines. Google's current guidance is that the host site is responsible for preventing third-party content from being used to manipulate rankings, and policy enforcement can apply at the site or section level when abuse patterns are detected.

NEGATIVE SEO

For some time, there was consternation about a tactic dubbed "Negative SEO." It was a method of revenge against a well-ranking website, so it was suspected that a competitor was engaging in Negative SEO. Unfortunately, some say that it still exists.

What Is Negative SEO?

Negative SEO does not directly affect the target website, making it difficult to detect. Here are some examples.

- **Negative Reviews** – The attacker might arrange to bombard review sites with 1-star, negative reviews so that the average star rating will drop, and soon, the site will no longer have its star ratings shown on Google.
- **Review Bombing** – If the site gets thousands of 5-star reviews suddenly, a search engine algorithm might flag it for a staffer to check for buying fake reviews.
- **Link Spam** – Thousands of random, low-quality links can be organized from comments left on blogs and any site that will accept a comment with no oversight.
- **Link Bombing** – Thousands of links could be purchased from questionable sources for a low price, which assures poor quality, but they would be done in a single day. This sudden surge in link acquisition would trigger a tripwire at a search engine, and the site might receive a manual review, as there are very few genuine cases in which a site could be written about in thousands of articles and blogs in a single day.

Should You Worry?

No, and yes. Negative SEO can affect a website in two ways:

- **Effect on Google rankings** – Google has said that you are not penalized if someone links to you; your link target choices assess you. That makes sense because you have no control over who decides to link to you, whereas you choose your link targets.

Google can say this because it knows that the kind of sites that are the victims of Negative SEO tactics seldom engage in dubious linking schemes. They usually rank well on their own merits.

- **Effect on customers** – If there are many 1-star reviews for a restaurant website, a casual visitor might be misled and will not make a booking. If this happens on a large scale, the business will suffer and perhaps close down.

If You Are a Victim of Negative SEO

Imagine this scenario. Your SEO team has confirmed that Negative SEO has taken place. They can itemize the causes and lay out a course of action. Whether you recover fully cannot be guaranteed, but it is worth engaging one of the few consultants specializing in this area.

YOUR LINK PROFILE

Search systems evaluate the collection of inbound links pointing to your site as part of your **link signals**, often referred to collectively as your link profile. Google no longer treats low-quality links as a binary trigger for penalties; instead, its link-spam systems may **discount, ignore, or devalue links at scale** when manipulative patterns cross an internal threshold. This is why site owners can struggle to diagnose performance drops when legitimate links—such as those earned during a news event—are silently ignored along with lower-quality ones.

BAD LINKS

Say, at some point in the past, your website acquired some questionable, low-quality backlinks that now embarrass you. You might not have been responsible for them. Perhaps a predecessor cut a deal with some agency to get many links and gave no instructions about quality. Perhaps those "carefully selected, blogger outreach" links in their articles have turned out to be webspam?

Some low-quality linking pages can be algorithmically flagged based on content quality signals, templated language, and patterns consistent with scaled manipulation. If the articles do not exhibit the classical signs of Expertise, Authoritativeness, and Trustworthiness, then the links on those pages are of low quality. Google might consider these links to be "manipulative."

Perhaps, Google saw the links as an attempt to manipulate rankings and issued you a manual penalty.

Once upon a time, all links could confer a positive or neutral value because there weren't many low-value or dubious websites. Then came some entrepreneurs who decided to make money by providing links from sites they had just created. They could easily create thousands of domains on a single server, using a single IP address and a common directory interface. A single input entry could create hundreds of directory entries on hundreds of domains. The search engines got savvy and could see what was going on, so manipulative directory-style links were suddenly rendered worthless.

Disavow File

Your SEO team will create a text file of URLs or domains you want the search engines to disassociate from your website. You can disavow an entire domain or specific URLs. Take the utmost care lest you disavow links that are beneficial to you.

Example of a disavow file (from Google):

```
# Individual pages to disavow
https://spam.example.com/stuff/comments.html
https://spam.example.com/stuff/paid-links.html
```

```
# Whole domain to disavow
domain:example.com
```

I recommend avoiding it unless a search engine has issued a manual penalty for unnatural links. The notification will include instructions on how to exit the penalty and mention the use of this disavow method. You could try contacting the linking sites; for example, if you purchased those links without realizing that Google could issue a manual penalty. They might charge a fee to do it, but this option is often unavailable because the individual has long left the scene, and the links are no longer under their control. A disavow file is the only option if you cannot reach the link provider.

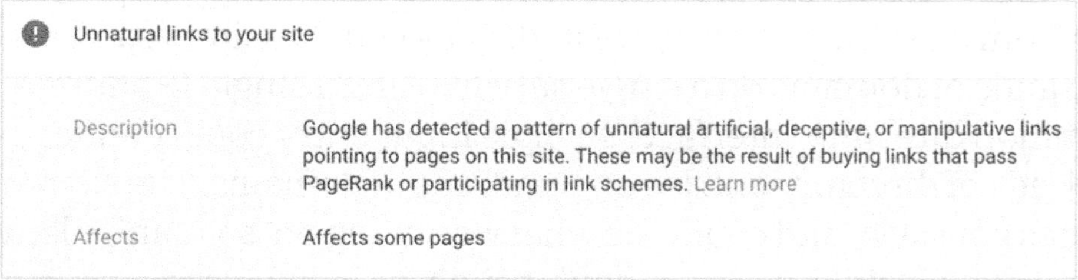

Figure 91 Unnatural Links notification in Google Search Console.

Reconsideration Request

If your site has been issued a manual penalty in Google Search Console, you are allowed to rectify the alleged "offense." Unfortunately, if "unnatural" links are the transgression, you are left to guess what they are. Suppose you bought them. Good luck trying to get them deleted. Some link providers charge a hefty fee to remove the links, while others keep the link site alive but don't check their email.

Over time, Google's link-spam systems have become better at discounting manipulative links at scale, which can make outcomes harder to diagnose. Even so, if you have a manual action for link spam, you should follow the remediation steps and document what you changed before filing reconsideration. I'd rather file a preemptive disavow file than wait for a manual penalty once I become aware of unnatural links.

If you get a manual penalty, you must file a reconsideration request, and sometimes, you might get rejected. You could be waiting many weeks or months for a reply. Clean up what you can and keep resubmitting that reconsideration request until you are exonerated.

Some SEO tools use the term "toxic domains," but Google has said it doesn't have this concept in its algorithms.

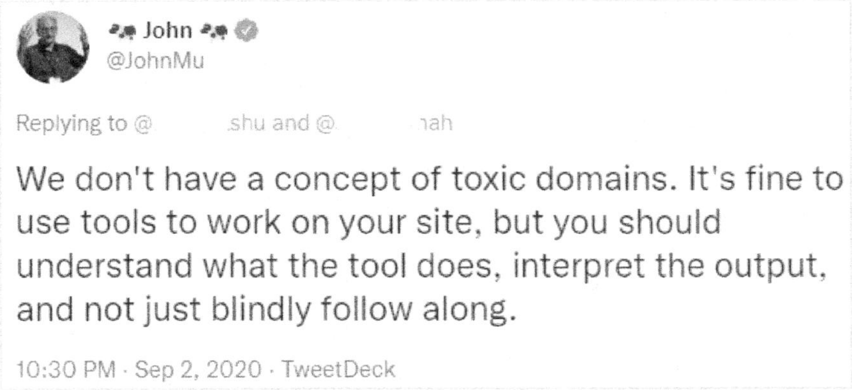

Figure 92 Google does not have a concept of toxic domains.

Google does not have a concept of "toxic links, yet there are backlink analysis tool providers who use that expression. They are street slang for what Google considers "unnatural links," – contrived links that did not happen for any plausible reason.

Figure 93 Google does not have a concept of toxic links.

Pro Tip: Some specialist consultants can help to recover from a manual penalty. If your SEO team is inexperienced, you might want to engage such a consultant.

INTERNAL LINKS

Internal links are the ones within the website – the navigation links are the most obvious, but you can also have them in the body text. But, again, this is an often-overlooked technique, and it is best done when the site is mature.

Anchor Text in Internal Links

"Anchor Text" is the text used in a link to signify the clickable link. Many pages underline the anchor text as a best practice for accessibility. Others show the anchor text in a different color. They are a ranking factor from the earliest days of Google, whether used internally or to link to an external website. The phrase "anchor text" features 13 times in the seminal article by Google founders Sergey Brin and Lawrence Page: *The Anatomy of a Large-Scale Hypertextual Web Search Engine*.

The abuse of spammy (excessive and reckless) anchor text links has ended with Google using AI technology, so doing it internally at a spammy level isn't going to help you. Elsewhere, I stress the importance of not using a mega nav bar, as it dilutes link juice and its flavor across a site. A well-structured information architecture goes hand in hand with an internal linking strategy.

Internal Links in Body Text

When you link related content within your website, you are helping to concentrate link juice – what I call "link juice flavor." For example, your banking website has product pages about your home loans. At regular intervals, your blog posts can mention home loans and other products. Such blog posts are good candidates for at least one mention of "home loan" or "mortgage" as the anchor text that links to your home loan product page. This should be done judiciously, as you don't always want to "lose" the reader to another page instead of finishing with this page.

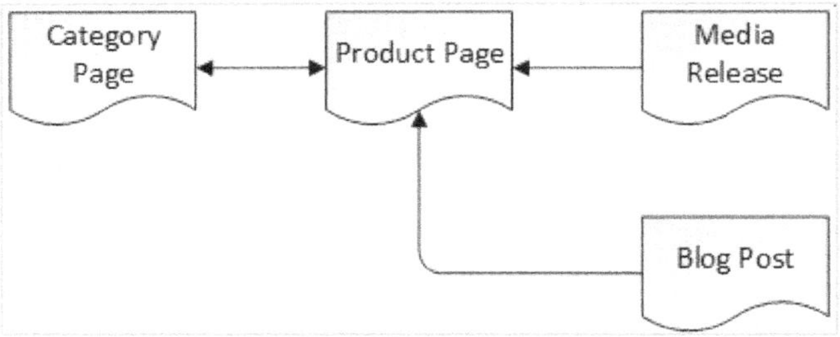

Figure 94 Internal linking concentrates "link juice" on important pages.

If you automate internal linking, say, a brand name that might occur more than once on a page, then don't link more than once from a page. This tactic will dilute that link's impact and also annoy visitors who click the next instance of the link, only to discover that they have already seen the destination page.

Contextual Text in Links

The anchor text is usually the relevant keywords, but try to vary them across different pages. Make them contextual where possible, to send the desired signals of topical relevance to the algorithms. The anchor text should be better than "Click here" or a button with such a label, and should give the visitor a sense of what to expect at the end of that click.

Using a brand name, e.g., "Apple iPhone 15" as the anchor text will strengthen brand recognition and increase the relevance of your internal page for that product. If the page is about some deeper topic, then using that keyword, say, "factory reset for the Apple iPhone 15," will improve its chances of ranking for that phrase, assuming that you have also optimized the destination page for that topic using other SEO tactics.

Chapter 8

MANAGING RANKINGS

Let's look at keyword ranking analytics—how to collect it, interpret it cautiously, and use it as one diagnostic input alongside broader visibility indicators such as impressions, surface coverage, and engagement. Rankings remain useful for trend analysis, but they are no longer a definitive measure of search success on their own.

SEARCH ENGINE ALGORITHMS

Search engines operate through multiple interconnected systems rather than a single, static algorithm. These systems discover billions of webpages, interpret their content and context, and retrieve results that best satisfy perceived query intent. Google remains the dominant general-purpose search engine in many markets and continuously updates its search systems, often without a single identifiable "update" event.

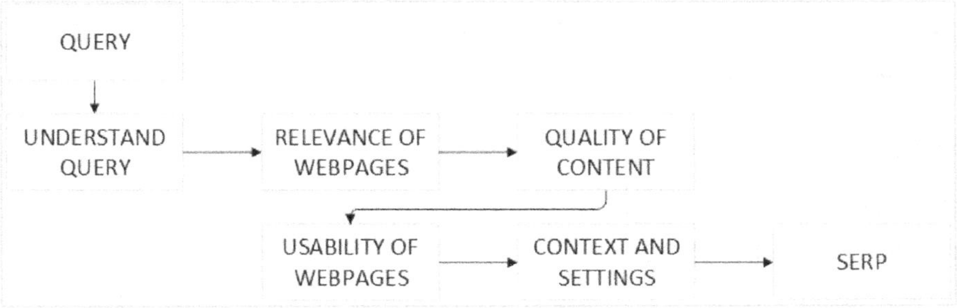

Figure 95 A simplified view of Google ranking systems.

Rankings vary by personalization, location, device, language, query context, and SERP composition. Because different users can see materially different result layouts for the same query, single-position rankings should be treated as directional indicators rather than precise measurements. Rankings are **one signal among many** used to assess overall search visibility.

Understanding the Query

Humans can ask the same question in many ways, sometimes as words, sometimes as phrases, and very rarely as complete sentences. Finally, they find a style that works for them. The search engine needs to get smarter at understanding the typed words and the intent behind them. Sometimes, for ambiguous queries, the user is asked, "Did you mean (something else)?" for clarification.

Relevance of the Webpage

Superficially, the presence of the exact words from the query on the webpage suggests a relevant match. That is how the early search engines worked. Modern systems routinely use AI to determine whether a page that does not contain the exact query text may still better satisfy the underlying intent.

Quality of the Content

Many quality signals are considered, such as the types of webpages that link to the page. PageRank remains one of many internal inputs, but it is no longer publicly exposed and is heavily transformed in modern ranking systems.

Usability of the Webpage

The page needs to be usable across all popular platforms in terms of appearance, loading speed, and other factors.

Context and Settings

The searcher's browser settings, location, and search history affect the SERP. For example, two searchers in different cities or countries typing the same query might see a slightly different SERP.

WHO ARE YOUR SEO COMPETITORS?

It's important to appreciate that for a given search query, the number of traditional organic results visible in a SERP varies widely and is often fewer than ten. Nowadays, many SERPs contain other kinds of results, so the number isn't always ten, but it's a convenient one for illustration. These results include your competitors.

Business Competitors

Business competitors are easily understood – for-profit or not-for-profit organizations targeting your primary audience. However, the SEO work must also include competitors for your keywords.

There is a second group of competitors, but they are not traditional businesses. They are small entrepreneurs who use SEO extensively, sometimes recklessly. They are prepared to see their sites banned by search engines after their "black hat" tactics are picked up, as they have new, "burner" sites waiting to take their place. These sites are often in the "PPP" (pills, poker, porn) space, and they find it hard to remain visible or buy ads, so they take such extreme steps.

Non-Business Competitors

Your non-business competitors should be appreciated, for they can sometimes be your ally. But unfortunately, they can also frustrate you.

Search engines analyze a query and serve results that best address that query. Many queries are imprecise, so the search intent is unclear. For example, if you sell cameras, you would like your catalog to appear in the SERP. The search engine algorithm might return non-business results, such as ratings and reviews pages, news stories, magazine articles, photographers' personal blogs, and Wikipedia pages.

Take heart – such disappointing rankings usually occur for vague searches without clear intent, such as searches for a model number. Once the searcher looks for specifics, such as the price, stalwarts like

Wikipedia are eliminated from the mix. The SERP might exclude ratings and reviews pages when users search for a specific feature or how to use it. Instead of your main product page featuring in the SERP, your supplementary pages, such as FAQs or blog articles, might show up. Thus, you can compete in non-business SERPs as well.

ENTITY (KEYWORD GROUP) VISIBILITY

I have been checking search engine visibility at the entity (keyword group) level for some years. I collected keywords and grouped them into their distinct entities, noting their preferred target pages. Then, once a month, I ran Rank Tracker from the *SEO PowerSuite* package. (Rank Tracker seems to be a common name and is found in other products, too.)

Monthly tracking remains useful for trend analysis, but should be interpreted alongside impression and visibility data.

Entity Visibility Matrix

For a small company with a few entities, it's feasible to track visibility manually, using Rank Tracker and an Excel or Google spreadsheet. For a large company, this task would take me a fortnight, between other work. I was the sole consumer, so the time did not matter. Eventually, I outsourced this work, and it was done in a couple of days. The percentage cells had a color gradient to indicate poor = red and excellent = dark green. After the sheet had been updated for several months, it became clear which entities needed SEO attention.

When significant changes were made to the website, such as a new design or changes to the tracked keywords, a horizontal, colored line helped me assess whether subsequent ranking performance could be attributed to them. Sometimes it can take several months for the high rankings to return, and sometimes they never do.

	Agfa	Kodak	Nikon	Sony	Fujifilm	Panasonic	Olympus	Leica	Rollei	Zeiss	
Summary											
Aug 2021	21%	27%	90%	35%	87%		0%	72%	98%		
Sep 2021	16%	30%	88%	35%	79%		0%	73%	97%		
Oct 2021	16%	21%	87%	70%	70%		0%	73%	96%		
Nov 2021	31%	20%	85%	44%	74%		0%	73%	97%		
Dec 2021	16%	27%	55%	0%	79%		0%	99%	0%		
Jan 2022	0%	21%	0%	0%	75%		0%	0%	0%		New website
Feb 2022	0%	28%	0%	0%	76%	0%	0%	0%	0%	29%	Refreshed keywords and competitors
Mar 2022	0%	26%	0%	0%	70%	0%	0%	0%	0%	29%	

Mar 2022 | About | Agfa | Kodak | Nikon | Sony | Fujifilm | Panasonic | Olympus | Leica | Rollei | Zeiss

Figure 96 Entity Visibility Matrix - Summary page.

Each tab was linked to its respective detail page, showing visibility compared to competitors. This type of tracking made it easy to identify topics the SEO team could investigate, work with the content team on, or look into for technical issues.

Company	2/09/2021	4/10/2021	4/11/2021	2/12/2021	7/01/2022	25/02/2022	8/03/2022	6/04/2022
Our company	90%	88%	87%	85%	55%	0%	0%	0%
Competitor 1	69%	70%	73%	75%	76%	75%	75%	75%
Competitor 2	44%	46%	48%	45%	48%	55%	63%	45%
Competitor 3	49%	58%	51%	43%	63%	60%	61%	62%
Competitor 4	75%	73%	10%	9%	0%	0%	0%	0%
Competitor 5	18%	18%	18%	19%	18%	0%	0%	0%

Mar 2022 | About | Agfa | Kodak | Nikon | Sony | Fujifilm | Panasonic | Olympus | Leica

Figure 97 Entity Visibility Matrix – Entity detail page, with competitors.

DATA VISUALIZATION

Google Looker Studio is a dashboarding tool that can take and combine data from several sources. Your SEO team will enjoy finding new uses for it, and other users share many free templates.

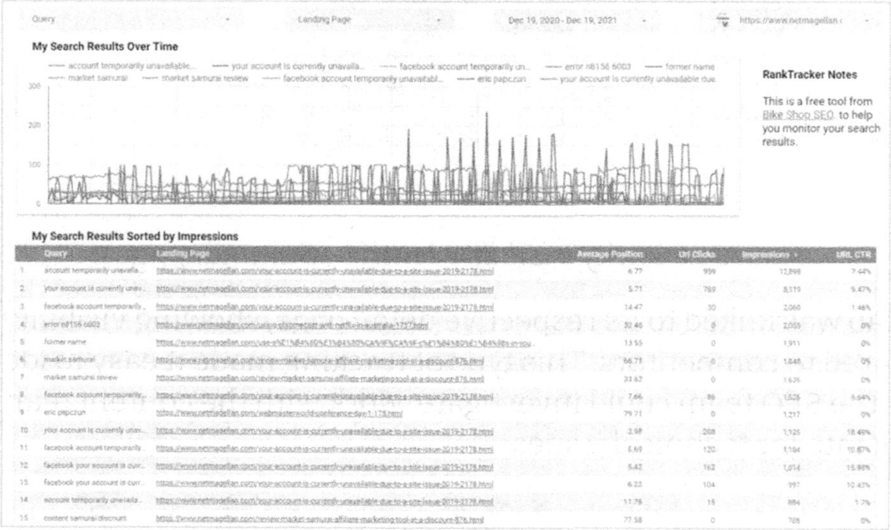

Figure 98 Google Looker Studio is used for visualizing keyword rankings.

CHECKING SERPS IN ANOTHER CITY OR COUNTRY

If you are casually curious about rankings in another city or country where you operate, there are a few ways to do it. Please use your browser's Incognito or InPrivate mode for ranking checks so that a previous search does not influence the new search. The Incognito mode will not store session cookies and other debris that the search engine can discover. Do not log into the search engine, such as their email service.

If your SEO team checks rankings frequently, they may use a reliable Virtual Private Network (VPN), as some VPNs can distort or block search results. For example, I once worked for a company whose headquarters were in another city, and all our offices were on an internal VPN, so our SERPs consistently showed results (particularly ads) for that distant city. The VPN will assign them an IP address corresponding to another city or country.

Changing Your Location in Google Chrome

Google offers a free location-change feature in the Chrome browser. The Search Settings pathway keeps changing, but is usually a gear icon at the top right after you do a Google search (using the Google instance of the target country, such as google.co.uk). Look for the Region Settings and select the country of interest. This feature lacks the granularity of a good VPN, but it's fine for a casual check.

Figure 99 Default location for me.

Figure 100 Location changed to India.

If you want to try something else in Chrome to view regular websites in addition to search engines, use the Console (Ctrl+Shift+I) and use the 3-dot menu on the left to invoke Sensors. Then choose a location or add one by providing the Latitude and Longitude coordinates.

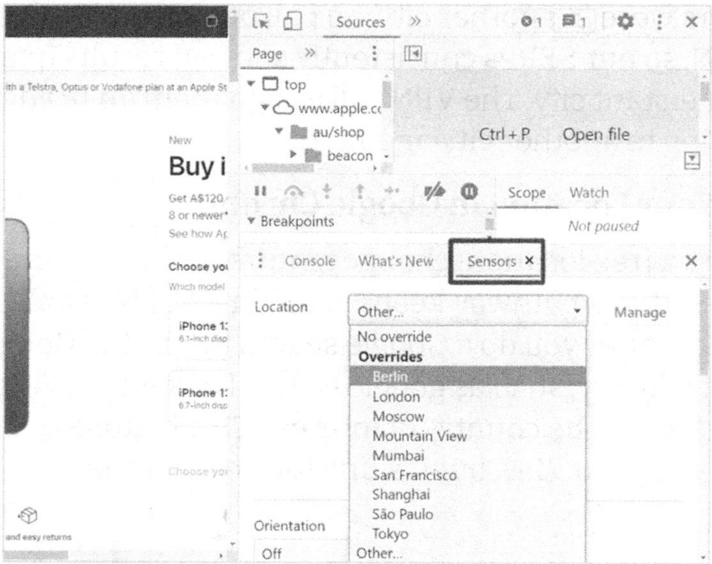

Figure 101 Changing location in the Chrome Console.

Changing Location in Opera

In addition to the better-known browsers – Chrome, Edge, and Safari - there are others worth checking out, such as Vivaldi, Brave, and Opera. Opera has an integral VPN, so you should always leave it on if you want to obscure your location. In addition, you can choose a general virtual location for the VPN, such as "Americas."

LOCAL SEO AS A GOVERNANCE DISCIPLINE

Local SEO is often misunderstood as a narrow tactic focused on "near me" queries. In practice, it governs how an organization appears to search systems when resolving *location-qualified intent*, which may or may not be geographically close to the searcher. Increasingly, users search with layered qualifiers that combine location, timing, availability, attributes, and identity.

Common patterns now include queries such as:

- A service or product "near me."
- A service or product "now" or "available now."
- A service or product "along the route" in navigation systems
- A service or product associated with specific attributes (for example, ownership or specialization)
- A service or product in any nominated location, regardless of the searcher's current position

For managers, the implication is straightforward: local visibility is no longer a niche SEO problem. It is a discoverability and credibility issue that sits at the intersection of data accuracy, content governance, and brand trust.

THE THREE PILLARS OF LOCAL VISIBILITY

Google describes Local SEO as three pillars: proximity, relevance, and prominence. While these are often framed as ranking factors, they are more usefully understood as *ownership domains* inside an organization.

Proximity — Data Integrity and Infrastructure

Proximity reflects how confidently a platform can determine where a business operates and serves customers. This is less about physical distance alone and more about the consistency and reliability of location data across systems. When addresses, service areas, or operating hours drift out of sync, visibility degrades silently.

Relevance — Content Completeness and Clarity

Relevance depends on whether a platform can confidently match a searcher's intent to a business's offerings. Missing attributes, incomplete menus, or vague service descriptions weaken this signal. If detailed information exists only in images or unstructured formats, systems may fail to recognize a match—even when the business is an ideal fit.

Prominence — Reputation and Brand Signals

Prominence reflects how well-known and trusted a business appears across the wider ecosystem. Reviews, citations, local media mentions, and consistent brand presence all contribute. This is not an SEO-only responsibility; it is the cumulative result of marketing, communications, and customer experience.

Manager takeaway: if no one explicitly owns each pillar, Local SEO performance degrades even when "SEO work" is ongoing.

GOOGLE BUSINESS PROFILE AS OPERATIONAL RISK

Google Business Profile (GBP) is often treated as a marketing asset. In reality, it is an operational dependency. Unclaimed or poorly maintained profiles regularly display incorrect hours, outdated addresses, or misleading service information—creating customer frustration before any marketing or sales interaction occurs.

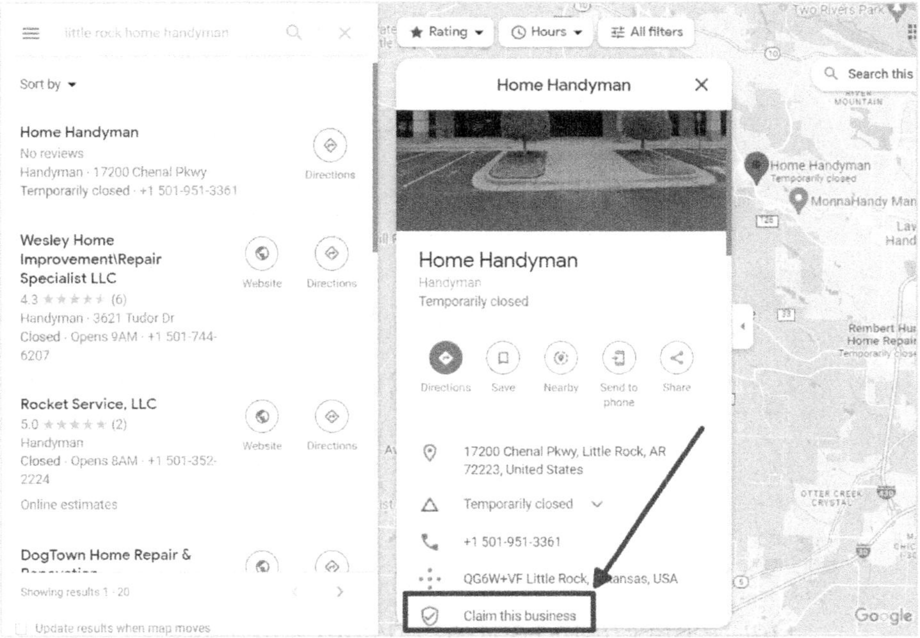

Figure 102 Example of an unclaimed listing in Google Maps.

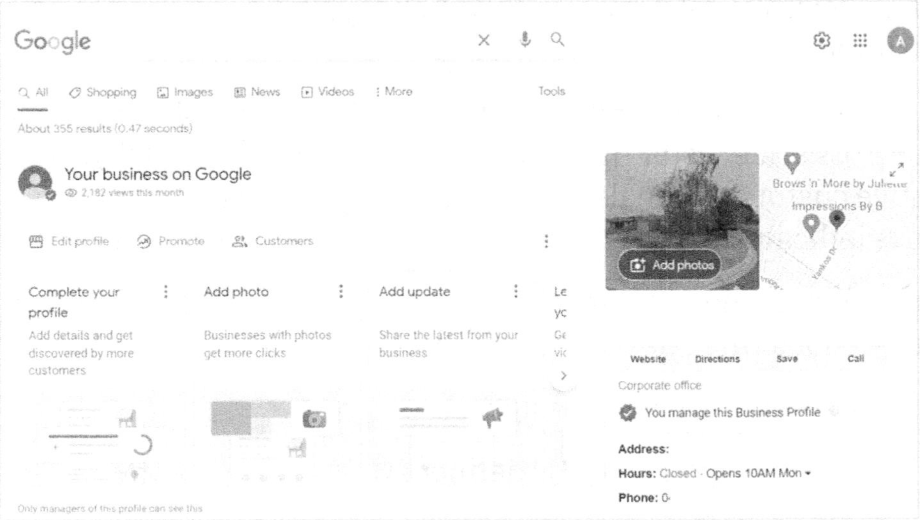

Figure 103 Edit Google Business Profile in Google Search.

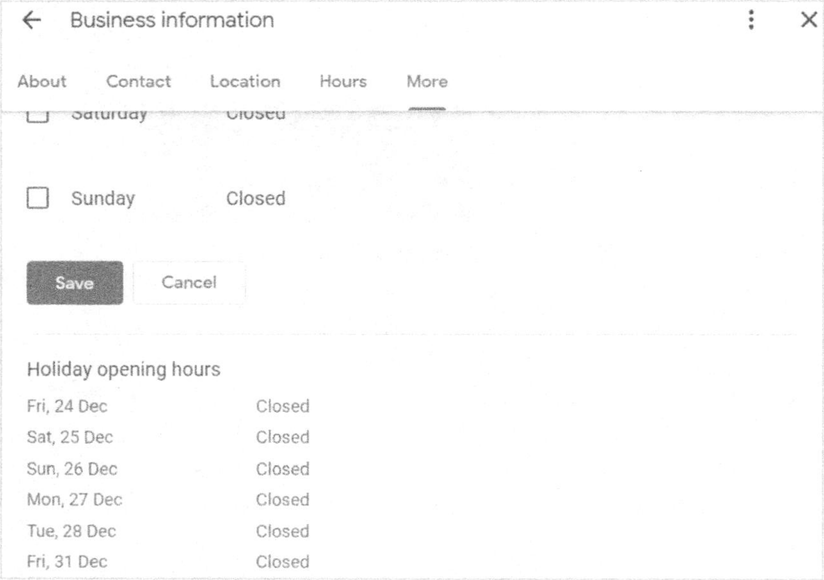

Figure 104 Editing operating hours on holidays.

Figures 105–107 illustrate how easily inaccurate listings can persist and how operational details such as holiday hours are surfaced directly to customers.

For large organizations with multiple locations, the risk compounds. Data errors scale faster than they can be corrected manually, and negative customer signals accumulate long before performance reports indicate an issue.

From a management perspective, the question is not whether GBP exists—it does. The question is whether:

- Ownership is clearly assigned
- Update: responsibility is defined
- Accuracy is reviewed as part of normal operations

LOCAL SEO ABUSE AND VENDOR RISK

Local SEO is particularly vulnerable to unethical shortcuts. Businesses are often exposed not through deliberate misconduct, but through vendors pursuing short-term gains without regard for platform policy.

Common abuse patterns include:

- Using residential or unrelated addresses
- Leveraging virtual offices without eligibility
- Creating multiple listings to simulate geographic coverage

These practices may produce temporary visibility but expose the organization to removal, suspension, or reputational damage. Importantly, enforcement consequences apply to the business—not the agency.

Managers should treat Local SEO abuse as a governance risk, akin to compliance or brand misuse, rather than a technical edge case.

VISUAL SIGNALS AND SEMANTIC INTERPRETATION

As search platforms rely more heavily on machine interpretation, images are evaluated for what they depict—not how attractive they appear. Clear, unambiguous photographs that accurately represent products, premises, or services reinforce credibility. Generic stock imagery weakens trust signals and reduces the likelihood of meaningful engagement.

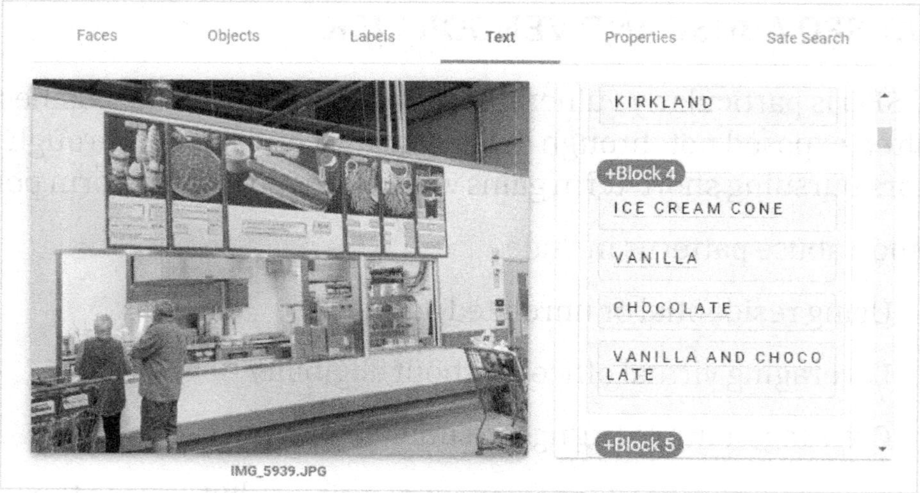

Figure 105 AI has read the text on the food menu.

Figure 106 AI can see this is a tour bus.

Figures 108–110 demonstrate how systems can interpret menus, vehicles, and environments visually. The managerial implication is not about tooling, but about intent: visuals should confirm reality, not decorate it.

LOCAL JUSTIFICATIONS AND DECISION SHORTCUTS

In local search results, platforms often surface "justifications"—short explanatory snippets that indicate *why* a listing appears relevant. These may reference website content, menus, reviews, or recent updates.

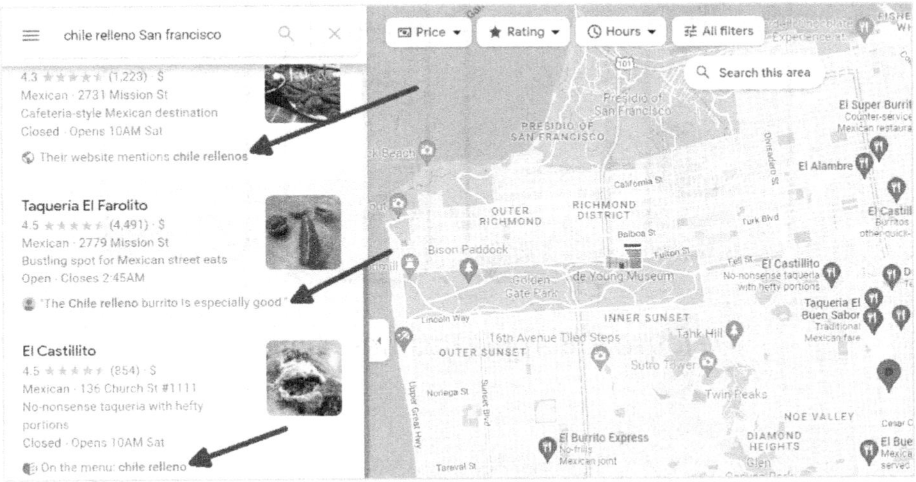

Figure 107 Local Post justifications.

Figure 113 shows how these justifications act as decision shortcuts for users. They are not directly controllable, but they are influenced by content clarity, review quality, and consistency across sources.

For managers, justifications are a reminder that visibility is being explained on your behalf—often using fragments of your own data.

PLATFORM COVERAGE BEYOND GOOGLE

Local visibility extends beyond Google. Apple Maps underpins Siri and is used by privacy-focused search engines such as DuckDuckGo. Businesses that neglect Apple's ecosystem may be invisible to a significant audience segment by default.

Figure 108 Apple Business Connect.

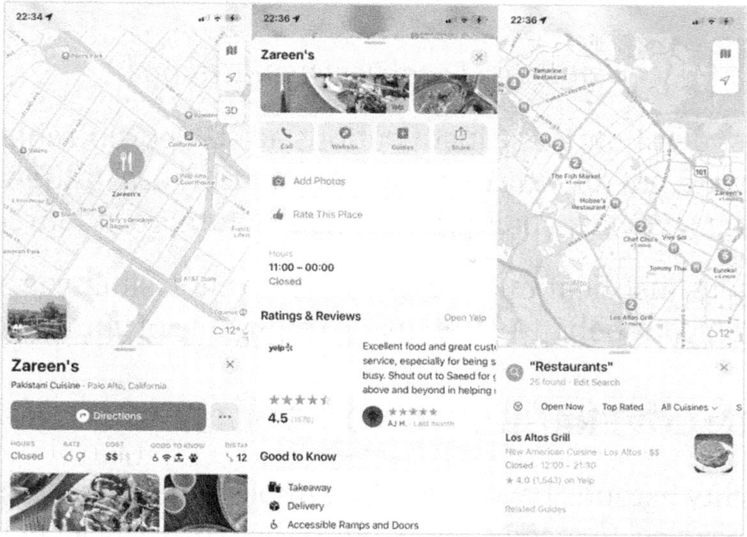

Figure 109 Business details in Apple Maps.

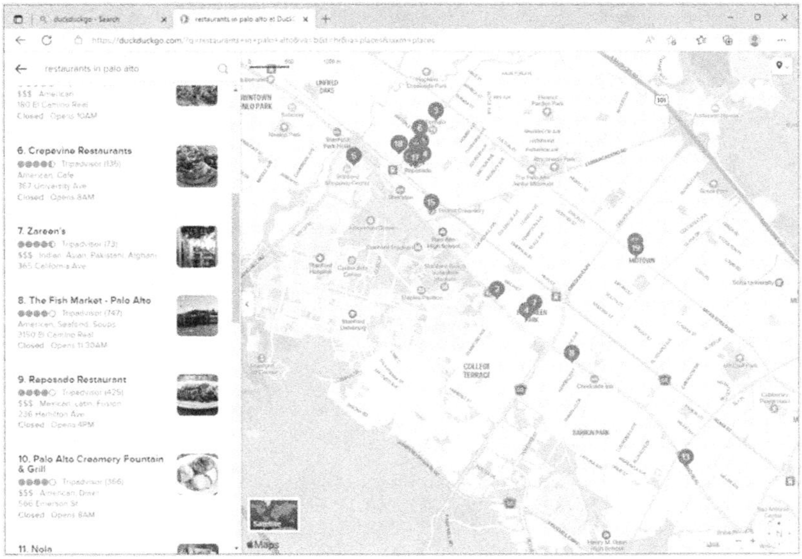

Figure 110 Apple Maps is seen in DuckDuckGo.

Figures 114–116 illustrate how business information appears across these platforms. The operational insight is simple: local data governance must be platform-agnostic.

LOCAL SEO AS ONGOING MAINTENANCE

Local SEO does not fail because algorithms change. It fails because ownership lapses. Data drift, staff turnover, vendor shortcuts, and neglected updates create gradual erosion that is rarely flagged as an SEO problem until customer complaints or revenue impact appear.

For accidental SEO managers, the practical lesson is this: you do not need to master Local SEO tactics. You need to ensure that location data, reputation signals, and platform listings are treated as maintained assets—with clear accountability and review cycles.

When that discipline exists, Local SEO becomes predictable. When it does not, visibility loss is inevitable—and usually goes unnoticed until it becomes costly.

Chapter 9

MANAGING YOUR ONLINE REPUTATION

Online Reputation Management (ORM) gets less attention than it deserves, or gets it when it's too late. In many cases, lawful and factual content cannot be removed or suppressed; it can only be displaced.

I once had a would-be client who ran a medical practice. He said that a search for his name brought up a negative story about him as the first result. It was from a leading newspaper during the time he was taken to court by a patient. The judge subsequently dismissed the case, so this doctor felt that Google should not prominently display it and came to me for help. When I told him what was involved and what it would cost him, he chose to do nothing, and that article still ranks #1 for his name.

A veteran who had been to prison came to me for the same kind of help – a negative story about his crime would rank high when searching for his name. So, I gave him free advice as outlined below, being a fellow veteran.

SOME TYPES OF NEGATIVE ONLINE REPUTATION

- Negative Personal Reputation
- Negative Brand, Product, or Service Reputation
- Bad Neighborhoods

Fixing Personal Reputation

My two examples were negative personal reputations. Being factual and appearing in mainstream news media made them difficult to fix quickly. Most individuals will not have the money to do what is necessary. Here are some tactics to try:

- Buy a domain of your full name, e.g., johndoe.com, and, if budget permits, buy the .net, .org, and other top-level domains. Make it a substantial website about yourself – perhaps make it your blog and fill it with positive stories at regular intervals. Make the content share-worthy and link-worthy. Links will come, and this new site will slowly reach page 1. Then you need to keep at it until this site ranks #1 for your name, but you must not stop adding content.
- As there is a limited number of traditional organic results visible on page 1 of the search engines, you want the negative content off the first page, so you need to tackle the remaining results. If you are a newsworthy person, be sure to get in the news for the right, positive reasons so those stories get on page 1.
- Implement Plan B. The doctor mentioned above had a fairly common name. By a stroke of good fortune, another doctor in the same city with the same name was an academic. The third person with his name was a historical figure of some notoriety. Getting the namesakes to a top-ranking position might be possible, thus dislodging the negative news story. Feature them in blog posts, and they might eventually take over page 1.

Although you might dislodge a negative story from the first position or even from the first page, that is for a search of the person's name. A search for this name with a qualifying phrase, e.g., "John Doe sued for x," is most likely to bring up every negative story about the incident. Also, keep in mind that a few online archives, such as the Wayback

Machine, keep copies of websites. Many other mentions, such as in privacy-enabled tweets and Facebook posts, might go unnoticed.

FIXING BRAND, PRODUCT, OR SERVICE REPUTATION

Many organizations receive negative product ratings and reviews on social media platforms and review websites. Address genuine negative reviews by resolving complaints when feasible and ensuring that positive reviews outnumber negative ones.

Fake reviews are a different matter. If a competitor or mischief-maker commissions a fake review, you might be able to get the review site to remove the review, perhaps with the help of a legal notification. It's always a good move to encourage lots of reviews and honest, 5-star ratings, particularly from happy customers.

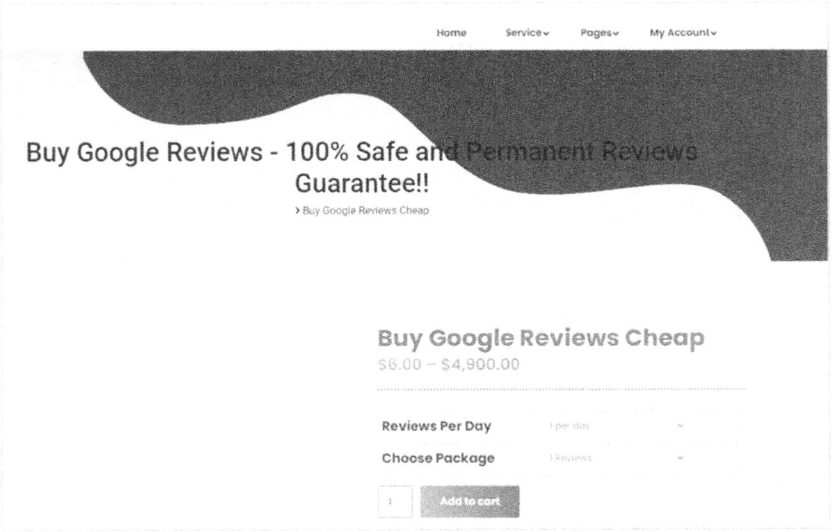

Figure 111 A site that offers fake reviews – please avoid such offers.

FIXING A BAD NEIGHBORHOOD

Only a small business is likely to use shared web hosting, and it may end up on a machine shared by many nasty websites. This is one type of bad neighborhood. At some point, the search engine might associate the shared hosting environment with abuse or spam signals, and you are better off finding a reputable web host or getting a dedicated IP address.

"OWNING" PAGE 1

Large companies have little trouble owning most of the entries on page 1 of the SERPs for their brand name. However, smaller entities can try a few tactics to achieve this goal.

Regularly setting up and using YouTube, X (formerly Twitter), Instagram, TikTok, Pinterest, Facebook, and other social platforms is an easy way to get more space on page 1 of a SERP. A Google Business Profile (map) listing is another quick win. A Google Business Profile (map) listing is another quick win. Increasingly, branded results are also influenced by knowledge panels

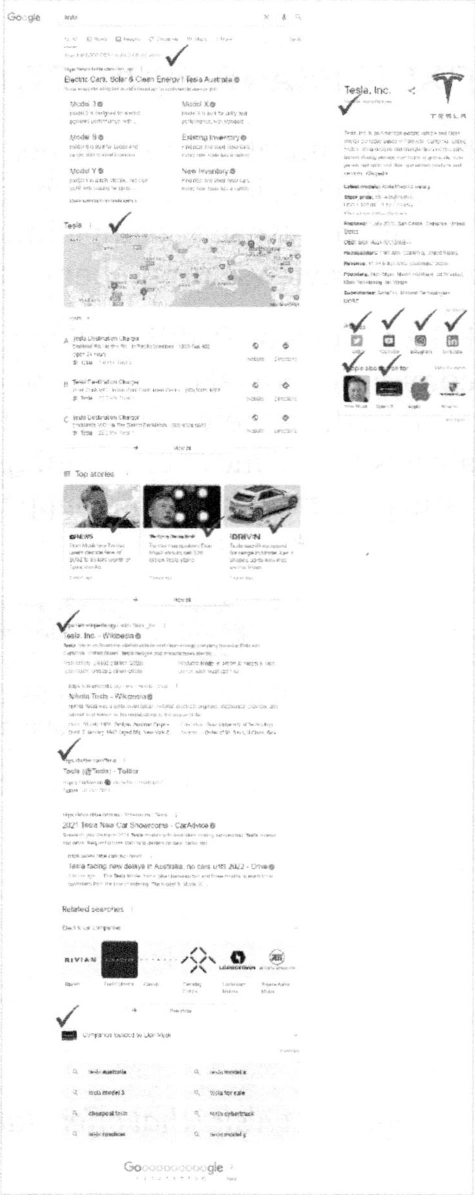

Figure 112 Tesla's brand "owns" most of Page 1.

and AI-generated summaries, which cannot be directly controlled.

Don't forget to optimize content on ecommerce marketplaces such as Amazon, eBay, and elsewhere, if relevant.

A search query phrased as a question often invokes a "People Also Ask" area in the SERP and might include a question about a problem with your product. If this happens, create a page or two to address the issue. That might earn you a featured snippet or inclusion near prominent SERP features.

BE ALERT

Many paid services can monitor all mentions of your brand across social media platforms and websites, but a good free option is Google Alerts. Perform the search you feel is best for your brand, e.g., "(brand name) sucks," and if the preview looks right, set it. You will receive emails when Google detects newly added results in its index.

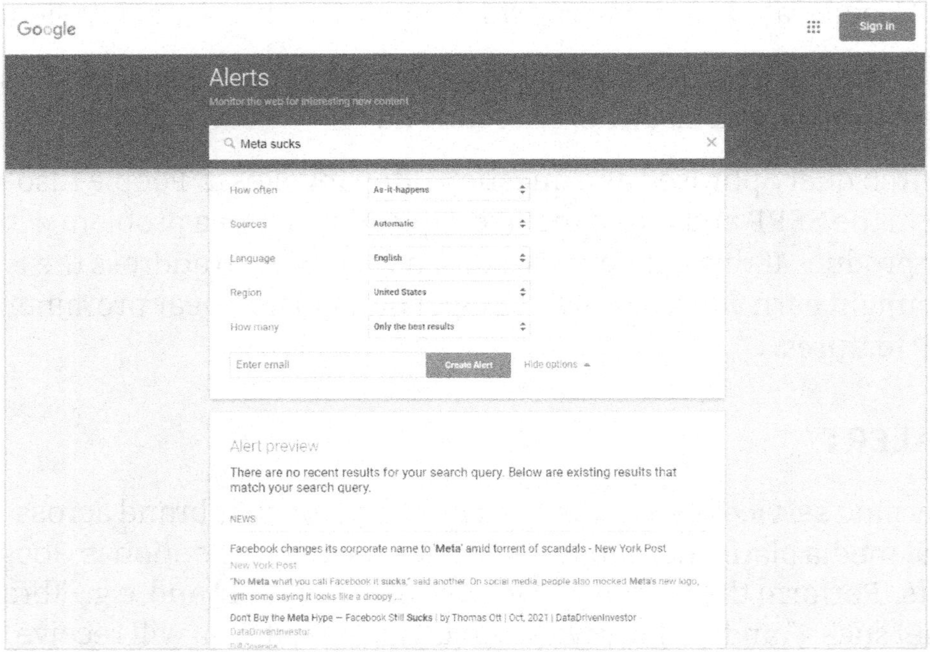

Figure 113 Set up a Google Alert for a brand mention.

Google Alerts offers high granularity, and you can choose a manageable number of notifications.

A WIKIPEDIA ENTRY

An unsolicited entry is best, as Wikipedia frowns upon self-submissions. Of course, Wikipedia has featured most large companies by now. Still, new entities should only pursue an entry once independent notability is clearly established, taking care not to look like a piece of advertising – a common rookie error.

You and I can edit any page, with verifiable facts, in Wikipedia, so be aware that your dirty laundry, such as litigation, failures, and the like, can and will be added to your page. Wikipedia editing should be approached cautiously and in accordance with its conflict-of-interest guidelines.

If your organization is quite old, check your entry for accuracy, as this is the most common issue with outdated content. Wikipedia "bots" discover and create many entries so that they might be worth a human edit.

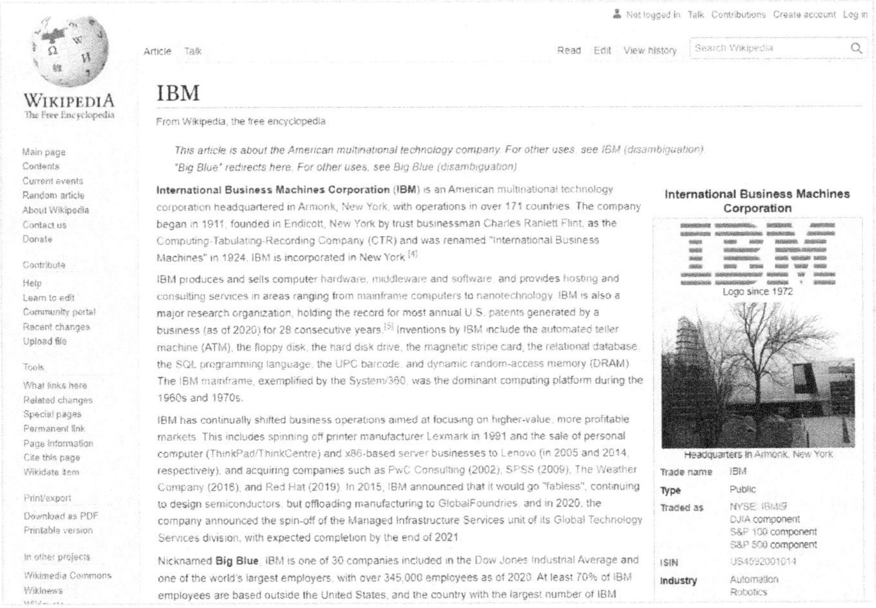

Figure 114 Wikipedia page for IBM.

You should check for changes in information, such as the CEO's name, the latest financial data, and product names, and update if warranted.

Does Wikipedia Benefit Ranking?

In a word, no. Google has said as much. A "nofollowed" link from Wikipedia does not confer any link-juice value. So why discuss a Wikipedia entry? Wikipedia content usually ranks on page #1, so it helps put your brand out there. A well-written page will rank for several keywords, providing an additional source of visibility.

Whether Google regards your Wikipedia entry as a positive signal (a "citation") is unclear, but I still recommend getting a page in it. Google says a nofollow link is treated as a hint, but any ranking impact is speculative and indirect.

BUYING AND RENEWING DOMAINS

If you are buying a domain name for a new business, brand protection, or any other reason, engage a specialist. Buying a domain name is not a trivial task for "someone in IT," as the pitfalls go far beyond the mechanics of purchase.

If you don't have a professional domain management company looking after your renewals, put your domains on backorder with your registrar. If you forget to renew and their reminders go astray, or your auto-renewal fails for some reason, this may help you recover. Still, it is not a substitute for proper renewal management.

Brand Protection

Brand protection is also SEO protection. It involves buying numerous similar domains to avoid misrepresentation or accidental confusion. In the early days of the internet (for business use), companies used to take the ".com" extension for the "commercial" connotation, the ".org" for non-profit organizations, ".net" for internet companies, etc. That didn't last long.

Those extensions are known as generic top-level domain names (gTLDs). They apply internationally, whereas countries issue their own country-code top-level domain names (ccTLDs).

Unless protected by a trademark, anyone can buy any available gTLD or ccTLD, subject to certain rules. However, even trademarked domains that are briefly encroached upon are recovered by their rightful owner through legal process. Therefore, buying as many similar domains as your budget allows is best. For example, I have worked for companies with a single primary domain but more than 1,000 domains on their renewal list.

Consider buying the following types of brand-protection domains, if applicable:

- gTLDs and ccTLDs
- misspellings and alternative spellings
- hyphenated
- "www" prefix without the dot, e.g., wwwexample.com
- disgruntled customer sites, e.g., ihateexample.com or examplesucks.com

Such domains rarely perform well today but may still be worth defensive registration in limited cases.

You can see how you could potentially buy hundreds of domains if the budget permits, but we are looking at the SEO angle here. If you only operate in one country, there is no need to buy more than the gTLD and ccTLD variations for one country. Perhaps buy others if they could be used to deceive your customers or deter potential customers. For example, you are unlikely to use a word like "scammers" or "sucks" in your brand name, but a disgruntled customer domain might rank high for one of those negative phrases.

Used Domains

I caution against buying "used" domains with unknown provenance. Many domains are bought and populated with questionable content (such as spam or adult content) that search engines do not like, which can lead to severe penalties, including suppressed visibility until trust is re-established. In addition, a change of owner and content might not earn it the visibility it might otherwise get on a virgin domain.

You could look for the domain on The Wayback Machine. However, it is possible that the site blocked the Wayback Machine crawler, or the crawler never discovered it.

Unsearchable Domains

I strongly caution against rebranding to a generic dictionary word. Not all organizations have the web clout of Alphabet (parent company of Google) to rank #1 for a generic name (its URL is https://abc.xyz). I will not name and shame here, but the new owners of an established NASDAQ-listed company decided to rebrand to a verb that occurs in daily speech and news items. A search for its name would bring up dictionary and wiki sites for the generic word. Now I see the company name has disappeared and the product moved to the website of its new parent company.

Unusual Domain or Product Names

By "unusual," I mean in the English language context. Although made-up words are highly brandable – Google is a case in point – they should be checked thoroughly. The legal team can engage a trademark law firm to check for that angle, but what about foreign languages? Never mind the impact on sales, which is bad enough, but there is a search angle, too. Is it such a nasty word that it will get filtered out by platform moderation and SafeSearch systems?

Chapter 10

MANAGING AN IN-HOUSE SEO TEAM

If you have the budget for an in-house SEO team (small or large), you're in a happy place for SEO. You can control your SEO sales outcomes better with an in-house team than if you paid someone on the outside to look after your SEO exclusively.

HIRING THE RIGHT MIX

SEO All-Rounder

A small company with a small budget needs an all-rounder, but finding an ideal candidate will be challenging because the salary offered won't meet expectations. Instead, look for SEOs who have worked in your industry or a similar one. They will be experts in some areas and not much in others. You can help them improve on some weaknesses through learning opportunities, but other shortcomings might be more challenging to overcome, such as geographic familiarity or language skills.

New to SEO

In my early SEO career, I was the manager of an SEO agency about to be closed down (I found out later). My technical resource quit at short notice, and I had to hire a developer. In those days, people either did not know about SEO or thought it was a big con. There were no suitable applicants, so I did the next best thing: I hired someone with potential. As I expanded my team, I repeated that formula, and today at least three of them are at the top of their game in corporate SEO.

Over the next 20 years, I recruited people with the potential to learn SEO. Often, they were employees from other parts of the company seeking a career change, bringing strong business knowledge with them. I asked them to sit with an experienced operator for a while until they found their groove.

SEO Specialists

An SEO Specialist has three to five years of experience, perhaps as a sole all-rounder in a small company. They have seen projects from start to finish and may have experienced adverse ranking situations.

Technical SEO Specialists

When you have several SEOs in your team, someone will be more "technical" and less "content" centric. They will be the ones who dig into HTML, CSS, JavaScript, PHP, and other areas of web development. They might not be able to code, but they will be able to communicate clearly with the developers.

SEO Strategist

A larger company should have a designated SEO Strategist, typically the senior-most SEO Manager. They look at the bigger picture, such as where the company is headed, and plan the SEO steps to get there. They also conduct audits to assess the strategic pulse rather than the minor issues that come up from time to time.

Writers

Whether the writers sit in the SEO team or a separate Content team depends on the company. They need a career path, so they should be an independent team reporting to a common manager. SEO content writers are also known as SEO copywriters.

UX Writers

User Experience (UX) writers overlap with SEO writers in their duties, and sometimes they are the same people. In larger companies, they are part of the UX team and write for more than the website. They write text for phone apps and microtext for forms, error messages, and help text. UX writers focus on users who are using the app or are already on the website, while SEO content writers focus on the words search engines can interpret to send the right audience to the website.

SEO TEAM SKILLSETS

In order of importance, the in-house SEO team should include people with these skills, though no single person is likely to have all of them. As a result, you might have to outsource some tasks.

- **Hard skills** – Hard skills are about proficiency in the SEO discipline.
- **Soft skills** – Soft skills are people skills – managing, collaborating, mentoring, communicating, etc.
- **Self-starter** – SEO is a mix of reactionary and strategic, planned tasks. They can plan work for the day, week, and quarter with little or no oversight.
- **Good listener** – Listening is a life skill we all need to develop, but SEO is about listening to the stakeholders' needs and to their feedback.
- **Calm and patient under pressure** – An SEO's daily routine is rarely predictable. Many tasks arrive with an impossible deadline. Then, Murphy's Law might step in and cancel a planned task. This requires a cool head and the ability to handle the matter without escalating unnecessarily.
- **Quick, analytical thinker** – If rankings dropped, was it a Google algorithm or something we did?
- **Multi-tasker** – Numerous SEO tasks are implemented in parallel by different teams. The SEO needs to be in all those places simultaneously.

- **Long-term visionary** – While a quick solution seems attractive, the SEO should consider the long-term implications.
- **Open-minded** – Sometimes, a junior SEO might have a contrary view, and the senior SEO should not shut them down. If the risks are low, it might serve as a learning opportunity for the junior team member.
- **Diligent with documentation** – All technical disciplines are guilty of not documenting enough, but an SEO needs to document diligently. They can reverse errors quickly and repeat their successes.
- **Excellent grammar and spelling** – Google can often cope with typos, but getting the language right the first time gives you one less potential worry.
- **Voice of the Customer** – The SEO needs to understand how customers talk about their products to give the right keywords adequate prominence.

The following technical skills are highly valued:

- HTML
- JavaScript
- PHP
- CSS
- Accessibility
- Regular Expressions (RegEx)
- Python

SEO JOB DESCRIPTIONS

Recruiting for SEO positions is as important as any other mission-critical role in the organization. Hiring the wrong person will end in the proverbial tears.

Write up the job description to fit the template used by the organization, but consider including the following points:

Job Description – Junior SEO Role

- Monitor Google Search Console and analytics daily
- Investigate anomalies as directed by a manager
- Monitor backlinks monthly
- Work with the Content team to optimize content

Job Description – Senior SEO Role

- Conduct regular audits
- Supervise and mentor the junior SEO
- Prepare reports for the SEO Manager

Job Description –SEO Manager Role

- Manage the team
- Analyze competitor sites for signs of their SEO tactics
- Present key metrics to upper management
- Collaborate with peers to achieve common goals
- Train and mentor the SEO team

WHERE TO FIND TALENT

Genuine SEO talent is scarce, so be prepared to hire someone based on their potential. Internal candidates should always be the first to be interviewed. Most organizations make this a part of their recruitment and career growth policy. Internal candidates might come with some relevant experience, such as:

- Marketing
- Customer Care
- Technology

- User Experience
- Product Management

Many high schools offer work-experience programs that allow students to gain workplace experience. Some university students might look for vacation jobs. Graduates might look for internships. These are all entry-level opportunities.

You can use the well-tried recruitment agencies to filter the applicants for SEO Specialist and SEO Manager roles. They will use one or more public recruitment platforms. The organization's employees should be encouraged to refer their connections and earn a finder's fee – this will be a lot cheaper than the fee charged by an employment agency.

Keep some budget to hire an external consultant annually or periodically. It is always good to have a fresh eye on your work.

SHORTLISTING THE CANDIDATES

If you don't have a well-briefed recruitment agency to filter out the applicants, you might be inundated by ineligible candidates, such as those without a valid visa. SEO teams are increasingly multicultural, including recent migrants. For in-house roles, I preferred candidates who had worked in-house, as those from low-priced agencies tend to be formulaic and tool-reliant in their approach. They might not have experience with corporate work practices. Someone who worked in a high-end agency with enterprise clients might be a suitable fit.

Avoid Discrimination

It is crucial to convey the organization's hiring ethos, such as equal opportunity employment, which should include mature-age candidates. I was working in my 60s with over 20 years of SEO experience – slightly less than the age of the WWW. Many experts I know in their 40s, 50s, and 60s are less likely to be hired than those in their 20s. It's unfortunate for the hiring company that is more concerned with what's called a "cultural fit" than with getting people who will achieve their sales targets without needing much business training.

Cover Letters

Cover letters help candidates express their interest in the position. I would not ask for specific information in them, but I would check whether the recruitment platform offers the option to request it.

INTERVIEWING

Conduct interviews at a time that suits candidates in employment, which means lunch-time and after-hours interviews. Otherwise, some worthy applicants might withdraw from the process.

Interview Panel

The SEO Manager and the Senior SEO Specialist should conduct the first interview if possible. If the vacancy is for the SEO Manager, a senior manager should do it with another SEO team member.

The second interview might include someone from Human Resources (HR) to observe candidates' interpersonal qualities, as well as a more senior manager. But, again, try not to have large panels that might intimidate candidates.

Interview Questions

As impromptu questions may arise during the interview, it is essential to know which questions are legal and which are illegal. The HR team can guide you on that score. If you have never interviewed, an HR associate could run you through a mock interview and give you feedback afterward. Printing the questions ensures that you ask all candidates the same questions.

For most SEO roles, you don't need to see their educational qualifications in detail. Their experience (for non-entry-level positions) is enough to separate those who will get to the second interview. I ask questions that show me their diagnostic skills, such as:

- Our organic traffic dropped on July 1 and has not returned to the same level – what might be the cause, and how would you investigate?
- Which tags do you consider essential for a home page, a product page, and a contact page?
- What recent Google Search ranking or spam update have you been following, and what practical changes did it imply for site owners?
- What are your views about linking, and how did you obtain them in the past?
- How do you approach the "directory versus subdomain" dilemma, and how can it be solved?

I used an "Interview Pack" for each candidate, consisting of a printed copy of their résumé and a sheet with the questions. The sheet enabled me to write notes on the resume before the interview – I would ask the questions while a colleague in the interview panel would take notes. Likewise, if they were asking a question, I would take notes.

I would shred the used interview packs after the successful candidate was selected – usually after the final interview.

Conducting the Interview

Find a quiet interview room that is free of distractions – corporate meeting rooms are perfect. Candidates should be made comfortable and offered a drink of water. A round of introductions will let the candidate know the names and roles of the people present.

Ethics of Assignments

Many companies ask candidates to conduct an SEO audit, write a strategy document, and explain their logic. Such a task might please some keen candidates, but is also likely to cause ill will among the unsuccessful ones. You don't need accusations of stealing ideas from them, so you are better off asking for the assignment to be based on a neutral, non-commercial organization, such as a not-for-profit website.

After all, you cannot expect external candidates to know your organization, and they don't need to wade through a hundred automated audit reports from the same tool.

Asking for References

There is no need to ask for references before the first interview. Experienced candidates should provide a reference for an SEO role they have held, while new SEOs can provide a more general reference. Your in-house or agency expert might wish to inspect the websites the candidates have worked on. That's the best way to check their technical competence. The reference checks can then focus on their interpersonal qualities.

My last corporate role involved applying through a recruitment platform that needed seven – yes, seven references! Fortunately, I was able to provide them, and the hiring manager apologized. If your platform allows it, please ask for a more reasonable number.

SUBSEQUENT AND FINAL INTERVIEWS

My last role involved four interviews, but most earlier ones required two at best. The first is with the hiring manager, while the second is essentially a "rubber stamp" interview with a more senior person.

TRAINING AND LEARNING

SEO learning is mostly self-taught and partly learned through the shared experience of others.

Training Courses

Where does one find SEO training courses? I owned an SEO training business for seven years, where we imparted knowledge in the classroom and online. It offered a one-day Basic SEO course and a two-day Advanced SEO course. There were a handful of other SEO training providers in my city, but in general, I found that individuals were not interested in paying for training. If their employer were footing the bill, they would come, but most wanted a half-day course. Very few wanted to do the two-day course.

So, here's a problem. SEO is not a subject where the trainer can impart meaningful learning in half a day. Yet most major cities offer such courses, provided by people with unverifiable SEO skills.

The other problem is that many workplaces cannot spare their staff more than a day to do such courses. Dwell on this for a moment. So those employers want their untrained staff to "do SEO" without much training? Perhaps they think that SEO is just "meta tags and keywords"?

Yes, SEO is a tool in your sales armory that can potentially bring in 30-60 percent of new online sales in an e-commerce organization. The rest comes from advertising and direct (or bookmarked) visits to the website. Can such organizations afford not to provide their staff with more than 8 hours of training?

What, then, should be the minimum length of SEO training courses? An initial SEO course should last about two days, and an advanced SEO course should be longer – at least three days. My ideal course would be delivered on company premises, customized to suit the unique mix of students.

Some small universities and colleges have attempted to create SEO courses. There might be some value in doing them, but remember that SEO is best taught by current SEO practitioners rather than by educators who have never worked on websites. Look for trainers who can tailor a course to your needs.

Self-Education Is Best

Self-education is the best way to learn SEO, so please encourage your team to do the same. Only a rare individual will self-educate in their own time, so make sure their daily routine includes time for self-education.

Here are some ways to acquire that knowledge:

- Online SEO portals that offer news and opinions about the profession
- SEO-specific forums and Facebook groups
- Following prominent SEO personalities
- Building and maintaining personal websites

Self-education also means the SEO team should be allowed to browse LinkedIn and Facebook during short breaks, as it is a quick way to get a filtered view of SEO articles worth reading. Opening the individual SEO newsletters in my email inbox takes longer.

There are many free and paid resources for learning HTML, CSS, and JavaScript. Of course, knowing HTML5 should suffice, but understanding the basic concepts behind CSS and JavaScript will enable better collaboration with the web developers.

I mentioned Python earlier. While it is a programming language, your SEO team isn't going to turn into web developers. However, knowing Python will enable them to speed up routine data-gathering and analysis. This is a skill worth acquiring by your more technical team members. It is available for Linux, Mac, and Windows. On Windows, they can install Python through the Microsoft Store or directly from the official Python distribution.

Kaizen is a team culture: rewarding small improvements accelerates capability growth and reduces rework.

Defining and Measuring SEO Skill Sets

SEO skill is not an easily defined concept. No syllabus defines the knowledge an SEO needs or the level of proficiency. There are a few "Full-Stack SEOs." You might not see this term much outside the developer context. Still, it describes some talented individuals who can read and write a programming or scripting language in addition to the other common SEO skills we cover in this book series. They are "part-time developers" but also "full-time SEOs."

An in-house, full-stack SEO might feel frustrated in a large company, as they will not be allowed near the website code. That's the job of full-time web developers. However, this full-stack SEO will thrive in an agency or as a self-employed professional.

Another reason is that the programming and scripting languages used on enterprise websites differ from those used on small businesses' free platforms. So, we're talking Java versus PHP, for instance.

A full-stack SEO is not a sustainable, repeatable model. Almost everyone in SEO has had an accidental pathway into the profession, so they have picked up atypical skills that are unlikely to be repeated. Good luck to those who can pick up new technical skills outside their comfort zone. Such individuals are worth hiring and retaining.

My SEO learning was entirely self-taught before my first SEO job, unlike many nowadays who learn on the job from experienced colleagues. My background was accounting, marketing, and computer science – an unusual combination where my first degree gave me no advantage in SEO. I built my first computer from a kit, and later founded an ISP for my computer user group. This experience included self-taught website-building skills, which still come in handy.

Many SEO tasks require no coding and very little knowledge of scripting or tagging. Some operatives work entirely with a tool and interpret its output in monthly reports or audit documents. If they work in a multi-talented team, such as in an agency, they will remain in an SEO role for many years, but they will only have partial knowledge.

No certifying bodies can say that a practitioner is "fully skilled" on a given date. Yes, some self-serving educational institutions have come and gone, purporting to issue "SEO Certification." I once owned such a training college and issued certificates. Guilty as charged.

Figure 115 I once issued such certificates to my students.

There are two reasons why SEO certification has never become durable:

- Search systems evolve continuously, making static syllabi obsolete quickly.
- There is no independent standards body with authority over training, assessment, and ongoing revalidation.

Retaining Corporate SEO Memory

Although SEO techniques are relatively universal, implementation is unique to an organization and sometimes to specific platforms within it. Therefore, an intranet-based wiki should be created, with write access granted to SEO team members and read-only access to anyone interested. When team members leave, the incoming replacement can pick up where they left off.

The SEO wiki does not replace project documentation, which might or might not document the details of specific tasks. However, I have worked in a few multiple-brand companies, where a well-documented wiki made it easier to repeat certain tasks, such as a platform migration, and to add and modify the wiki with new learnings.

The SEO implementation process generates numerous documents that will have a permanent home in the network folder system. The SEO wiki should link to the important ones.

Major website milestones should be documented for each website, so you can consult them if you're trying to debug an anomaly in Google Search Console later on. Examples include the following:

- Launch dates
- Platform migration dates
- Significant content addition/deletion dates
- Major Google algorithm update dates, if they affected you.

Suppose your organization does not provide a secure password repository. In that case, you may want to store low-value passwords in a protected document here because they are no more or less safe than keeping them in a notebook or in your email folders.

Build and Maintain an SEO Wiki

A shared internal wiki—such as Atlassian Confluence, Notion, or SharePoint—acts as the team's long-term memory. By documenting workflows, checklists, SEO tactics, experiments, and lessons learned, teams make knowledge easier to search for and reuse. This reduces reliance on individual memory, speeds up onboarding of new hires, and ensures consistent execution even when people move on.

Upskilling for the AI Era

Encourage every team member—not just writers—to understand how AI systems interpret content. Provide short internal sessions on structured data, entity optimization, and prompt crafting for branded queries. Your developers, legal reviewers, and product owners all influence how well AI systems describe your business.

Building shared literacy today prevents future "visibility shocks."

HANDLING SEO DISPUTES

The HR department can best prescribe the framework for handling interpersonal disputes, but here we are referring to professional SEO disagreements. There are perhaps as many opinions on tackling an SEO challenge as there are SEOs, and while we can ignore the "wrong" solutions, there are often many "right" solutions.

Better, Rather Than Perfect

Usually, there is insufficient time or resources to get the "perfect" outcome. Looking for a "better, rather than perfect" option often works, but sometimes you must choose between doing nothing and doing it perfectly. Usually, the SEO Manager can deal with such dilemmas, but sometimes you are asked to adjudicate between an external consultant and the internal SEO Manager.

As we don't have an actual example to dissect, let's say it is about link acquisition because you have tried "everything," but you are not moving the dial on traffic or conversions. The agency wants to acquire links through (paid) blogger outreach, while the cautious internal team doesn't want a Google penalty if Google discovers the purchased links.

I once faced that situation when a senior executive outside my chain of command asked if we were getting any paid links from a major news company's regional brands. I replied that we were already getting daily citations and links from sponsoring sports stadiums and teams, as well as mentions in the stock market and the business press, so we did not need to buy links.

Pressure was brought to bear upon me through three company layers, so I relented. After all, I had done my job to point out the risks. We acquired 60 advertorial articles with "dofollow" links, but there was no change to any of our rankings. Absolutely nothing happened. There was no Google penalty. The "perfect" solution here was "don't buy links as you are a household brand," but the "better" solution is to keep the management happy if you value your job.

Had the pressure come from an ill-informed source, such as buying 500 links for $5 (yes, such providers exist), my manager would have backed me up to refuse the request.

So, there will be instances of SEO disagreement that are escalated to you. You will need to start with the do-nothing option and flip a coin if there is no best option.

WRITING EFFECTIVE TECHNICAL REQUESTS

The clearest SEO strategy fails if technical teams cannot implement it. One of the most common bottlenecks in SEO execution is poorly written technical requests. A ticket that seems simple to an SEO specialist often reads as confusing, resource-intensive, or low-priority to developers and IT teams who lack SEO context.

The result? Your critical canonical tag fix has been sitting in the backlog for 3 months while developers tackle what they perceive as higher-priority work. Meanwhile, duplicate content issues compound, rankings suffer, and you explain to executives why improvements are delayed.

Why Technical Request Quality Matters

Developers and infrastructure teams triage incoming requests based on clarity, urgency, and perceived effort. A poorly written request might languish in the backlog because it sounds complex or resource-intensive, when the actual fix takes only 15 minutes once someone understands what you need.

Common patterns that delay implementation:

Unclear scope leads developers to estimate high to protect themselves against scope creep. SEO jargon without context makes the request sound more complicated than it is. Missing acceptance criteria means developers cannot verify their work is complete. The absence of urgency context means the ticket competes equally with everything else, regardless of its business impact.

Your role as manager is to ensure your team writes requests that are understood, prioritized appropriately, and implemented the first time correctly.

Pre-Ticket Collaboration

Before writing the ticket, have your SEO team member spend five minutes talking with a developer or IT representative. This brief conversation accomplishes several things:

It confirms the request is technically feasible and identifies potential implementation approaches. It surfaces technical constraints you may not know about that could affect your approach. It builds relationship capital that makes future requests smoother. It lets you adjust the request based on technical reality before formal submission.

These conversations need not be formal meetings. A quick Slack exchange or hallway chat often suffices. The goal is to confirm shared understanding before the ticket enters the queue.

Using AI to Test Clarity

Before submitting a ticket, use an LLM to test whether your request is clear. Ask the AI to role-play as a developer who knows nothing about SEO and have it explain back what it thinks you're asking for.

Example prompt: "You are a web developer with no SEO knowledge. I'm going to give you a technical request. Please read it and tell me: (1) What you think I'm asking you to do, (2) What you're confused about, (3) What information is missing that you'd need to implement this."

Then paste your draft ticket. The AI's response will reveal gaps in your explanation, ambiguous language, and missing context. Revise the ticket addressing these issues before submission.

This technique costs thirty seconds and dramatically improves ticket quality. It catches problems before they delay implementation.

Essential Ticket Components

Every technical request should include:

Business context: Why does this matter? What breaks if we don't do this? Connect the technical change to business outcomes developers care about—page speed, user experience, revenue impact.

Specific action required: State exactly what needs to change. Avoid SEO jargon or define it inline. "Add canonical tags" means nothing to most developers; "Add a <link rel="canonical"> tag pointing to X URL on page Y" is actionable.

Scope boundaries: Be explicit about what's included and excluded. "Fix canonical tags on product pages" is vague. "Add canonical tags to all product detail pages in the /products/ directory, pointing to the primary URL for each product" is clear.

Examples: Show a specific page URL and the exact code change you need. Developers work better with concrete examples than abstract descriptions.

Acceptance criteria: How will you both know the work is complete? "Canonical tags implemented" is weak. "All product pages in /products/ directory have canonical tags in the <head> section pointing to their primary URLs, verified via view source" is testable.

Testing approach: Explain how you'll verify the change works. Include URLs to test, tools you'll use, or specific scenarios to check.

Before and After Examples

Bad example: "We need to implement canonical tags on product pages to fix duplicate content issues. This is affecting our rankings."

Why it isn't good: Assumes the developer knows what canonical tags are and why they matter. Doesn't specify which product pages or what the canonical should point to. No clear acceptance criteria or testing approach. Vague urgency without context.

Good example: “Request: Add canonical tags to product detail pages

Context: Our product pages are accessible via multiple URLs (with and without category paths, with tracking parameters). Search engines index these as separate pages, diluting ranking signals. This affects approximately 2,000 product pages generating $400K monthly revenue.

Required change: Add <link rel=‘canonical’ href=‘[primary-url]’> in the <head> section of all product detail pages, pointing to the primary URL without category paths or parameters.

Example: For a product accessible at both /products/widget-123 and /category/tools/widget-123, both should have canonical pointing to /products/widget-123

Scope: All pages in /products/ directory (approximately 2,000 pages)

Acceptance criteria: Every product page has exactly one canonical tag in <head>. Canonical points to the primary product URL without category paths or tracking parameters. No product pages have self-referential canonicals with parameters.

Testing: I’ll check five random product pages via view source and use Screaming Frog to crawl 100 pages to confirm the canonical implementation.

Urgency: High—this is affecting search visibility for our highest-revenue product category. Would like to do it in the next sprint, if possible.”

Common Mistakes to Avoid

Using unexplained SEO terminology: Terms like "crawl budget," "link equity," "schema markup," or "hreflang" are meaningless to most developers. Either avoid the jargon or define it clearly in context.

Assuming SEO priority is obvious: What seems urgent to you may not register as important to developers who juggle many priorities. Explain the business impact in terms they understand—user experience, page performance, revenue at risk.

Vague scope: "Fix the meta descriptions" could mean five pages or five thousand. Be specific about what you're asking for.

Missing examples: Developers implement faster and more accurately when they see exactly what you want rather than having to interpret abstract requirements.

No acceptance criteria: If you cannot explain how to verify that the work is done correctly, the developer cannot either. This leads to an implementation that misses your actual need.

Bundling unrelated changes: Keep tickets focused. "Update robots.txt, add canonical tags, and fix breadcrumb schema" is three separate tickets. Bundling them makes estimation difficult and increases implementation risk.

Training Your Team

Make ticket quality a team standard, not individual preference. Provide your team with:

A ticket template that includes all essential components. Examples of good tickets they can reference and adapt. Regular feedback on ticket quality, particularly when implementation is delayed or incorrect due to clarity issues. Encouragement to do pre-ticket technical conversations and LLM clarity checks.

Review tickets before submission and provide initial coaching on improvements. As team members demonstrate consistent quality, reduce oversight while maintaining the standard through periodic spot checks.

Measuring Success

Track metrics that indicate ticket quality improvement:

Time from ticket submission to implementation start—better tickets get prioritized faster. Number of clarification requests or ticket rejections—clear tickets need fewer back-and-forth exchanges. Implementation accuracy—correctly written tickets get implemented right the first time. Developer satisfaction—ask technical teams periodically whether SEO tickets are getting clearer and easier to work with.

When ticket quality improves, you'll notice faster implementation cycles, fewer misunderstandings, and better relationships with technical teams. The investment in clarity pays dividends in execution speed.

UNDERSTANDING SEO FRUSTRATIONS

Managers need to understand the types of professional problems faced by their SEO team members. Both in-house and agency-side SEOs have these frustrations. The central message is that the SEO specialists are experts in their craft but not in other specialties. Therefore, they need their manager to help them give their best.

The Manager Doesn't Know Best

- **"No, we don't need links"** – Some managers don't understand the importance of backlinks or don't want to think about the challenge of acquiring them. My advice is to let the SEO team be the experts in such matters. Some of the decisions that SEOs have to make draw upon experience and intuition, so a non-SEO manager should not pull rank unless budget is the sticking point.

- **"You need help"** – More than once in an in-house role, I had managers who insisted on hiring external SEO "experts" to help me. It's pretty easy to check my credentials online, but better experts were always out there, at least in their minds. Once, I was part of the agency selection process, which was great. We had a good outcome. Another time, my managers hired an SEO agency without consulting the in-house team or disclosing the terms of the arrangement.
- **"You don't need help"** – The other extreme is the manager who thinks that the SEO team is in place, so all SEO work has to be done in-house. There are a lot of mind-numbing, repetitious tasks, particularly reporting, that will cause staff to leave, and that cannot be a good thing. Sometimes, there is no budget to buy the necessary tools.

Impossible Asks

- **"The customer is always right"** – I had a manager (when I worked in an agency) who wanted every SEO client to get what they asked for and not cancel the contract. For example, one customer had a new Flash site that was impossible to rank because the entire website was essentially one Flash file. We ended up recreating the appearance and functionality in a conventional HTML website. The work was so tedious that my developer completed it and, with a flourish, got up and walked out, never to return.
- **"Pleasing the customer"** – I had a self-inflicted variant of the same problem, although not a Flash site. I should not have agreed to make "small changes" to the website design while I was on an SEO contract. Instead, I spent so much time making

"one more change" that I stopped consulting with one-person businesses, other than to deliver audits.

Trust Your Team

- **"You need to work out a compromise"** – There are inter-team situations where the manager does not want to create conflict at their level, so they ask their team to "sort it out," even if it means a compromise. For example, a friend at a catalog-driven site did not get their manager's support to add content to catalog pages to improve their ranking. The product manager was unconvinced that this would add value, so they abandoned that initiative. Folks, the product manager isn't the SEO expert here, and their opinion needs to be corrected by higher-ups if necessary.

Check Yourself

- **"No, our rankings still suck"** – A friend describes a workplace where they outsourced their SEO and the agency only delivered audits at regular intervals. They did no implementation. Everyone presumed rankings were "good" because an agency was being paid "to do SEO," but nobody checked personally. Instead, they filed the unread audit reports away.
- **"SEO is under control"** – A similar situation occurs when the SEO reports are glanced at or skimmed but not understood. For example, the SEO team might be reporting something of concern. If the manager fails to appreciate the gravity of the problem, they will demoralize the SEO team.

Career Path

After you have created one or more SEO roles in the organization, please document a career path that leads into this team and out to other parts of the company.

- **"How do I join the SEO team?"** – In large companies, people will be curious about SEO and wonder if it is a career option. I used to invite them to spend a day with different team members, and so did other teams in that company. At least two such curious employees later joined my SEO team.
- **"There are no vacancies"** – Even in a large company, the SEO team is tiny and rarely has more than three levels. If people do not move out of their positions, the career path seems nonexistent, and ambitious staff will leave. On the other hand, if you show career paths outside of SEO, particularly for senior positions, then the organization will be the winner.

I wrote this book as an outcome of such frustrations. SEO generates significant online revenue, so it deserves a fair hearing. However, frustrated staff will leave, and so will the ones who replace them.

Chapter 11

MANAGING A REMOTE SEO TEAM

Remote SEO teams are not new, but the COVID-19 pandemic, associated lockdowns, and work-from-home mandates and policies encouraged more employers to consider hiring remote employees, including SEO team members. These employers can be agencies or companies with an in-house team. Your SEO agency or consultant will face the same hurdles for remote access as if they were remote employees. These employers can be agencies or companies with an in-house team. Your SEO agency or consultant will face the same hurdles for remote access as if they were remote employees.

Companies in many countries now allow their permanent staff to work from "anywhere," which is usually interpreted as within the same income-tax jurisdiction. In addition, some let their existing staff work from another country on a case-by-case basis. Working from another country is easier for individual contributors than senior managers. Still, I have seen instances where the C-suite team is scattered across a few countries and a handful of cities.

SKILL CONSIDERATIONS

The main reason for hiring remote staff is to access a larger skill pool than you can find in your city. This is particularly true of technical and native-language skills. In the high-tech industries, many companies have used offshore employees or contractors for decades. Some companies set up subsidiary companies in Asia, while others use staffing contractors, some of which have set up subsidiaries in their client countries.

Offshore SEO Skills

Using offshore workers for SEO tasks is a different matter. Some types of SEO tasks are better done at home or close to home than others that anyone can do.

An Australia-based company that offers white-label SEO implementation services sent me to India three times to train their offshore SEO team. My training course helped the offshore team to deliver best-practice work. However, they were working to a formula set by this agency's Australian customer, so there was no scope to offer unique solutions.

Figure 116 Training a remote SEO team in India.

If you are an employer needing to bolster your in-house SEO team, can you hire an overseas team member? Yes, you can, but it depends on the size and make-up of your team. If it is a technical skill requirement, it's a definite "yes."

If it's an SEO strategist role, it's better filled by candidates from countries that are a closer cultural fit for yours. "Culture" here refers to the subject matter of the company's business and certainly not to the individual's ancestry. So, for example, if your business involves winter sports, then a remote worker who lives in a winter-sports country is more likely to write an SEO strategy that would work well than if they lived in the hot tropics with no snow in winter.

For specific business models, the best content creators are more likely to live in your city than across the country or another state. For example, a car magazine that needs a constant flow of car reviews and video clips will find good remote workers who live close to car factories or importers and to proving ground tracks. If they also feature foreign cars, they could hire freelance content providers in the countries of manufacture.

Other non-technical tasks, such as link acquisition, can be done worldwide. For example, they can use templates to send link requests in the target country's language.

Search engines deliver rankings tailored to the searcher's location, so a remote employee in another country will need a VPN connection into your city before they do any visibility checks. In addition, search engines such as Google differ across many countries, so a new SEO will need a period of adjustment and a good level of presence of mind before making such checks.

LEGALITIES

Countries have laws that touch on employment, such as:

- Visas and employment rights for non-citizens or permanent residents
- Taxation
- After-hours obligations by employers
- Insurance
- Employee benefits
- Data protection and privacy
- Employee rights and protections
- Employee unions

You should consult your legal counsel on all such matters.

TIME ZONES

Employees in significantly disparate time zones must work some hours outside their local business hours to work remotely. Examples include regular live video meetings with colleagues or a company-wide town hall presentation, possibly once or twice each month. When they are in the same country or time zone on the same continent, the adjacent time zones offer a wider window of opportunity. Daily stand-up meetings cannot be avoided and must be convenient for most of the SEO team. When I worked for the Australian office of a US company, the country CEO reminded all staff never to point out the time zone difference to headquarters.

Some countries now recognize a formal "right to disconnect" or similar workplace protections that limit unreasonable out-of-hours contact, so be alert to these rules and build expectations into team norms, on-call processes, and escalation pathways.

NATIONAL AND LOCAL HOLIDAYS

What would you do if your overseas workers took a long summer break at a different time from your country's norm? For example, this happens if you are in the Northern Hemisphere and your workers are in Australia or South Africa. Other countries have long religious festivals that occur at different times each year because they are based on a lunar calendar. Another issue I have observed is that personal leave (annual leave) is taken at short notice, causing consternation among the affected teams.

The answer is simple – you work around the issues rather than avoid hiring the right people who live in other time zones or legal jurisdictions. For example, I know of at least one outsourcing company whose contract staff agrees to take only the national holidays of the customer's nation. At one overseas subsidiary of a multinational company, the country head would remind the local team regularly never to say or do anything that would remind the staff at the head office of the distance between them.

TECHNOLOGY, SECURITY, AND DATA PRIVACY

Countries in the EU and Australia, for example, have well-defined laws to protect the security and privacy of their citizens. However, in the remote SEO worker context, you must be mindful of whether personal information crosses international borders. Careful workflow design and regular training sessions can help avoid such issues.

Your network operations team will also need to help arrange secure access to your network, such as VPNs, project management tools, and video conferencing.

RECRUITING CONCERNS

Be aware that your internal recruitment team might not want to take on something unfamiliar, such as remote employees. For example, the United States has an E-3 visa category for Australian citizens, with an annual statutory cap of 10,500 principal visas, and it has historically often issued fewer than the cap. Perhaps American recruiters don't want to learn how to process their documentation to sponsor an Australian employee? What matters is the outcome for the whole organization.

I would not dismiss the Recruiting team's concerns out of hand, but a compromise is possible. Hiring outside the country is perhaps best done on a contractor-client basis, so you don't have to deal with issues such as retirement fund contributions, health insurance, compliance training, etc. But again, your legal team can contribute to this decision.

INTERNAL COMMUNICATION

Your dispersed SEO team will need to communicate regularly with the rest of the organization. These days, video conferencing tools are ubiquitous. I join Zoom or Microsoft Teams calls with colleagues in three countries for scheduled meetings on a typical day. We use Slack for informal, textual communications and for lightweight audio when a quick voice discussion is faster than a thread. We use email for more formal communications, mainly when sending attachments. Slack also has a voice conferencing feature. We use email for more formal communications, mainly when sending attachments. Since most staff do not have company phones, the laptop becomes the central point for all communication.

Chapter 12

MANAGING AGENCIES AND CONSULTANTS

You will consider hiring an SEO agency or independent consultant at some point in your SEO journey. You should do so if the budget permits, as they will bring experience, expertise, and a fresh perspective. However, please involve your in-house SEO team (if any) from the beginning.

WHAT IS OUT THERE?

You will see many ads offering SEO services. If your LinkedIn profile shows that you are in an organization (at any level), you will get connection requests and unsolicited email approaches, sometimes from others in your company. That is how many kinds of service businesses look for new clients.

Independent Consultants

Independent consultants are one person short of being a small agency. Still, there are many variations of this model, such as the consultant who sub-contracts some work to others or asks others to contract directly with the client.

Many consultants are genuine, cutting-edge experts. Many of them are active in the SEO community and speak at conferences. Some write for marketing publications and websites. They compare notes and analyze website data to see if Google has quietly unleashed a new algorithm. Such consultants are my tribe, and we stay in touch through regular meet-ups or phone calls.

How do you find the best consultant who can help you? If you are a large organization, an independent consultant should be brought in to solve thorny problems that the in-house SEO team has not managed to overcome. Your team might be able to name such a consultant. Their initial deliverable is usually an audit report.

If you need help implementing an SEO strategy, you need a consultant who can handle all of that work, or someone who can bring in other experienced people to handle some of it.

Small SEO Agencies

A small SEO agency might be a consultant with a handful of team members, with enough clients to pay the bills. They are likely to have some subcontracted web design and coding offerings. It's impossible to generalize about their quality without a detailed inspection of the agency.

There are also a few small-to-medium-sized agencies that are entirely profit-driven and invest little in staff training. Learning is on-the-job and perhaps checklist-based. They might use outdated, therefore ineffective techniques, mainly to give the illusion of working for the client.

Large SEO Agencies

Large SEO agencies are similar to small ones, except they have larger staff counts. There is no hard-and-fast definition in terms of numbers, but large agencies will look for enterprise clients likely to pay six- and seven-digit sums in management fees per annum. In addition, they are likely part of a global digital agency and have been acquired/merged a few times over the years. Enterprise clients are likely to hire such agencies, perhaps for billing convenience and a belief that a large agency can "scale" to more extensive requirements.

The large staff size is often misleading because they allocate each client the number of SEO specialists (or hours) listed in the contract.

Usually, they work for just one client per industry, but if that is not clarified, you should check that they don't work for a direct competitor. For example, one agency I know used to hire replacement staff from people on short-term visas and did not draw from its own "large" staff pool, as they mentioned in their initial pitch. Instead, they hire employees as required.

Offshore and White-Label Agencies

An offshore agency sells its services directly to businesses or acts as a white-label provider to a small or large local agency. You might not be aware of such an arrangement in the latter case. The ones that sell directly sometimes have a virtual address in a Western nation and display local phone numbers to seem "local." A white-label agency can also be in the same country as you, and "offshore" does not always mean in a developing nation. For example, I started my SEO career based in Australia, contracting to a NASDAQ-listed American company.

Is offshore work a concern? Here are some possibilities I have noted over the years:

- Cultural differences make it difficult for an overseas writer to write credible content for your audience. It's not just a case of a writer in Asia writing for Europe; a native UK English writer based in the UK wrote a page about Victoria in British Columbia, Canada, instead of my state of Victoria, Australia, where the company operates.
- Many offshore and white-label providers operate under tightly defined checklists set by client agencies, which can limit strategic flexibility and visibility into ongoing professional development.

HOW MUCH DOES OUTSOURCED SEO COST?

Choosing an SEO provider is not easy, but let me break it down for you. First, the "cost" is not just what you will pay; if you make a poor choice, the cost will include lost sales if they fail to spot an opportunity to optimize, and it will be worse if something breaks.

It is near-impossible for a company to identify a "good" SEO provider, as they are not hiring a specific individual but are usually buying a brand based on its website pitch. Some SEO brands cost more than others. The agency will not yet have hired the SEO specialist assigned to you. The solution is to perform due diligence.

A professional agency will charge you a decent fee for an audit and a strategy. Please don't waste time with those who offer free audits to get their foot in the door.

A bad agency will sell you a formulaic solution based on the number of keywords. This formulaic approach is at least 15 years out of date. If you sell 10 products, they will suggest 10, 20, or more keywords. Then they will "write content" that uses those keywords. They will submit it to article sites and say you are getting value from those article links. This is a worthless tactic nowadays. Next, they will submit your URL to "bookmarking" sites. It is all a waste of effort and money.

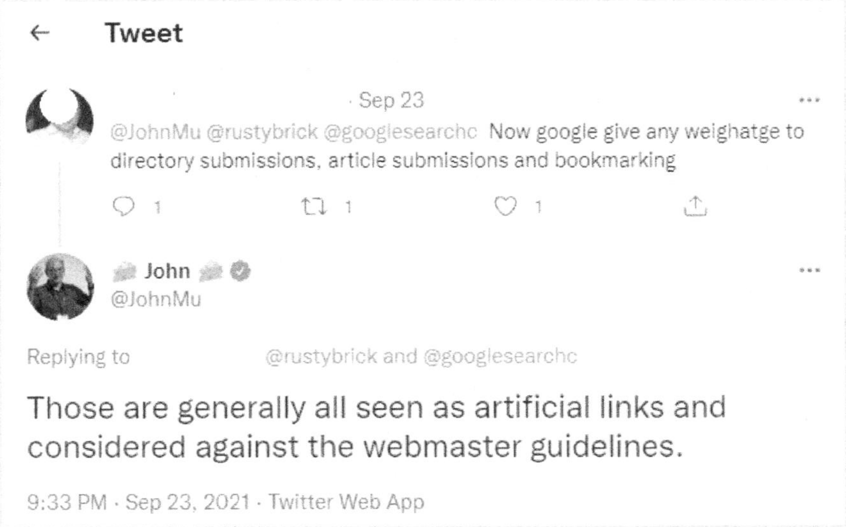

Figure 117. Google's spam policies warn against link spam and link schemes, including manipulative directory-style links.

A competent SEO will take at least one day to analyze a small site and write you an audit report. Writing a "strategy" can require some back-and-forth with stakeholders, so that the task could take one or two more days. How long it takes for someone to understand your business will determine the length of that task. Then someone has to implement the strategy, which is open-ended - how much can be done by you and how much by someone else. An audit of a large corporate site could take a few weeks, followed by time to write a strategy. I have done it in three months for two clients.

PAYING FOR SEO SERVICES

Consultant Prices

There is no way to gauge how much to pay an independent consultant other than asking a few to quote on the opportunity. You'll find that pricing starts around US$200/hour, with no upper limit. Some cheeky consultants charge much more when they see little resistance to a high hourly rate in a particular industry. Some might drop their hourly rate for an extended contract, or you might be a strong negotiator. For example, I used to charge $1,500/day for a short audit and strategy assignment, but $1,000 for a more extended implementation contract. I did not bill by the hour because SEO work is a series of short bursts and much idle time. Hence, I had a small number of clients at any given time.

Agency Prices

I see three broad groups of agency rates, which are usually per person/day. Price is no indication of quality.

- Low
- Reasonable
- High

I won't mention the site where people claim to perform SEO for a single-digit sum. The "low" agency prices range from the low hundreds per month to the low thousands – in your currency (USD, CAD, UKP, AUD, EUR, etc.)

Most agencies fall in the "reasonable" group. They might have started with low prices and learned quickly that price-sensitive customers are not worth the trouble. Instead, they begin their monthly billing in the low thousands, with rare exceptions.

The "high" prices cannot be generalized but tend to be higher than ten thousand in your currency. I know of two companies that paid more than $100,000 per month. I worked in a company that allegedly paid more than $1 million per month, but that is hearsay. Some might do more work than is needed to maximize billable hours.

Each agency has its unique set of circumstances that determines its pricing model. The best agencies have some of the best-known experts on their staff, who command high salaries. Some of these individuals shut down their own consulting practice to join a high-end agency.

Pay-for-Performance Contracts

Where I have read about pay-for-performance, there is an existing relationship between the two parties; hence, there is trust. Such arrangements are likely to arise in startups without a budget for SEO. It isn't easy to pick a metric because you cannot say whether an increase in traffic or conversions was entirely due to SEO work. Perhaps it is easier with a brand-new domain for a limited time, because in due course, new conversions occur for non-SEO reasons.

SOFTWARE DEVELOPMENT SERVICES

Many large companies have long-term software development contracts in which the supplier presents itself as a Jack-of-all-trades. Often, they have large teams that work full-time on your premises, with many more people offsite or offshore. They write code for custom software and mobile apps, and, by the way, they can also build websites.

Accounting teams that pay invoices don't like having more suppliers than necessary. If you are in a large company, such a situation might be inescapable, but remember that there are software developers who only build websites, which might be a better choice. At a minimum, state your SEO needs and the potential implications if they cannot be met.

WEBSITE BUILDING AND MAINTENANCE CONTRACTS

Any mention of contracts implies that lawyers will be involved in their drafting, but the requirements will have to come from the business owners. In this book, we focus only on the SEO aspects of the contracts. It's best to assume that your web developer knows little about SEO than that they will "get it right." It's also likely that you might have to compromise on some points.

Scope

In addition to the business requirements and website functionality, your SEO team or consultants will need to list their requirements and reach a consensus before the RFP is issued. Sometimes, a product owner might want a feature like infinite scrolling on pages, which isn't search-friendly. Such examples can be addressed depending on the underlying platform.

Information Architecture (IA)

If the SEO team wants the IA built a certain way, the RFP is the place to specify it; otherwise, the designer will build as they see fit. Mega navs are implemented in most cases because they are applied site-wide and require less coding and testing time than flat navs. But, in one fell swoop, this can reduce internal linking clarity, making it harder for search systems to prioritize key pages.

Code Standards and Quality

Does the contract specify any quality metrics, such as compliance with HTML5 and CSS3 standards, as measured by https://validator.w3.org/ or another page performance tool? Consequently, the website will probably "work," satisfying most non-technical stakeholders but possibly not Google (or people with disabilities). Accessibility should be well-defined, for example, "WCAG 2.2 Level AA" as a minimum standard.

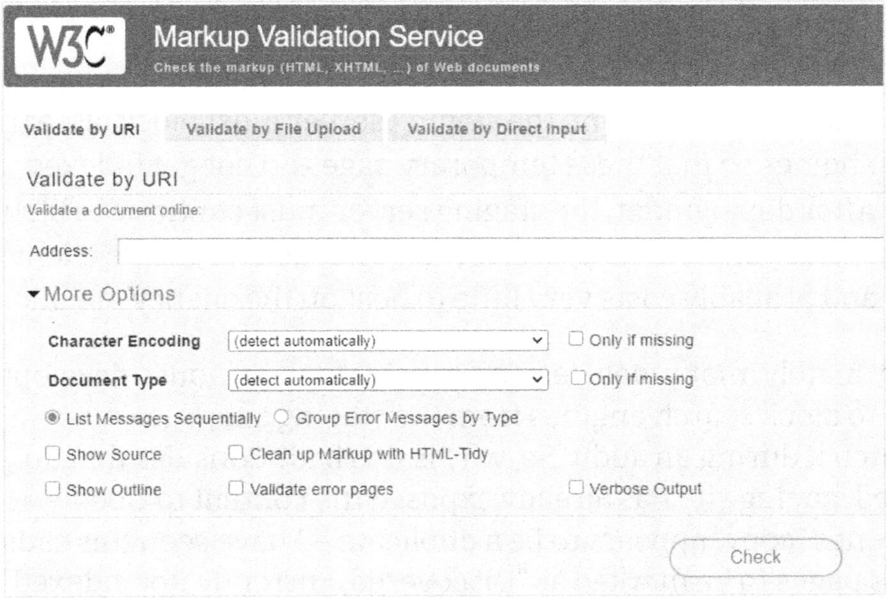

Figure 118 Online HTML validator by W3C.

Timing

The delivery schedule is likely to be longer than you think, and you might have to make compromises for the SEO requirements. In addition, pressure from your Sales and Marketing teams will be ever-present.

Staging Servers

Special mention must be made of staging servers, which the agency usually owns. They try to create a similar environment to the final home for the website. Usually, they will include all pages they will deliver for the website launch. Once the client approves the work, the agency will copy the staging site to the client's domain.

Notice the word "copied." If poorly done, it can cause significant SEO problems in the future:

- During development, the staging server must block all search engines so that these temporary pages do not get indexed.
- After deployment, the staging server must continue to block all search engines, as above. It will be needed for future client work and probably costs very little to host on the agency's subdomain.

Unfortunately, many web design agencies (and in-house developers) forget to block search engines from the staging site, but a diligent SEO will catch it during an audit. So, why is this bad? Consider that an indexed staging site has already exposed the content to Google. Hence, the client's "copy" appears to be a duplicate – I have seen this cause the client's pages to be marked as "Discovered, currently not indexed" and "Crawled, currently not indexed" in Google Search Console. In one recent case, the staging site had more indexed pages than the client's production site.

CONTENT PROVISION SERVICES

You will need external content services if you don't have someone in-house to write copy, create videos, or produce other website content. Many such companies and individuals would like to sign your contract, but few will be a perfect fit. Here are some considerations.

Industry Experience

If you sell consumer products or services, many writers will either have recent experience with similar products and services or be able to write about them with little effort. Many other companies are in specialized niches, where finding a credible writer is more challenging. You need to be convinced that your potential content supplier can deliver the content you can put online without much back-and-forth that would otherwise make you want to do it yourself.

Time and Effort

You should know how much time the agency would need to prepare each type of content and whether the agreed price would deliver a result you can host on your website.

Professionalism

You can define "professionalism" in your content provision relationship with the customer. Plagiarism is a widespread hazard, so what can the supplier do to compensate you if the supplied content leads to a copyright lawsuit? What keeps their staff honest? For example, if your business is a global travel agency, how will the writers deliver accurate content about the destinations at the agreed price? You cannot fly them to each location.

There are online plagiarism checking tools you can subscribe to and use diligently before publication. Additionally, your contract should have a penalty clause if the agreed-upon checking tool rejects the supplied content.

You would want your SEO team to be part of the selection process, and they should ensure they have conveyed all SEO requirements for the deliverables. People sometimes forget about Accessibility features until it's too late. Don't rely on a new content provision agency to know much about SEO, as your experts will convey those requirements. Over time, they will understand your needs and require less scrutiny.

Sub-contracts

You need to know about the subcontracts the content agency has made. Not everything can be created in-house, such as photo shoots, special video processing, etc. If the written content is outsourced, you need continued and consistent quality assurance.

SITE SUBMISSION SERVICES

Some low-end SEO agencies still try to sell "search engine submission services." Manual submission to search engines has not been a meaningful SEO service for many years, as modern search engines discover URLs through crawling, internal linking, and XML sitemaps.

Google Search Console provides a URL Inspection tool that allows you to request indexing for individual URLs on a verified property. This is a diagnostic and troubleshooting feature, not a scalable submission mechanism.

At the top of a GSC page, you will see an "Inspect any URL" field where you can enter an address from that domain. If it is not in the Google Index, you can request indexing. Treat this as a diagnostic tool for a recalcitrant page that Google isn't crawling or indexing, and see if you can force it to crawl and index. It is not a scalable tool for bulk page submission, but the sitemap.xml route is available.

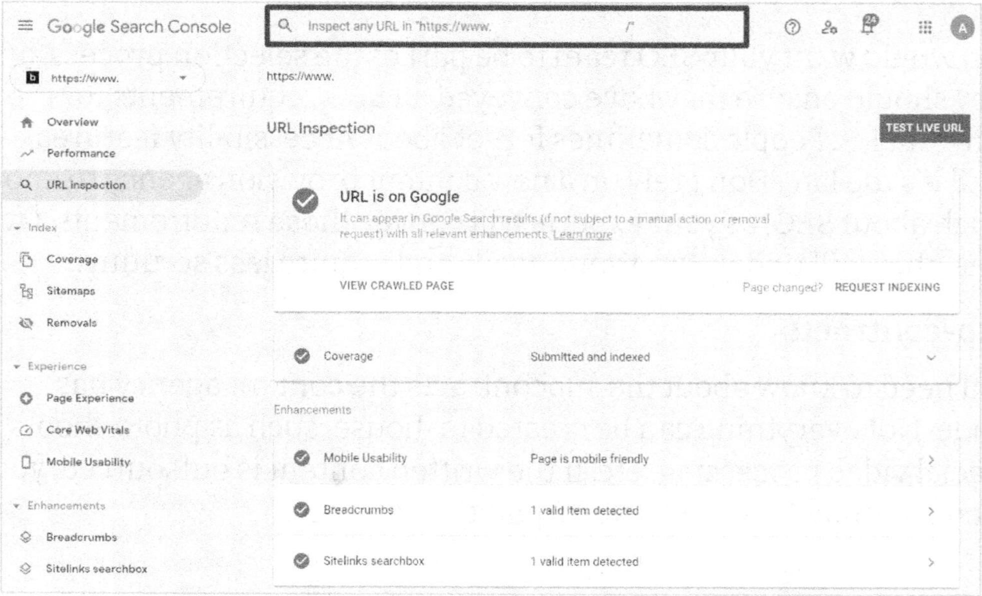

Figure 119 The new way to submit a page.

WRITING GOOD RFPS

A Request for Proposal (RFP) or Request for Quotation (RFQ) is a common legal mechanism for describing your needs and providing the same information to all interested bidders. I have also seen them written as Purchase Orders (POs). In many organizations, it is a governance requirement to use this process to engage an external provider.

Be mindful that some potential service providers may not respond to RFPs for reasons that are not stated. For example, your RFP process may preclude them from asking detailed questions because the other bidders would not be responding to the same criteria. If you have a likely agency in mind, you can talk to them before issuing the same RFP to all contenders. In addition, some agencies recognize their limitations and will not respond to RFPs that do not align with their service model. For example, one agency declined my employer's request to place staff on our premises, preferring to deliver the service remotely.

RFP ELEMENTS

Your Request for Proposal (RFP) must give agencies the context and constraints they need to bid accurately and deliver what you expect. The clearer you are at this stage, the smoother the engagement will run.

Organization Profile

If your brand is not well-known or your site structure is complex, the agency needs to understand it. Include a list of corporate sites, sub-brands, or legacy domains that may still be indexed and affecting SEO.

Key People

List contacts involved in the selection process, including the person who will act as the day-to-day owner once the contract begins.

Maximum Budget

Include a realistic maximum budget. This prevents mismatched bids and avoids wasting time with agencies that typically serve much different budget tiers.

Past SEO History

A summary will help set expectations. Your shortlisted agencies will dive deeper later.

SEO Requirements and Deliverables

Describe what you need the agency to accomplish:

- Fix existing technical SEO issues
- Improve content quality and velocity
- Support structured data, analytics, and UX
- Influence authority and earned-media coverage

Be explicit about whether SEO is part of a wider initiative, such as a CMS migration or rebrand.

Project Timing and Engagement Structure

Specify contract type:

- Fixed-term project
- Retainer support
- Multi-year agreement with individual statements of work

Include target start dates or phases if known.

Agency Information

Request details such as:

- Founding team and notable clients
- Experience in your industry and average engagement duration
- Staff resourcing is available to you if they win
- Insurance coverage such as Professional Indemnity and Cyber Risk

Technical Requirements

Ask agencies to identify:

- Whether development capability is in-house or outsourced
- Expertise with specific platforms (Shopify, Magento, Adobe Experience Manager, WordPress)
- Experience with JavaScript rendering and performance optimization
- Collaboration and project-management tools they use

SEO Approach and Methodology

How will they:

- Diagnose and prioritize issues
- Drive improvements across technical, content, and authority
- Ensure compliance with search-engine guidelines
- Report progress tied to business outcomes

Look for answers framed around your objectives — not just rankings.

Pricing Model

Specify how you expect pricing to be structured:

- Hourly, daily, or monthly rate

- Retainer vs. deliverable-based work
- Package inclusions and exclusions

Ensure all bids use your requested pricing format for side-by-side comparison.

Response Length and Deadline

A practical limit (for example, 10 pages) prevents excessive boilerplate. Set a clear submission deadline — noon is better than the end of the day when chasing last-minute questions.

Evaluation and Selection Process

Explain how submissions will be evaluated and who is involved. It should be clear that the process may result in no award if proposals do not meet the criteria.

Service Level Expectations

Add a request for **proposed SLAs** as part of the RFP submission. This shows you expect operational discipline — not loose promises.

Ask agencies to define:

- Response times for critical SEO issues
- Structured-data updates with new templates
- Redirect and link integrity during releases
- Monitoring of Search Console alerts
- Human review of automated or AI-generated content
- Communication cadence and dashboards

The goal is to **protect visibility during change**, not just optimize it when convenient.

The SLA acts as your safety net: visibility declines must be detected and corrected before they affect customers and revenue.

INVITING AGENCIES TO PITCH

Large companies usually know the type of agency that can help them, so they should send the RFP invitations to a small, manageable number of potential partners. Publicly advertising is guaranteed to generate hundreds of responses, many from completely mismatched agencies. If you feel you have no option but to advertise publicly, consider requiring applicants to deposit "earnest money" into an escrow account. This step will filter out most of the time-wasters.

RED FLAGS

A large organization is unlikely to come across a dodgy or genuinely incompetent agency, but everyone should do their due diligence when evaluating potential contenders. Here are some red flags.

Recognized by Google

Google does not certify or recommend any agency. Therefore, beware of agencies that might misuse their Google Partner credentials (if any) or claim a Google blessing. For example, some agencies claiming to place you on the first page might use ads or obscure keywords with low competition.

Figure 120 A misleading claim by an SEO agency (redacted advertisement).

Guaranteed Page 1 Results

Offshore SEO service providers are more likely to "guarantee" rankings on the first page of search engine results. On the other hand, a local company might be more guarded in their ads, e.g., they "help" you to rank #1.

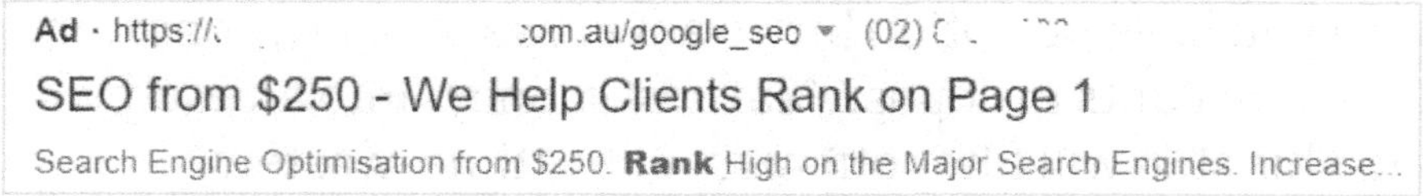

Figure 121 "Rank on Page 1." (Redacted advertisement)

So, what's the catch? Any competent SEO could achieve this result, but not necessarily for the keywords you had in mind or keywords that would increase your conversions. Instead, you could rank on the first page by selecting obscure, uncompetitive keywords.

Then there's the unknown about how many keywords they will rank on the first page – many companies I have worked with have thousands of keywords. Online marketplaces can have millions of products, which means millions of keywords. Hundreds of them are likely to rank #1 with no SEO effort.

Such providers usually offer low prices in their ads, but you have to wonder what they can do for you unless they outsource to a low-wage country. They tend to be formula-based in their assembly-line approach. They apply the same formula to all clients.

Mumbo Jumbo

Watch out for people who post tips that look impressive at first glance. This is a common tactic of some consultants on platforms such as LinkedIn. One long post included this tip, "Focus on 'information gain score.'" It caught my eye for a couple of reasons. It's not a common phrase in SEO circles, but it is very common in academic papers.

Superficially, it's easy to understand – when many pages are presented in the Google SERPs, a reader gets a diminishing return from subsequent pages that they open because many will say the same thing, with a little bit of additional information. Although Information Gain is an interesting concept raised in a Google patent, when it is dropped in an article without explanation, the writer is simply trying to impress.

In reality, nobody outside Google has a formula to calculate it, let alone focus on it. Each variation of a search term produces a slightly different SERP, and there are a zillion other search terms that could target the same pages.

It's disingenuous to use a buzzword as part of a content strategy, unless it's to baffle the audience.

In short, this is spam, dressed as an information piece.

Who Owns the Accounts?

Sometimes, a new, small business starts from scratch and asks an agency to do "everything" to get its website and online marketing underway. The agency – possibly a one-person operation – will arrange the following:

- **Domain name registration** – in the agency's name for expediency, perhaps to be transferred to the client later?
- **Website/email hosting** – often installed on the agency's server, which might not be the fastest at that price.
- **CMS** – Is the content management system open source and well-known, such as Drupal or WordPress, or is it on a proprietary platform built by the agency?
- **Advertising platforms** – if the agency manages advertising on Google or Microsoft Ads, they might run your ads in their account for "simplicity."

- **Raw data** – the agency might send you monthly summary reports, but would they hand over the raw data each month or when they are terminated?

I have seen sad outcomes for SMB clients who had their first SEO experience with such operators. Their website was relatively mature, running on an in-house, proprietary platform, so there was no option to migrate it to a new web server or an open-source CMS. Instead, the new agency had to rebuild it from scratch. This tactic held the client hostage by design. Similarly, if their ad campaigns were within their agency's account, that data could not be exported to their account for historical comparison. Finally, if the agency owns the domain name, it can become a legal quagmire when the client wants to retrieve it in a hostile "divorce" situation.

What Do Monthly Reports Cover?

Ask for some actual (but redacted) reports they have done for their other clients. You need to see if they cover both failures and wins. Do they mention conversions at all? High rankings mean little if your online sales aren't improving. If the reports smack of "See how much work we have done," it could be smoke and mirrors. The makeup of the reports will show whether the agency treats you as a partner or a service provider.

Some reports (and services) might be unnecessary or pointless for your needs. For example, "Local SEO" at a suburb level is meaningless when nobody searches for your product with a locality qualifier. On the other hand, a Local SEO report showing that a Google Business Profile (GBP) map listing generated new leads is convincing. You can measure calls through a custom phone number and unique UTM tags used only in a GBP listing. Even if a customer stores it and reuses it later, the agency that set it up earns the kudos.

The reports will usually include information from GA4 and Google Search Console (or equivalents). The agency has not added value if they repeat what you can see for yourself by logging in. They must explain unusual or unexpected variances before you ask the question. Delays in implementing earlier SEO recommendations are one example of results falling short of expectations; more often, external factors are the cause.

Keyword traffic reports need to cover unbranded queries; otherwise, the results will be rosier than they are. Brand keywords usually rank #1, or else it's a poorly chosen brand name (which happens all too often). A separate report might be appropriate if the brand name competes with a generic dictionary word and does not rank well.

Do the reports cover the next steps the agency proposes to deliver even more SEO success? Again, a partner will do it proactively, and the client will pay attention.

How Is Time Billed?

Some agencies have an hourly rate, perhaps with a minimum monthly spend. Others have a daily rate. You should ask whether the invoices are granular enough to identify the nature of the work performed clearly. Having been at the agency end a few times, I should point out that many SEO tasks take less time than it takes to document them. Opening your Google Search Console, for instance, and looking at the charts for any anomaly can take a minute if everything is normal. So, you do not want a minute-by-minute accounting.

I used to charge a daily rate, but the work might span several days, totaling eight hours. When I consulted through another agency, I had to document time by the hour.

Agreed Success Metrics

You need an agency that agrees to modest success metrics. These need to be based on conversions and not just traffic, which is easy to fake. If, say, a 1% increase in conversions is more than the cost of the SEO agency, it's a good outcome for the first year.

These metrics should be checked regularly, not just once a year. Depending on the extent of your existing SEO challenges, it might take a short time or a very long time to see tangible improvements. For example, if you had a manual action imposed for violating a policy, you might not regain a previous ranking level, even after remediation. In some cases, recovery is slow and incomplete. A reputable agency would not make rash promises of success to win the business. Scrutinize the proposed methods before you choose an agency.

Non-Disclosure Agreements

Most agencies struggle between bragging about their blue-chip clients and hiding them behind real or made-up non-disclosure agreements (NDAs). In Australia, I have never heard of a client imposing an NDA on their agency, so I don't understand why agencies are reluctant to name their current or past clients in an RFQ. By all means, this can be disclosed in confidence.

As a potential client, you can and should ask for references – the applicant agency cannot say that some privacy clause protects all their clients. They might not have any clients if they are new to the game. So, ask them to approach their clients and request a phone call with you. Of course, they will not want you to talk to their fussy or unhappy clients. A successful, reputable agency will be happy to get you those references.

To prevent being trapped in the agency's NDA requirements, make it clear in the RFP that you will not sign an NDA about some aspects of this contract. After all, if things don't work out, you should be free to leave an honest review in the appropriate context. Conversely, if things go well, then you should be free to recommend this agency.

SHORTLISTING THE APPLICANT AGENCIES

Some responses might be eliminated by the RFP criteria, leaving a short list for you to interview. There is no magic number for the shortlist. It might be two, five, or more. It depends on the quality of responses and the importance you attach to the process. Sometimes, your organization will set the rules for this process.

PITCHES BY THE SHORTLISTED AGENCIES

The evaluation process should be detailed in the RFP to avoid any misunderstandings. The corporate purchasing team can explain the process to the stakeholders if this is their first RFP interview.

Interview Panel

The panel should include the SEO manager and the senior-most SEO specialist. There is no need for spectators if they will not participate in the interviews. Perhaps you can invite others for the second round of interviews with the two finalists.

Ask the applicants to bring their technical SEO specialist, so your specialist can ask technical questions.

The Pitch Process

The pitch is important to both parties, so don't set an unreasonable, arbitrary duration. For example, it might take two or three hours – I'd be a little concerned if the agency only asks for 30 minutes.

Each applicant will want to go through a slide deck. I would tell them to omit the "What is SEO" introductory slides and go straight into their capabilities and track record. Each presentation could include the maximum number of slides and the time for questions. I suggest that you provide a skeleton slide deck so that all presentations contain at least the headings you wish to see, for example:

- Introduction to the agency, its size, and locations
- Names of staff who will work on the account and their focus, such as technical, content, linking, etc.
- Experience in similar businesses to yours
- One-page case study
- Notable achievements
- SEO challenges they see for your website
- How will they begin the engagement, and how will they work with you month by month?
- Their internal project management process

Question Time

You could ask questions as they arise, but ideally ask them at the end, where possible. You should hear their presentation and not waste time on a specific point if it is not a show-stopper.

EVALUATING RFP RESPONSES

The RFP response should include all elements listed in the RFP. Any omission should be questioned and clarified in writing. Look for signs they are up to date with terminology and recent Google updates, for example, mentions of entities.

Evaluating AI-Powered SEO Tools

Many agencies now embed AI in their deliverables—content scoring, predictive ranking, and automated reporting.

When reviewing proposals, ask three questions:

1. What data trains their model, and is it compliant with your privacy policies?
2. Does the system disclose when output is AI-generated?

3. Can results be validated independently?
   Use AI as an assistant, not an authority. Human judgment still defines strategy.

Choosing the Winner

I use a scoring sheet in two parts. The first part is the RFP itself. Each item in the Scope gets a score out of 10. The second part of the sheet is subjective, with elements such as (as applicable):

- Understands our business and SEO challenges
- Frank and honest, or saying what they think we want to hear
- Staff expertise:
    - SEO knowledge is up-to-date
    - Content
    - Linking
    - Technical
- Has staff or needs to recruit
- Will work on-site, remotely, or in a hybrid model

ONBOARDING THE WINNING AGENCY

An outgoing, professional agency will cooperate in the handover process. However, if you are parting on bad terms, you will not receive anything beyond existing correspondence and reports.

Logins

These days, large companies have various internal systems that require logins, so it's easier to provide corporate email accounts and a process for remote login, such as a VPN. It avoids confusion when the agency needs to reach out to people outside the core SEO team. Some of those internal systems cannot handle external email addresses by design.

Logins with higher privileges need to be granted to the existing search engine accounts and to other relevant internal analytics and reporting platforms. Such logins can take a few days to organize, so they are best anticipated and arranged internally before you announce the winning agency.

Formal Briefs

All relevant teams working with the website – product owners, IT, analytics, sales, and marketing leaders, etc. - should provide the agency with one or more formal briefs. The internal SEO team or notional accountable manager is the logical liaison point. These meetings should cover SEO-related tasks already in flight so that the new agency can hit the ground running or speak up if there is a concern.

FIRING AN AGENCY

Sometimes you need to fire the agency before a contract renewal date. Think of this possibility before you first sign the contract – big-brand agencies want you to sign their contract, while large organizations have the clout to dictate the terms for all their contractors. Usually, there are compromises made on both sides.

When to Fire

Terminating a contract must be done in accordance with its terms. Usually, it is for non-delivery of agreed work or a manual penalty imposed by a search engine due to an agency's work. When I have been in in-house roles, I have not needed to fire an agency, but I have worked with the account director to change their staff. As a consultant, I advised more than one client to terminate their contracts when they were not receiving value for their money.

BEING FIRED BY AN AGENCY

Your contract might allow the agency to legally end the relationship. For example, some clients are impossible to work with – in my agency days, after closing the sale, a client would fail to provide the essential information we needed to deliver the service. After a few failed attempts to get the information, we would terminate the contract.

TRANSITIONING AGENCIES

Changing Passwords

Just as you would change the passwords when your staff members with privileged access leave, you must do this just before you terminate an agency contract, again, you will need to delete the agency accounts and any names you don't recognize on the Google and Bing webmaster platforms.

Handover

The circumstances of the handover will dictate whether it makes sense for the incumbent agency to hold a handover meeting with the incoming agency. If, for example, you have a process of documenting all SEO work, then it will be easy to share it with the new agency.

CO-MANAGED SEO SERVICES

Large enterprises that outsource SEO should consider hiring an independent SEO consultant to co-manage their SEO contract and its implementation. It's one thing to check a box and tell your manager that "SEO is under control" because an agency is on the case, but it's quite a different matter if you have no idea what they are doing to get their monthly payment.

The Value of a Second Opinion

Two companies initially hired me to assess the incumbent SEO agency and make recommendations to the ecommerce manager. In both cases, the agency worked from its own offices and communicated via email, video conference, and telephone. In addition, they sent large, software-generated reports each month to show that significant work was underway. Unfortunately, the recipients did not know what to make of these large reports.

The companies sought a second opinion because they felt they were not receiving value from their service provider. You don't need to be a large enterprise to feel that way. A second opinion from an experienced consultant is likely to be worth the investment.

Hiring the Independent Assessor

The assessor mustn't be placed in a position of temptation, namely, an opportunity to badmouth the incumbent agency to create an opening for themselves. If you can hire two assessors and make that fact known to both, you will get better value from each of them.

Scope of the Assessment

The SEO services contract should be the main scope of the independent assessment. Is the agency delivering on the terms of the contract? The evaluation should follow the contract sequence and make a graduated scale "score" against each clause. For example:

Contract Clause	% Delivered	Comment
3a. Provide a list of high-ranking keywords that have dropped, with possible reasons for the drop.	20%	The monthly report fails to mention 30 high-value keywords that have declined steadily since Google implemented the Panda algorithm update.

Other observations should be welcomed, but should not form the basis of judging the agency. At best, the next annual iteration of the contract can be worded better as a result of the independent assessment.

Evaluating the Assessment

Each assessment report should be kept confidential and circulated only when necessary. However, the individual comments can serve as the basis for your next catch-up meeting with the agency, and you should emerge from that meeting with a list of action items for the service provider.

A FRACTIONAL SEO

A slightly different option is to hire a part-time SEO, also known as a fractional SEO. They have an employee status in the company, not that of a consultant. They can represent the company. To be effective, they should be employed at least half-time. They should be free to work for other employers who are not competitors.

A CO-MANAGED CONTRACT

If you are in the happy position of engaging an SEO agency for the first time, hiring an independent consultant will enable you to word the RFP/RFQ perfectly. However, if you have no in-house SEO capability, the external consultant can be given a part-time role to represent the company's SEO interests continuously.

Keep in mind that the agency might not like being supervised by an expert, so you should define professional boundaries, rules of engagement, arbitration, and lines of communication.

TWO-WAY COMMUNICATION IS CRUCIAL

Once you have established a relationship with a consultant or an agency, you need to inform them of every detail that might affect the website. If in doubt, tell them more, rather than less. All parts of the company that work on the website need to be aware of this requirement. Often, people working on the "back end" think that it is not visible to the public, so it does not concern SEO. While that might be the case, let the consultant or agency decide.

Chapter 13

STRUCTURING THE SEO STRATEGY PROCESS

The term SEO strategy is widely used – sometimes too casually in conversations and internal documents. Here, we take a more structured approach to SEO strategy and how to guide it. The detailed tactics of the SEO strategy will be determined by your SEO experts – agency-side or in-house. Still, you must ensure that it aligns with the organization's objectives and contributes to its key results.

THE IDEAL SEO STRATEGY

The ideal SEO strategy is rarely realized in practice because it must align with C-suite objectives, yet SEO is often not directly represented in executive planning discussions. The C-suite might plan for five years or even longer. They would know the competitors who need to be beaten, or who are nipping at the heels. Instead, the SEO team sees a filtered-down version of the master plans and has to identify competitors based on keyword rankings. Therefore, in this book, we will discuss the single-year, or even quarterly, SEO strategy.

SEO STRATEGY FORMAT

The tasks required for an SEO strategy will depend on the challenges identified in the SEO audit and the subsequent tactics determined by the SEO consultant or the internal SEO team. Outside of an audit, they will complement the Company's annual and quarterly conversion goals. At a very high level, they usually include the following tactics:

- Content approach
- Links
- Technical SEO

When you break this down into individual tasks, they will overlap across all three tactics, say, if articles need structured data tags and links; therefore, the three groups are not independent.

If an agency is preparing the strategy document, it will have some more sections that you might not need in a mature organization, for example:

- Identifying the audience
- Keywords

AGILE, SCRUM, AND SEO

Agile

Agile is a project management approach used by many organizations and governments. Scrum is a heuristic framework within Agile and comes with a vocabulary.

Scrum

Scrum can adapt to changes in requirements and handle imprecise requirements. Therefore, SEO tasks align nicely with a Scrum environment. A classic Scrum Team consists of a Product Owner, a Scrum Master, and Developers. In Scrum terminology, an SEO representative (like QA, writers, or designers) participates as part of the Developer role, regardless of job title.

The details of the addressed issue are called a User Story, or simply a Story. When a significant project involves several related stories, they can be placed in an Epic. A Product Backlog is a repository of identified tasks and is often re-prioritized. Finally, a Sprint is a period during which a scrum team agrees to complete a set number of tasks from the backlog, likely to be completed within that period.

Scrum Boards

Scrum tasks are managed in a visual environment called a Board. They used to be whiteboards in the early days, and tasks were written on cards or sticky notes. Now they are online and enable collaboration across multiple workplaces or among people working from home. Consequently, many old timers refer to user stories as Cards. Most of the large companies I have worked for use Atlassian Jira, but I have also used Monday, Trello, and Asana.

The board software is highly customizable, so the layout, colors, and labels can vary, but the columns depict a timeline. Sample columns could be:

- To Do
- In Progress
- Quality Assurance (QA) or Code Review
- Done
- Backlog

During the daily Standup, the team will report on the progress of each story, and the story is moved to the next column as appropriate. Sometimes a blocker arises, and the story is returned to the backlog.

ASSURANCE OF RESOURCES

An all-too-common frustration for the SEO team is preparing for a business-as-usual (BAU) SEO task or a more significant initiative, only to be told that resources have been diverted to another team. As a result, the SEO task has been "deprioritized."

Whose Priorities?

At one workplace, the corporate culture was to express task requests in "Sales Dollars." I'd find that an SEO task had been deprioritized in favor of another "revenue-generating" task. Hello? They asked me to show how many Dollars we would earn if (some SEO task) were implemented first, rather than some widget that a product manager wanted.

Yes, product managers are always asking for new widgets on the website or fixing things that didn't work as well as expected, but someone needs to look at the bigger picture – constantly.

That company got 60% of its online revenue from SEO traffic. I was new to the company, and my manager, who was new to SEO, did not speak up at the right time. So, I evolved my corporate survival skills and began showing the revenue impact of delaying SEO tasks.

Dedicated SEO Squad

The SEO team can perform many minor tasks without involving anyone outside the team. However, for good reasons, access to the website infrastructure is limited to a few people.

Many Agile-enabled organizations, such as Spotify, operate in a hierarchy of Tribes, Squads, Chapters, and Guilds. The SEO team is housed in a squad that appears to "need SEO" the most. Fair enough, but there's a strong case for a dedicated SEO squad.

The SEO team will find itself working on tasks owned by all product owners (POs). Some POs might never ask for SEO help because their page content is a static, minor part of the website. Others will need SEO help but not realize it, possibly because an SEO audit has not covered their product area. The product squad that co-houses the SEO team is likely to get the lion's share of SEO attention – but is that fair to the organization?

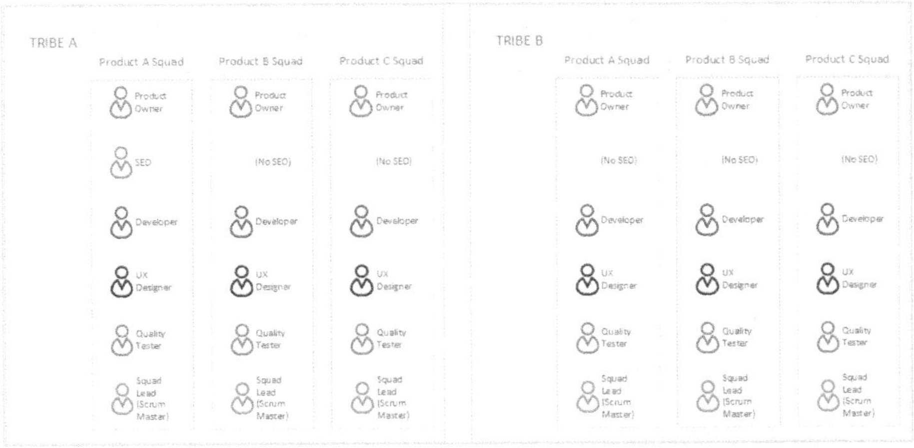

Figure 122 SEO is in a single squad (top left).

Another possibility is an SEO team member in each squad – if the organization can justify the cost. The SEO members can form an SEO chapter – a term introduced by Spotify.

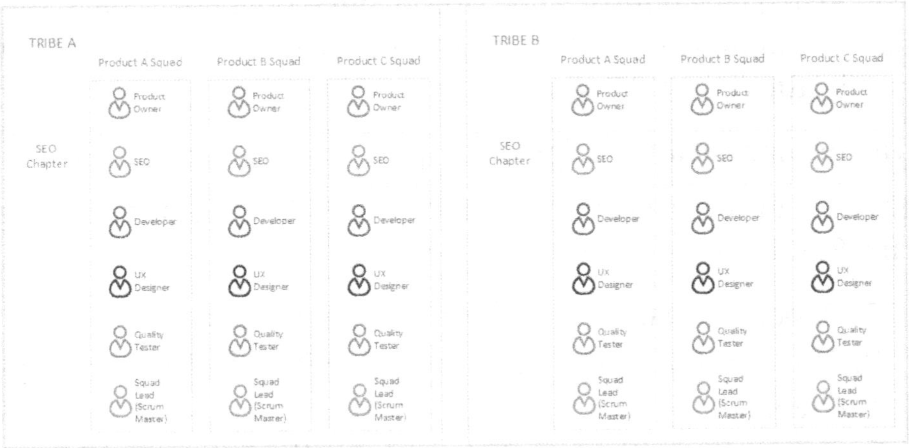

Figure 123 A mature Scrum structure – SEO in each squad.

Consider creating a separate SEO squad. Now the SEO squad can do specific work without waiting for the developer or UX resources from another squad. Of course, larger tasks would still need resources from other squads who know their products well, while the SEO squad can look after squad-agnostic tasks such as sitemaps and, in quieter moments, be an additional resource to the other squads.

Figure 124 An SEO Squad in each Tribe.

A larger, multinational organization might have an SEO Tribe, with an SEO squad in each country. The Tribe leader would be based in the company headquarters and close to the relevant decisions that could eventually affect the SEO squads.

SEO Implementation Budget

An SEO budget consists of much more than salaries or the cost of an external SEO agency. The SEO team will need:

- SEO tools and subscriptions to paid resources
- VPN access for secure remote connectivity and location-specific diagnostics
- Laptops with sufficient administrative flexibility for SEO tooling, subject to corporate security policies
- Separate internet connection for the SEO laptops
- Conferences and training
- Books

- Contractors, if internal resources are not available for a Scrum task

SEO TEAM BOARD

While the Product Owner will run their squad's board for product-wide implementation work, the SEO team should consider running an SEO Team board. Creating an SEO user story in the Jira environment is easy from the SEO team's perspective, as there are often tasks for the SEO team members. The SEO team can complete some of these stories independently.

As most stories need to be worked on by the product squads, an SEO board story can be cloned, moved to the product squad board, and a two-way link inserted at each end. Then, when the task is completed, the SEO user story is marked as done. Such a hook-up is great for reporting on the SEO team's work in each sprint.

SEO User Stories

The user story should describe the desired outcome, not dictate how to perform the technical steps. Further clarification should be listed in the Acceptance Criteria. If the developer team asks for more information in the comments, it is fine to provide the technical steps, if known. Links to external articles can help here.

OBJECTIVES AND KEY RESULTS (OKRS)

Many companies, including Intel, Microsoft, Google, Twitter, and Uber, use a management methodology known as Objectives and Key Results (OKRs). Some government departments also use OKRs. It is a goal-setting and team alignment framework, and the SEO team will find itself an active participant in the company's OKRs. This book looks at its relevance to SEO's contribution to the company's goals.

Some other similar management frameworks, such as Key Performance Indicators (KPIs), exist, but the broad principles still apply. For example, Google describes KPIs in the context of a customer journey in four stages, as defined by Avinash Kaushik. Each of them is an SEO opportunity that leverages Commercial/Investigation Intent.

1. See – a target audience with specific attributes
2. Think – the target audience that is actively searching for a solution
3. Do – the target audience that is ready to buy
4. Care – the target audience that has bought

Recap of Search Intent

We covered earlier the four types of search intent we see in the SEO world:

- Navigational
- Informational
- **Commercial/Investigation**
- Transactional

This framework places particular emphasis on Commercial/Investigation intent, though the terminology and boundaries between intent stages are fluid.

See

The target audience, say, a car buyer, has gone past the information-gathering stage and is almost ready to buy, so the SEO response would be to have content for that state of mind.

Think

The car buyer needs specifics to make a decision. Therefore, some detailed content that overcomes doubts is optimized on the website – perhaps comparison charts, FAQs, etc.

Do

The car buyer is ready to transact, so the SEO checks that the order pages are optimized and searchable.

Care

Customers need ongoing support and represent an opportunity to up-sell, enabling the SEO team to optimize such content.

CONVEYING THE PRODUCT VISION

SEO teams should be invited to product management meetings, as their research skills can be helpful. For example, studying competitors, keywords, and search volumes relating to the new feature set might be beneficial. Once the product vision is finalized, it should be shared with the broader product team and the SEOs.

Goal Setting for SEO Teams

Small companies can use metrics such as Sales or Leads (perhaps filtered to exclude organic search-acquired), but in a large company, the SEO team might feel they are not in a position to improve outcomes. There are many other teams whose decisions can adversely affect sales, and pinpointing why sales improved isn't easy.

Some like to use Customer Lifetime Value (CLV), but how can a new organization measure this, and which generation of SEOs can take the credit or blame for the customer's lifetime? One can measure CLV, but it's another area where the SEO team might not agree that such a metric can measure its role.

I prefer SEO goals to have clear Yes/No outcomes, as percentage-based targets often drift into vanity metrics when search behavior is unpredictable. It's meaningless to set a goal like "Get 70% of keywords on page 1 of Google," not simply because you don't know how many keywords to include in that count, but because the team might pick "easy" keywords like brand terms. If you require the keywords to be non-branded, the SEO team might choose a small number – say, 10.

The OKR philosophy requires goals to be easily measurable – ideally by people outside the core SEO team. In addition, the results should have well-defined, objective success criteria.

OKR Tools

A good performance management tool should enable upper management to cascade the top-level organizational goals down the hierarchy. Individuals should be able to track the completion of their fraction of the overall goal. For example, a top-level goal might be to launch a new product by a specific date. The SEO team will work with many parts of the company towards that goal, so their tasks being shown as completed on time will flow up the line.

Format of an OKR

The **Objective** of an OKR should be clear and succinct, and in this format:

> <verb> <task>
>
> Example: <Implement> <internal backlinks for product pages>

It should address what needs to be done and, if it is not obvious, why it needs to be done.

The **Key Results** should list 2 – 4 measurable results that demonstrate the achievement of the objective. Additionally, they should suggest how the results can be achieved. Not all results can be measured numerically.

SEO OKRS

Here are some sample thought starters to get you thinking about SEO OKRs. Each of them should be linked to a higher-tier goal so that it is seen as contributing to the company's objectives for that quarter.

SEO Objective	Key Results
Identify keywords for a new product	• Identify 50 primary unbranded keywords • Identify 100 long-tail unbranded keywords
Write website content for a new product	• Writers use SEO keywords in product pages • Writers use SEO keywords in blog posts
Create accessible content for a new product	• Provide Alt text for all new product images • Color contrast of normal text above new product imagery is at least 4.5:1, and of large text, it is 3:1.

New Visibility Metrics for AI Search

Traditional analytics miss traffic from AI Overviews or chat results that mention your brand without a click.

Track **implied visibility** by monitoring brand mentions in LLM outputs and referrals from emerging search partners. Tag these as **"AI-**

Assisted Discovery" in reports. Over time, treat this channel as a measurable contribution to organic share, not as "dark traffic."

This monitoring relies on controlled testing, referral analysis, and third-party observation tools rather than direct access to proprietary models.

Chapter 14

SUMMARY

Let's summarize what we have covered in this book. First, in the Managing Rankings chapter, we saw this simplified diagram of the Google Search algorithm.

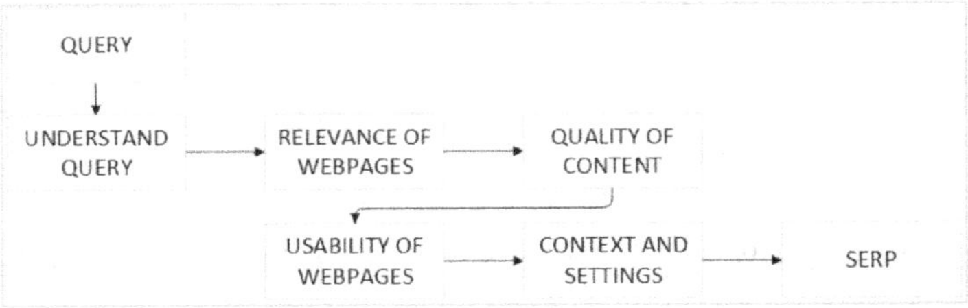

Figure 125 Simplified diagram of the Google ranking algorithm.

Now, let's pick some topics we covered and insert them into the previous diagram.

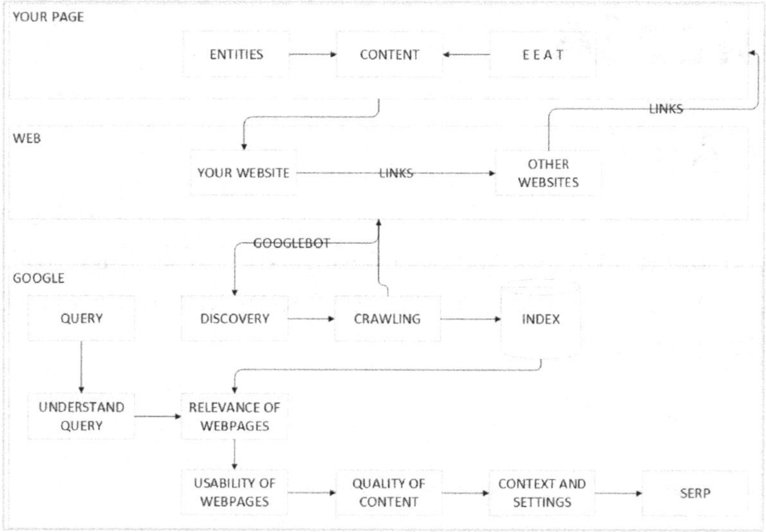

Figure 126 How the Google search systems join the dots.

Search engine systems try to understand the search term (as best as AI and machine learning permit) and serve a high-quality, relevant set of URLs and AI-mediated results based on the user's known context and privacy settings. Your job is to create expert, authoritative, and trustworthy content that is better than your competitors and serve it in the most technically speedy way.

LOOKING AHEAD

As AI reshapes how information surfaces, your team's role shifts from keyword optimizer to **visibility strategist**. You're no longer competing for ten blue links—you're competing for **machine understanding**. Keep learning, document your governance, and stay curious; that mindset keeps you visible when algorithms change.

Connect with Me

I welcome connections that mention this book (please edit the default text in LinkedIn). I am happy to offer a quick answer to your SEO governance questions.

WHERE TO NEXT

This book introduces the practical foundations of managing SEO—the people, processes, and priorities that shape how your organization becomes discoverable.

If you're ready to deepen that understanding:

- **For governance and compliance leadership**, read Book 3 ***AI Visibility Playbook*** to learn how visibility, ethics, and automation intersect.
- **For measurement and ROI evaluation**, explore Book 4 ***Is Our SEO Working?*** to quantify impact and communicate results across departments.
- **For executive-level strategy**, see Book 5, The C-Suite Blind Spot, to understand how visibility, governance, and funding decisions affect long-term enterprise growth.

Together, these four volumes form a complete roadmap—from operational SEO management to boardroom-level accountability in the AI era.

INDEX

Made in the USA
Monee, IL
08 November 2026

67378322R00181